D0820290

Capitalism and the Third World

Capitalism and the Third World

Development, Dependence and the World System

Wil Hout
Department of Political Science
University of Leiden, The Netherlands

Edward Elgar

Published by
Edward Elgar Publishing Limited
Gower House
Croft Road
Aldershot
Hants GU11 3HR
England

Edward Elgar Publishing Company
Old Post Road
Brookfield
Vermont 05036
USA

A CIP catalogue record for this book is available from
the British Library

ISBN 1 85278 785 6

Printed and Bound in Great Britain by
Hartnolls Limited, Bodmin, Cornwall.

Contents

List of Figures and Tables

Figures

Tables

Preface

During the writing of this book, the manuscript has benefited from the comments of many people. Of all these I would like to single out a few and express my thanks to them. First, I thank professors Fred van Staden and Galen A. Irwin of the Department of Political Science at Leiden University for the extensive discussions we had about earlier versions of the text. I would also like to thank Frank van Beuningen and the members of the Leiden Department of Political Science's *promo-groep*, whose comments helped to sharpen the argumentation contained in the first two chapters. Furthermore, I thank Frits Meijerink, who assisted with the LISREL analyses, which unfortunately did not provide a solution for the present purposes. Finally, I express my thanks to Mariet Overeem, who commented upon the text of the entire manuscript and prepared the index.

An earlier version of chapter 2, section VII appeared in *Acta Politica* of January 1992. Parts of chapter 9, section III were published before in *Acta Politica*, October 1988.

Rotterdam, October 1992

1. Introduction

I THE RISE OF DEPENDENCY THEORY

Since the beginning of the 1970s, the orthodox views that dominated the study of international relations have increasingly come under attack from scholars promoting alternative perspectives. It was argued that the orthodox approaches, which focused on problems of war, peace and order in the relations among states, have overlooked other, equally or more important issues in international affairs. One of the most conspicuous perspectives that have been developed as an alternative to the orthodox approaches certainly was *dependency theory*.

Dependency theory holds that a so-called *world system*, comprising an ever increasing number of countries, has developed during the last several centuries. This world system is referred to as *capitalist*, meaning that the relations among the constituent parts of the system are characterized by the exchange of goods by means of the *world market*. It is argued that international relations - that is, relations in the context of the capitalist world system - enhance *inequality* among the countries of the world. This inequality is said to result in the creation of a dominant, wealthy *core*, and a subservient, impoverished *periphery*.

Over the last two decades, dependency theory has proven to be a successful theoretical approach to the study of international relations. It has gained substantial support from scholars all over the world and its ideas have been adapted into other, non-dependency theories. It is probably no exaggeration to say that dependency theory cannot be left out of any overview of the contemporary theoretical landscape of international relations.

The recent attention for the interrelationship between political and economic dimensions of international relations has stimulated the development of a *political economy of international relations*. As shown by Robert Gilpin's seminal work (1987, chapter 7), the concern with political-economic problems has created new interest in theories linking political and economic aspects of international relations, such as dependency theory.

Apart from the scholarly appeal, dependency theory has had influence in political circles as well. To a considerable extent, the ideology of *Third Worldism*, as Nigel Harris (1987, pp. 11-29) has called it, may be seen as the result of dependency and related theories. The critique of the existing international order has been one of the main results of this *Third Worldism* and it has found supporters both in the Third World and in the West.

All of this is not to say, however, that there is consensus about the *scientific value* of the dependency approach. Whether or not dependency theory can be seen as an advance in the knowledge about international relations has, to the present day, never been fully assessed. Usually, scholars pretending to perform such evaluations have only paid attention to the theoretical or the empirical implications of the theory, or details thereof. For a more complete evaluation, it will be argued below, it is necessary to look at both the theoretical and the empirical aspects of the approach. The object of this study is to perform an evaluation of the strengths and weaknesses of dependency theory, with respect to both its conceptual and its empirical dimensions.

II DEPENDENCY THEORY AND THE STUDY OF INTERNATIONAL RELATIONS

In the study of international relations several 'great debates' can be discerned. In a nutshell, these debates can be characterized as (1) the debate about the place of norms and values in international politics ('realism' vs 'idealism'); (2) the debate about the proper way to study international relations ('traditionalism' vs 'behaviouralism' or the 'scientific study of politics'); and (3) the debate about the nature of international relations and the appropriate level of analysis in the study of this domain. Although none of these debates has been decisively ended until the present day, the first two have been analysed and documented relatively well.[1] At this moment, the third debate is still at the centre of discussion in the academic study of international relations.

According to K.J. Holsti, the 'classical' state-centric approach to international relations is still dominant.[2] Yet, over the last two decades, several scholars have claimed to offer an alternative and, in their view, consequently better perspective on international relations. In his widely cited work on the development of theorizing in international relations, Holsti (1985, pp. 7-8) has presented a taxonomy of approaches on the basis of two or three questions or criteria. These are:

(1) the central problems with which scholars in the field are concerned;
(2) the essential actors and/or units of analysis under study;

(3) the image of the world, the international system or the society of states that characterizes the work of students of international relations.

Holsti has argued that, until recently, the field of international relations has known a fundamental consensus on these three questions. This means that scholars working in the classical tradition basically agree:

> (1) that the proper focus of the study is the causes of war and the conditions of peace/security/order; (2) that the main units of analysis are the diplomatic-military behaviors of the only essential actors, nation states; and (3) that states operate in a system characterized by anarchy, the lack of central authority. (Holsti 1985, p. 10; cf. Maghroori and Ramberg 1982, pp. 1-22 and Van Staden 1987)

In a recent attempt to characterize the study of international relations, Susan Strange has made a similar point by writing that '[a]lmost all the standard texts on international politics assume the maintenance of order to be the prime if not the only *problématique* of the study'. (1989, p. 14)

Apart from the classical state-centric approach, Holsti (1985, pp. 41-81) has distinguished between two groups of 'dissenters', one consisting of global society and transnational theories, the other comprising (neo-) Marxist and dependency theories. In their recent book on the state of the art of international relations theory, William C. Olson and A.J.R. Groom have supported Holsti's classification. In their view, the previous consensus on the classical approach has been replaced by 'an element of consensus in that there is general acknowledgement of the existence of three intellectual traditions in approaches to IR [international relations]'. (1991, p. 137) Using a nomenclature that is different from Holsti's, Olson and Groom (1991, p. 140) classify the three dominant intellectual traditions as: realism, world society approaches, and structuralism.

The dominance of these three intellectual traditions does not imply that all three receive equal attention from international relations scholars. At present - that is, at the beginning of the 1990s - regime theory and neo-realism appear to be the most vital branches of theorizing about international affairs. The concern with problems of international inequality and development has diminished since the first half of the 1980s. This reduced interest appears to have been caused by several important transformations that took place since, roughly, 1985: problems of the international political-economic order (such as the relative decline of United States hegemony, the rise of the Pacific Basin, and the troublesome trading, monetary, and financial relations among the developed countries), the end of the Cold War, and the subsequent disintegration of Soviet-dominated Central and Eastern Europe and, more recently, of the Soviet Union itself.

Holsti's criteria and the resulting taxonomy appear to contain two different ordering principles with the help of which approaches to international relations can be classified. The first ordering principle deals with the *object* under study (the question then is: '*what* is studied?') and is roughly equivalent to Holsti's first criterion. The second ordering principle is concerned with the *perspective* from which the study is performed (the question is: '*how* is the object studied?') and is the upshot of Holsti's second and third criteria. Referring to Golembiewski's analysis of the development of public administration (1977, p. 7), the two ordering principles might aptly be termed the *locus* and *focus* of a scientific theory.

Without the least difficulty more than two *loci* can be distinguished in the study of international relations. For the benefit of clarity, however, the discussion will be limited to two: problems of order, peace and security, on the one hand, and problems of international inequality, on the other. Holsti has already indicated the two main *foci* in international studies: the state-centric versus the systemic focus.

With the help of these two ordering principles a relatively clear and comprehensive picture of the diversity of theoretical approaches to international relations can be drawn, as figure 1.1 on page 5 makes clear.

In figure 1.1, the theories that were mentioned by Holsti as well as the ones that will be discussed in chapter 2 have been characterized according to their *focus* and their *locus*. Of the theories that focus on the problems of development and that have played a role in the genesis of the dependency theories, the traditional economic theories of imperialism and the theories of modernization have applied explicit state-centric perspectives on international relations, the former focusing on the Western countries, and the latter on Third World countries. Neo-Marxist theories of imperialism, the ideas developed in the framework of the Economic Commission for Latin America (E.C.L.A. or C.E.P.A.L.), and the (neo-) liberal free trade theory appear to contain state-centric as well as systemic elements.

The so-called 'theories of global society' are characterized by 'new conceptualizations of the world, a vastly extended problematic, and solutions which suggest that the norms of equality and justice are more important than order and stability'. (Holsti 1985, p. 48) Apart from the nation-state, non-state actors are to be studied as well: corporations, international organizations and international voluntary agencies (peace movements, human rights organizations, etc.) are among the most important of these. Because of the increase of contacts among peoples and the growing interdependence the global society theories no longer speak of anarchy but instead of global society.

The 'transnational theories' have stressed that the classical, state-centric perspective is inadequate for explaining contemporary international relations, since it mainly focuses on diplomatic and military affairs.

(Keohane and Nye 1971 and 1977) What is needed, is a supplementary conceptualization in order to explain 'new' issues. The transnational school has therefore introduced the concept of 'complex interdependence'. This concept stresses the fragmentation of present-day international relations into different issue areas, each of which is typified by distinctive relations of power and dependence.

The approach that has been termed 'neo-realism', exemplified by, among others, Kenneth N. Waltz (1979), focuses on the 'classical' problem of peace, security and order, but introduces an explicit systemic perspective. The position of states, defined by their relations of dependence and power, is seen as the most important factor in explaining the outcome of international politics.

	Focus		
Locus	State-centric		Systemic
Problems of inequality	Traditional theories of imperialism	Neo-Marxist theories of imperialism	Dependencia
		E.C.L.A. theory	Centre-periphery theories
	Modernization theories	(Neo-)liberal free trade theories	World system analysis
		Global society theories	Transnational theories
Problems of order	Classical, state-centric tradition		Neo-realism

Figure 1.1: Foci and Loci in the Study of International Relations

It does not appear to be a fruitful enterprise to study all different theories mentioned in figure 1.1. Moreover, this would be an enormously huge undertaking, which goes far beyond the scope of one book. The discussion in this book will be limited to dependency theory, which has attempted to present an innovative approach to international relations by studying problems of development from a systemic perspective.

III NOMENCLATURE AND SELECTION OF AUTHORS

Following Chris Brown's lucid interpretation of the development of dependency theory, the label 'dependency' has been used, in the preceding sections, as a general indication of a broad range of theories. Brown (1985, p. 63) has subsumed several variants under the general notion of dependency theory, in order to point out their relatedness and common heritage. He has distinguished dependencia theory, centre-periphery theories, and world system analysis. (Cf. Chase-Dunn 1989, p. 3) These three variants of dependency theory were developed in consecutive order during the 1960s and the 1970s, and were expanded and transformed during the 1980s.

Dependencia theory contains the original formulation of the assertion that most Latin American countries have obtained formal political independence during the nineteenth century, but have remained economically subordinate to outside powers ever since. The lack of development of these countries is attributed to their integration in the capitalist world system and the resulting exploitation by colonial powers, such as Spain, Portugal, Great Britain, and the United States. Among the scholars who developed the original dependencia position were: Theotonio dos Santos, Fernando Henrique Cardoso and Celso Furtado.

The centre-periphery theories may be described as the result of the spatial 'broadening' and theoretical 'deepening' of the dependencia position. The centre-periphery theories do not limit their analysis to the countries of Latin America. Instead, they claim to be more general, and applicable to the whole of the Third World. Centre-periphery theories emphasize the unequal and exploitative structural relationships that have developed between the different parts of the capitalist world system, that is, the centre and the periphery. They pay ample attention to the allegedly negative effects of the ties between the centre and the periphery on the latter. Representatives of centre-periphery theory are scholars such as: Andre Gunder Frank, Samir Amin, Johan Galtung and Giovanni Arrighi.

World system analysis is the third variant of dependency theory that is mentioned by Chris Brown. This variant is inextricably linked with the work of Immanuel Wallerstein. Wallerstein's work focuses on what he has termed the 'Modern World System'. His analysis is basically analytical-historical: he tries to determine which were the causes of the rise of the capitalist world economy during the 'long sixteenth century' and of its subsequent spread across the world. Instead of analysing the world system in terms of two categories (centre and periphery), Wallerstein distinguishes three parts, adding the so-called semi-periphery to the aforementioned two.

As a consequence of the wealth of literature on dependency and the world system, it is necessary to select a limited number of authors whose work will be studied in some more detail. It would be possible to either focus on some recent works and consider these to be the culmination of dependency theory, or choose the *oeuvre* of a limited number of scholars who can be deemed representative for the entire approach. The first alternative, however, is unsatisfactory, since the choice of authors would, of necessity, be rather coincidental. The second alternative is more promising, because more adequate criteria are available for the selection of authors. In the present study, the work of three established dependency scholars will be focused upon: Andre Gunder Frank, Samir Amin and Johan Galtung.

The work of these three theorists has been chosen for several reasons. First, their work is, to a high degree, 'paradigmatic' for the whole of dependency theory. Frank, Amin and Galtung have worked in the theoretical framework for over two decades, and their writings clearly reflect the development of the approach in reaction to changing international political-economic circumstances. Second, their work emphasizes structural international factors in the explanation of international inequality. This characteristic makes the writings of Frank, Amin and Galtung most relevant for international relations theory. Third, as these authors have themselves asserted, their work is not limited to one region or period in the development of the capitalist world system.

The traditional dependencia theory will not be considered in this study, since its pretensions were limited to analysing the economic situation of Latin American countries, and its explanations tend to focus on the internal consequences of external relations of dependence. It is, moreover, more a way of analysing concrete situations than an explicit *theory*.

The so-called world system analysis of Immanuel Wallerstein will be discussed alongside the work of Frank, Amin and Galtung. The treatment of Wallerstein's writings, however, will differ from that of the other three authors. In this book no attempt will be made to model Wallerstein's world system analysis, nor to subject it to an empirical test. Several reasons can be given for this difference of procedures. First, Wallerstein's work is less a dependency *theory* than a description and analysis of the development of the 'capitalist world economy'. Wallerstein's general writings, which have been published in collections such as *The capitalist world-economy* (1979) and, recently, in *Geopolitics and geoculture* (1991), are either too schematic or too detailed to be the source of an empirical model of international relations. Moreover, Wallerstein's work is mainly historical, whereas the focus of this study is on the present, post-World War II reality of international affairs. Finally, the part of his work that will explicitly focus on the recent developments in the international system (the final volume or volumes of his *magnum opus*, *The modern world-system*) has not yet been published.

IV THE AIM OF THE STUDY

The aim of this study is to investigate dependency theory's contribution to the study of international relations, in particular to the scientific knowledge about development and the differences in the level of development among countries. In order to assess the theory's contribution, two problems will be addressed. First, the question will be answered whether dependency theory can be considered theoretically 'progressive' in relation to its main predecessors and competitors. This problem will be dealt with in chapter 2. Secondly, the problem of dependency theory's empirical adequacy will be addressed in chapters 3 through 7. (See also subsection D below.)

In order to evaluate the growth of scientific knowledge embodied in dependency theory, it is necessary to have a framework accounting for scientific change and growth.[3] The philosophy of science has produced several of these meta-theoretical frameworks. The approaches of *Karl R. Popper*, *Thomas S. Kuhn*, *Imre Lakatos* and *Larry Laudan* will be discussed in subsections A, B and C.

A Interpreting Scientific Growth: Popper and Kuhn

Popper's revolutionary idea was that the classical problem of the philosophy of science, the relation between theory and reality, should not be solved by constructing meta-theories stressing the correspondence between theory and reality, but by taking theories as more or less autonomous phenomena. (E.g. Popper 1969) Although theories could never be said to reflect reality in all its respects, and therefore it would be impossible to *verify* them, it would nevertheless be possible to determine whether theoretical constructions do *not* correspond with reality: it would be possible to *falsify* theories. Scientific progress, in Popper's terms, then, is the ongoing process of the testing of theories: 'bad' theories - i.e., theories that are not supported by empirical findings - are to be rejected, while 'good' theories - theories that have not been rejected - are retained.

Kuhn (1970) reacted to Popper's depiction of the process of scientific growth as a succession of 'conjectures and refutations' with a more sociological and historical interpretation of 'scientific revolutions'. According to Kuhn, theories must be understood in the context of 'paradigms'. Paradigms are conceptualized as broad bases of knowledge containing shared values, methods, standards and generalizations used for studying reality and, among other things, for deciding about the rejection and retention of theories. The adherence of scientists to these paradigms is based not only on 'scientific' considerations, but also on 'extra-scientific' - or as some people would call them, irrational - ones. 'Normal science' is the situation in which one paradigm is dominant; if scientists lose confidence in the paradigm and criticism is widespread, a 'crisis' may result. The outcome might be a 'scientific revolution', meaning the replacement of the formerly dominant paradigm by a new one. In the context of Kuhn's theory it is difficult to speak of scientific *growth*; the supporters of the dominant paradigm will undoubtedly see themselves as scientifically more sophisticated than the supporters of paradigms that have become unfashionable. Yet Kuhn's theory does not offer criteria for deciding which theory offers scientific progress, since the rules and criteria for judging theories are inevitably part of a paradigm.

B Lakatos' Methodology of Scientific Research Programmes

Imre Lakatos reacted to both Popper and Kuhn. He could not accept Kuhn's claim that there could be no 'rational', 'objective' way to judge theories and, therefore, scientific progress. Lakatos (1970) started with Popper's idea of falsification and by stressing so-called 'sophisticated falsificationism' he tried to build his own 'methodology of scientific research prorammes'.

Lakatos has tried to present a methodology with the help of which a *rational* reconstruction of scientific change can be presented. Kuhn's approach, in which scientific revolutions dominate, leaves no room for this: in his theory, scientific change is brought about because of non-rational considerations. The importance of creating a rational reconstruction in the sense of Lakatos' approach is to be found in the consideration that without the assumption of rationality and the importance of rational argumentation there are absolutely no criteria on which scientific theories can be built. As Kuhn himself has argued, in the situation where non-rational arguments dominate the scientific 'discourse', adherence to theories can be compared to adherence to religions. Scientific argumentation will then be reduced to dogmatism.

Lakatos' conception of theories and of 'sophisticated methodological falsificationism', as he has called it, offers a means to evaluate the claims that theories represent scientific growth. Generally, theories are legitimized by stressing their value relative to other theories. If one does not possess criteria to judge this value, it remains impossible to assess the theories' contribution toward the growth of scientific knowledge. Popper's and Kuhn's approaches do not produce adequate criteria to perform such assessments. The central criterion presented by Popper is the *falsifiability* of theories. As Lakatos has argued, the scientific value of theories can only partly be determined by Popper's demarcation criterion: 'exactly the most admired scientific theories simply fail to forbid any observable state of affairs'. (1970, p. 100) Kuhn's approach is of even less use if one wants to judge the scientific value of theories, since he has argued that 'inter-paradigmatic' judgments are by their very nature impossible. Moreover, Kuhn's concept of 'normal science' appears to be inapplicable to the social sciences. According to Kuhn (1970, pp. 21-2 and 177-9), the maturity of sciences depends on the existence of a paradigm; a situation of Kuhnian normal science, in which one paradigm is dominant, clearly has not been reached in the social sciences.

The starting point of Lakatos' methodology of scientific research programmes is to be found in the realization that no undisputable proof or disproof can be found for any proposition (he rejects so-called justificationism and dogmatic falsificationism) and that, therefore, *all theories are fallible*. (1970, pp. 93-107) Sophisticated methodological falsificationism, according to Lakatos, 'realizes that if we want to reconcile fallibilism with (non-justificationist) rationality, we *must* find a way to eliminate *some* theories. If we do not succeed, the growth of science will be nothing but growing chaos.' (1970, p. 108)

The demarcation criterion proposed for sophisticated falsificationism is the following:

> [O]nly those theories - that is, non-'observational' propositions - which forbid certain 'observable' states of affairs, and therefore may be 'falsified' and rejected, are 'scientific': or, briefly, *a theory is 'scientific' (or 'acceptable') if it has an 'empirical basis'*. (Lakatos 1970, p. 109; cf. pp. 95-7)

The empirical content of theories is thus one of the central criteria in accepting or rejecting them. Lakatos has introduced this criterion in order to overcome the problem connected with the demarcation criterion in 'naive' falsificationism, which might lead to the acceptance of theories that prove to be falsifiable and the rejection of unfalsifiable ones. As Lakatos has made clear, *any* theory can be saved from 'disproof' by the formulation of auxiliary hypotheses. In order to avoid fruitless discussions about the acceptability of such hypotheses, he proposed to assess theories together with their auxiliary hypotheses.

Lakatos then arrives at the following criterion for scientific progress:

> [A] theory is 'acceptable' or 'scientific' only if it has corroborated excess empirical content over its predecessor (or rival), that is, only if it leads to the discovery of

> novel facts. [...] For the sophisticated falsificationist a scientific theory *T* is *falsified* if and only if another theory *T '* has been proposed with the following characteristics: (1) *T '* has excess empirical content over *T* : that is, it predicts *novel* facts, that is, facts improbable in the light of, or even forbidden, by *T* ; (2) *T '* explains the previous success of *T*, that is, all the unrefuted content of *T* is included (within the limits of observational error) in the content of *T '*; and (3) some of the excess content of *T '* is corroborated. (1970, p. 116)

In order to stress the centrality of scientific progress, Lakatos proposes to analyse *series of theories* instead of isolated theories. He defines series of theories as *theoretically progressive*, or as constituting a theoretically progressive problemshift, if the new theories have excess empirical content over their predecessors, that is, if they predict novel, previously unexpected, facts. Theories are *empirically progressive*, or constitute an empirically progressive problemshift, if some of the excess empirical content is also corroborated. A problemshift is considered *progressive* if it is both theoretically and empirically progressive. (1970, p. 118)

Mutatis mutandis, the same criteria can be applied to research programmes, which are series of theories characterized by a continuity connecting their members and by certain methodological rules. With respect to these rules, the 'negative' and 'positive' heuristics are most important. The negative heuristic specifies what kind of research is to be avoided in the research programme or, in other words, what is the incontestable 'hard core' of assumptions of the programme. The positive heuristic, on the other hand, tells the members of the research programme what is the long term research policy; it also anticipates 'anomalies' that do not fit in with the programme and teaches the researchers how to deal with them.

C Laudan's Problem-Solving Approach to Scientific Growth

In some respects, Imre Lakatos' methodology of scientific research programmes has paved the way for the development of a useful theory about the rational assessment of scientific change and growth. As Larry Laudan has made clear in his *Progress and its problems* of 1977, Lakatos' methodology is important, but several important characteristics make it less applicable to the concrete analysis of theoretical development. Laudan has not only criticized Lakatos, but he has also presented a new, useful criterion for judging scientific growth: the 'problem-solving capacity' of theories and so-called research traditions.

As Laudan has indicated, Lakatos' model of scientific growth is, in many respects, a decided improvement on Kuhn's. In Laudan's words:

> Unlike Kuhn, Lakatos allows for, and stresses, the historical importance of the co-existence of several alternative research programmes at the same time, within the same domain. [...] Lakatos insists that we can objectively compare the relative progress of competing research traditions. (1977, p. 76)

Despite these positive words about Lakatos' approach, Laudan (1977, pp. 77-8) has formulated several elements of critique. Of these, two deserve to be mentioned here in somewhat more detail.

In the first place, Laudan criticizes the fundamentally empirical nature of Lakatos' conception of progress. As has been indicated in the previous section, Lakatos proposes empirical corroboration as a *necessary* (but not in itself a sufficient) condition of progressiveness. Laudan argues rightly that not all progress needs to be empirical in nature, and that sometimes theoretical contributions may be (and, in the history of science, have been) more important for the growth of scientific knowledge.

In the second place, Laudan has indicated that Lakatos' approach implies that a theory in a certain research programme, in order to be counted as progressive, has to entail other existing theories (this is the second element of Lakatos' criterion of progress that was cited in the previous section). The criterion of entailment is one that has seldom, if ever, been met in the reality of scientific endeavour: the succession of theories usually involves both the elimination and addition of theoretical and/or empirical content. Connected with this, Laudan has pointed out that Lakatos' measure of progress requires 'a comparison of the empirical content of every member of the series of theories which constitutes any research programme'; for this reason, Laudan has termed this content measure for scientific theories 'extremely problematic if not literally impossible'. (1977, p. 77)

In the development of his own criterion for scientific progress, Laudan shares Lakatos' epistemological view that no conclusive proof or disproof can be found for any theory; the fallibility of all theorizing is also Laudan's starting point. From this realization, Laudan concludes that there can be no absolute criteria (such as 'truth' or 'falsity') with which the value of theories is to be judged. Therefore, his approach to scientific growth does not attempt to make such assignments of truth or falsity. Instead, it focuses on the 'problem-solving effectiveness' of theories and research traditions. (1977, p. 43)

Problem solving seems the natural focal point of Laudan's approach, since he considers science as 'essentially a problem-solving activity'. (1977, p. 11) This interpretation of the role of science is intimately related to Laudan's conception of theory:

> The function of a theory is to resolve ambiguity, to reduce irregularity to uniformity, to show that what happens is somehow intelligible and predictable; it is this complex of functions to which I refer when I speak of theories as solutions to problems. (1977, p. 13)

Laudan has defined progress in terms of increasing problem-solving capacity. In his view, scientific problems can be of two sorts, empirical and conceptual. (1977, chapters 1 and 2) A theory or research tradition can, therefore, be considered progressive if it provides a better explanation of empirical phenomena, or exhibits fewer conceptual difficulties than its competitors. The 'appraisal measure' formulated by Laudan is the following:

> [T]he overall problem-solving effectiveness of a theory is determined by assessing the number and importance of the empirical problems which the theory solves and deducting therefrom the number and importance of the anomalies and conceptual problems which the theory generates. (1977, p. 68)

Laudan has opted for a non-cumulative concept of scientific growth, because the history and philosophy of science have both demonstrated that the 'progress-by-accretion' view is historically and conceptually unsound. Laudan's is a concept of 'cognitive progress', which is in line with the fundamental intellectual inspirations of science. (1977, pp. 6-7)

Although Laudan's approach is more 'operational' than Lakatos' methodology, it is not entirely unproblematic to derive general criteria (that is, criteria that are not specific to a theoretical domain) from it with which theories can be judged. Because of the nature of the approach, empirical problems can only be said to exist if they are identified by theories. Empirical problems are first-order problems, relating to 'the objects which constitute the domain of any given science'. (1977, p. 15) These problems can be considered solved by a theory if this theory 'functions (significantly) in any schema of inference whose conclusion is a statement of the problem'. (1977, p. 25) This can probably be best illustrated in reference to the deductive-nomological model of explanation:

'fact'	
theory	*explanans*
problem	*explanandum*

Laudan's view implies that a theory has to indicate why something (here called a 'fact') must be considered a problem. Progress is, then, the situation in which one theory has not recognized a certain 'fact' as a problem, while another theory has identified it and has made it significant in the context of a complex of statements.

Roslyn Simowitz and Barry L. Price have indicated that empirical research can be a significant contribution to judging theoretical progress. The exposition of Laudan's views in this section indicates that, in the context of the presently discussed meta-theory, empirical research will not estimate whether a theory is 'truthful', but whether it is significant in the light of the problem it claims to address. As Simowitz and Price have put it, 'the theory must logically imply an approximate statement of the problem before the theory can be regarded as having solved the problem'. (1990, p. 450) As a consequence, empirical evidence is needed in order to determine whether a theory can rightfully claim its place in the 'explanans' of the model mentioned above.

Laudan's problem-solving approach implies that *testing*, in the Popperian sense, has to be rejected as a methodological principle. In line with the discussion above, in this study the position is taken that theories in the social sciences hardly ever lend themselves to falsification. Falsification is an unsound criterion of demarcation between scientific and non-scientific activity, since, as Lakatos has observed, the most important theories in the social sciences forbid hardly anything. In non-experimental research, the principles of verification and falsification appear to be equally inapplicable. In this type of research design, it is not possible to include all potentially relevant variables or the entire theoretically relevant population. As a consequence of the nature of social and political reality, it is not feasible to develop indicators that measure theoretical concepts to the full. For these reasons, so-called random effects cannot be kept completely under control, nor can they be estimated with absolutely reliable measurement tools. Some uncertainty will be an inevitable element of research in the social sciences.

The methodology adopted in this study is more open-ended than a falsificationist approach would be. Consequently, the conclusion of the study will not be the outright and unconditional acceptance or rejection of dependency theory. Rather, the outcome will be twofold. On the one hand, elements of the theory will be specified that appear to solve certain conceptual and/or empirical problems. On the other hand, elements will be pointed out that do not solve problems or create new problems.

D The Evaluation of Dependency Theory

The central problem of this study, as it has been formulated above, is to indicate what is dependency theory's contribution to the study of international relations. Laudan's problem-solving approach has been dealt with in the previous subsection, because it presents a means to assess claims of scientific progress. In the terms of this approach the research problem of the present study can be reformulated as: can dependency theory be interpreted as progressive - i.e., does it solve problems better than its predecessors and competitors? - and is dependency theory an acceptable 'statement of the problem'?

Using Lakatos' terminology, Javier A. Elguea (1984) has argued that dependency theory can be seen as a research programme with its own negative and positive heuristic. According to Elguea, dependency theory offers a *progressive problemshift* when compared with its direct predecessor, modernization theory. This implies that in his opinion, dependency theory is both *theoretically* and *empirically* progressive. In other words, the theory is considered to have pointed out and explained novel, previously undiscovered facts and it is assumed that some of the 'excess empirical content' of the research programme has been corroborated.

Elguea points out that the negative heuristic, which contains the 'hard core' of the research programme, directs the attention to the notion of dependency as a determinant of national development and underdevelopment and to the notion of the world system as an explanatory factor in understanding development, underdevelopment and the stratification of states in centre and periphery. According to Elguea (1984, pp. 82-5), the positive heuristic of dependency theory contains two methodological directives: the construction of dependency models and the analysis of concrete, historical situations of dependency.

Elguea's analysis illustrates that Lakatos' methodology is not suited for assessing concrete examples of scientific growth. One of Lakatos' criteria with which theories or research programmes are to be judged is the extent to which they contain 'the unrefuted content' of their predecessors or competitors. Elguea has not, however, addressed this problem, thereby failing to apply a - it might even be argued: *the* - crucial Lakatosian evaluation criterion of scientific progress.

Two things have to be done in order to assess the theoretical progress of the dependency approach. First, it has to be shown that dependency theory has solved (empirical and conceptual) problems better than its predecessors and competitors. This part of the study will, of necessity, be modest in its pretensions. Each of the theories or research traditions that will be discussed in the following chapters contains a wealth of generalizations and predictions. The focus will be on the most important problems they have addressed and have failed to solve.

Secondly, apart from assessing dependency theory's problem-solving capacity, ample attention will be paid to the empirical evidence. In the past, most researchers have evaluated the *conceptual and theoretical* characteristics of dependency theory, not so much the *empirical* content. Most empirical studies pretending to evaluate the strengths of dependency theory have been limited to testing specific hypotheses, which were assumed to be general dependency statements. There is hardly a study that has performed a relatively complete assessment of the central theses of variants of dependency theory with respect to the nature and features of the international system. (Cf. Hout 1984) It is felt that, in the light of the relative underdevelopment of the social sciences, attempts at confronting theories with empirical evidence are badly needed. In the present study, the emphasis will therefore be on the confrontation of dependency theory with empirical data.

V THE DESIGN OF THE STUDY

This study is organized along several broad lines, the object of which is to assess the extent to which the dependency approach can be considered a significant contribution to the study of international relations.

Chapter 2 will deal with the 'theoretical' background of dependency theory. In this chapter, an analysis will be presented of the theories that can be interpreted as the 'roots' of dependency theory, that is, the theories that have been a stimulus - either because of similarities or differences - toward its development. The object of the chapter is to determine what are the main theoretical innovations of dependency theory or, in other words, to what extent the theory has solved problems better than its main predecessors and competitors.

In the next four chapters, several variants of dependency theory will be described in more detail. There, the theories of Andre Gunder Frank, Samir Amin, Johan Galtung and Immanuel Wallerstein will be analysed. The object of the analysis is to derive, from the first three theories, a model containing the central relations among the crucial variables. This implies that the models will not necessarily contain all variables introduced by Frank, Amin and Galtung. Since the object of this study is to assess the contribution of the dependency approach to the study of international relations, the models will focus on the elements that are relevant to international relations. The discussion of Wallerstein's world system analysis serves a mainly heuristic purpose.

The respective models will be used to analyse to what extent the dependency approach is supported by empirical evidence. In order to permit this assessment, a research design will be presented in chapter 7. In that chapter, the units of analysis and the data will be presented. A discussion of the empirical analyses of dependency theory that have been undertaken by previous researchers will result in the choice of research techniques.

Chapter 8 will contain the results of the empirical analyses that have been performed on the basis of the dependency models. In chapter 9 the conclusions of this study will be formulated and the implications of the analysis for the study of international relations will be assessed.

NOTES

1. The debate among 'realists' and 'idealists' has been waged, among many others by Edward Hallett Carr (1939) and Hans J. Morgenthau (1948). An outline of the debate can be found in Dougherty and Pfaltzgraff (1981, pp. 3-9 and 84-133). The debate among 'traditionalists' and 'behaviouralists' has been waged by Hedley Bull, Morton A. Kaplan, J. David Singer, and others. Their first contributions to this debate have been collected in Knorr and Rosenau (1970). Dougherty and Pfaltzgraff (1981, pp. 28-38) offer a summary of this debate.
2. The adjective 'classical' is used in the sense used in Holsti (1985). In his overview of international theory, Holsti uses the term 'paradigm' to denote what is here either called a perspective or a theoretical framework. The use of the term 'paradigm' has been avoided throughout this study, since the meaning of this term is controversial and not at all clear, especially when it is applied to the social sciences. For a critical analysis of the concept 'paradigm' with respect to theories of development, see Elguea (1985).
3. This stand implies that so-called 'post-positivism' has to be rejected. In a recent article, Yosef Lapid (1989, p. 236) has argued that 'the empiricist-positivist promise for a cumulative behavioral science' has been proven to be unfounded. The thrust of Lapid's analysis appears to be that criteria which have hitherto been used to assess theoretical progress - and which are all lumped together under the epithet of 'positivism' - no longer apply. Lapid (1989, p. 250) advocates 'a more reflexive intellectual environment in which debate, criticism, and novelty can freely circulate. The international relations scholarly community - like all communities of inquiry - is communicatively constituted, and its success is partially conditioned by its ability to sustain and enhance the quality of argument in the context of deeply entrenched paradigmatic diversity.' Since Lapid does not present the reader with arguments for his expectation that 'freely circulating debate, criticism and novelty' will be realized, his plea in favour of post-positivism runs the risk of being mere 'wishful thinking'. In any case, Lapid does not offer criteria with which the value of theories is to be assessed. Holsti (1989, p. 257), in a response to Lapid, is therefore correct to ask whether the latter means that 'intellectual progress [is] measured solely by the accumulation of theories, a pluralism without purpose?'

2. The Theoretical Background of Dependency Theory

I INTRODUCTION

In the first chapter it has been argued that dependency theory is a quite distinct approach in the complex of theories of international relations. It has been demonstrated that it challenges the still dominant classical tradition, not only with respect to its central problems (subordination and exploitation vs diplomacy and war), but also to its unit of analysis (the capitalist world system vs the sovereign nation-states) and its image of the international system (hierarchy vs anarchy). Dependency theory can thus be interpreted as claiming to offer an explanation for international phenomena that is different from explanations provided by theories in the classical tradition, especially in respect of economic relations, development and the position of Third World countries.[1]

The origins of dependency theory are not as meta-theoretically inspired as the interpretation above is likely to suggest. The coming into being of the theory has mainly been induced by the rejection of the central concepts of other theories, thereby applying both its own and 'borrowed' concepts and approaches. The theories that have been attacked by dependency theorists are: liberal free trade theory, the E.C.L.A. approach and modernization theory. Concepts and approaches used in attacking these theories have for instance been derived from traditional economic and neo-Marxist theories of imperialism.

In this chapter, the focus will be on the relationship between dependency theory and these other theories which, all in their own way, deal with the connection between the presently developed and underdeveloped countries and/or the causes of the latter countries' lack of development. Sections II through VI will provide the background against which the theoretical progress of dependency theory can be assessed. Sections II and III will deal with, respectively, the traditional economic and neo-Marxist theories of imperialism, both of which have been important sources of the dependency scholars' theoretical insights. Sections IV through VI will analyse three kinds of theorizing that have been attacked by the representatives of the dependency perspective, that is, liberal theories of international trade, the so-called E.C.L.A. approach and theories of modernization. Section VII will contain the conclusions of the chapter.

II TRADITIONAL ECONOMIC THEORIES OF IMPERIALISM

To a certain degree, traditional economic theories can be seen as the archetypal formulation of explanations of imperialism. In many respects, D.K. Fieldhouse's characterization of these theories, and most notably of the Hobson and Lenin versions, as *The theory of capitalist imperialism* remains true until the present day. (1967, p. xv; cf. Fieldhouse 1984, pp. 3-9; Coppens 1980; Doyle 1986, pp. 22-30)

Many scholars, both those writing about imperialism *per se* and those dealing with the history of the study of international relations, have discussed the traditional economic theories of imperialism and its main representatives, such as Hobson, Lenin, Hilferding, Bukharin, and Luxemburg. (Cf. Brewer 1980, pp. 61-127; Dougherty and Pfaltzgraff 1981, pp. 213-50; Kiernan 1974; Mommsen 1980, pp. 11-49; Schröder 1973; Wehler 1972, pp. 104-54) Since much has been written about these theories, and since this is not the right place to dwell on specifics, the discussion of the contents of the traditional economic theories of imperialism will be limited to some of their most important representatives.

John Atkinson Hobson has analysed various imperialist relationships, most notably the relationship between Great Britain and its imperial possessions. Hobson himself summarized the central tenets of his work in the following way:

> [I]n nearly all cases where white peoples have brought under their sway lands peopled by coloured races, the earliest contacts have been of a commercial nature, and though considerations of political acquisition, colonial settlement and missionary services have been conscious supports, economic motives of trade and the exploitation of natural resources have been the dominant urges. (1988, p. [48])

From this it becomes clear that Hobson's explanation of imperialism is essentially economic in its orientation. The central element in the explanation is the alleged 'over-saving and under-spending' in capitalist economies. Since the effective demand is too low, due to the unequal distribution of the national income - according to Hobson the working classes receive too small a share of total income, and too much is saved by the owning classes - a substantial part of production remains unconsumed. As a consequence, the expectations of returns from investments become negative. Imperialism is the reaction to these two phenomena: it 'is the endeavour of the great controllers of industry to broaden the channel for the flow of their surplus wealth by seeking foreign markets and foreign investments to take off the goods and capital they cannot sell or use at home'. (1988, p. 85) Being a liberal, Hobson praises the benefits of international investment as 'sane' imperialism. (1988, pp. 223-37; cf. Townshend 1988, p. [29]; Cain 1979b, pp. 418 ff.)

According to Hobson, imperialism does not inevitably result from capitalism. The problems would be remediable, if only the capitalist state would diminish the huge inequality of economic and educational opportunities and raise its standard of consumption. (1988, pp. 86-8) Then they would no longer feel the need to 'fight for foreign markets'.

Rudolf Hilferding, in his book *Finance capital*, was one of the first authors to formulate a Marxist theory of imperialism. Finance capital means the 'unification of capital'. In Hilferding's words:

> The previously separate spheres of industrial, commercial and bank capital are now brought under the common direction of high finance, in which the masters of industry and of the banks are united in a close personal association. The basis of this association is the elimination of free competition among individual capitalists by the large monopolistic combines. This naturally involves at the same time a change in the relation of the capitalist class to state power. (1981, p. 301)

Finance capital is seen as the immediate result of the capitalist tendency toward the concentration of capital. The large enterprises, or, in the words of Hilferding, cartels, which come into being under capitalism, can realize huge profits and thereby stimulate the formation of large banks. In their turn, the banks encourage the cartelization of the economy in order to maximize the returns on money lent to the large enterprises. (1981, pp. 223-7)

Hilferding sees the export of capital as a condition for the rapid expansion of capitalism. (1981, pp. 311-36) Since the level of profit is argued to be higher in those areas where capitalism is less developed, finance capital will preferably invest in the pre-capitalist parts of the world. The opening of new markets is important not only for the level of profit realized by the capitalist enterprises: it also serves as a means for ending or moderating the recurrent crises of capitalism.

The state in capitalist countries has the function of pacifying the non-Western countries in order to create the conditions under which the export of capital can take place. (1981, p. 319) Inter-capitalist rivalry, and hence the potential for conflict, is enhanced by formal colonization. It is, however, not this rivalry that leads to the demise of capitalism. Capitalism will only be destroyed because the proletariat opposes the policy of finance capital and ceases to bear the burdens of this policy. (1981, pp. 364-70) With respect to the non-capitalist countries it is Hilferding's evaluation that, as they are reduced to being exporters of raw materials, the possibilities for a capitalist, as well as for a political and financial, development will be greatly limited. (1981, pp. 328-31)

Rosa Luxemburg has developed an entirely different view on imperialism. In her view, '[i]mperialism is the political expression of the process of capital accumulation in its competition for the rest of the non-capitalist world-environment which has not yet been taken into possession'. (1975, p. 391)[2] She explicitly focuses the analysis on the distinction between capitalist and non-capitalist modes of production. (Brewer 1980, p. 74) Luxemburg (1975, p. 307) visualizes capitalism as an economic system, comprising ever more parts of the globe until one single worldwide market comes into being.

The accumulation of capital is central to Luxemburg's inquiry of capitalist imperialism. In her view, capitalism needs to expand into previously non-capitalist areas in order to obtain sufficient means for accumulation, which is the prerequisite for its continued existence. As Luxemburg herself has phrased it:

> From the very beginning capitalist production, in its forms and laws of development, has been destined to comprise the entire world as a storehouse of productive forces. In its urge to appropriate productive forces for the purpose of exploitation, capital ransacks the entire world, provides itself with means of production from all corners of the earth, obtaining these from all levels of civilization and from all forms of society. (1975, p. 307)[3]

Luxemburg (1975, pp. 365-91) interprets imperialism as a distinct phase in the development of capitalism, in which foreign loans, the building of railways, the initiation of revolutions in the colonized areas and wars are the main mechanisms for the capitalist countries to serve their interests. Since it is her assumption that capitalist accumulation can only exist as long as there are non-capitalist territories that can be exploited, capitalist accumulation thus contains the seeds of its own decay.

According to Anthony Brewer, *Nikolai Bukharin* 'welded [Hilferding's slightly chaotic writing] into a coherent picture'. (1980, p. 103) Bukharin describes the development of a 'world economy', implying an international division of labour, in which all national economies are included. The main cause for the coming into being of such a world economy is 'the uneven development of productive forces in the various countries'. (1966, p. 20) International exchange of commodities is seen as the result of the international division of labour. Bukharin uses a modern-sounding vocabulary for the analysis of the 'world system', which is said to consist of 'consolidated, organised economic bodies ("the great civilised powers") on the one hand, and a periphery of undeveloped countries with a semi-agrarian or agrarian system on the other'. (1966, p. 74)

As a consequence of the development of capitalism, according to Bukharin, the world economy has shown an extraordinarily rapid growth. The internationalization of the economy leads to greater international interdependence: '[t]he growth of world market connections proceeds apace, tying up various sections of world economy into one strong knot'. (1966, p. 39) Capital becomes 'international': the number of international syndicates, cartels and trusts increases rather quickly, stimulated as it is by the finance capital of the capitalist countries.

At the same time, a parallel process of nationalization of capital takes place. According to Bukharin the national economy is transformed:

> into one gigantic combined enterprise under the tutelage of the financial kings and the capitalist state, an enterprise which monopolises the national market and forms the prerequisite for organised production on a higher non-capitalist level. (1966, pp. 73-4)

Subsequently, a conflict arises between the growth of the productive forces and the limits of the national economic system. Finance capital therefore induces the capitalist state to expand its territory, and this is how imperialism comes about. To Bukharin, imperialism 'is an integral element of finance capitalism without which the latter would lose its capitalist meaning'. (1966, p. 142) The expansion of the capitalist states is meant to relieve the tensions created by the lack of markets, of raw materials and of investment opportunities. Although for some time the proletariat will benefit by the imperialist policy of the finance capitalists, in the end the inevitable imperialist wars will hurt exactly this part of the nation. Then the proletariat will turn against imperialism and 'the dictatorship of finance capital'. (1966, pp. 161-7)

The pamphlet *Imperialism, the highest stage of capitalism*, written by *Vladimir Ilich Lenin*, is probably the best-known of all Marxist works on imperialism, even though Brewer argues that 'it makes little or no contribution to the development of a theory of imperialism [and i]ts theoretical content is slight and derives from Hilferding, Bukharin and Hobson'. (1980, p. 108)

Lenin starts from the insight that modern capitalism is characterized by a concentration of production in monopolistic enterprises. Banks also play an important role in modern capitalism. Finance capital is the result of these developments.

According to Lenin, the capitalist economy distinguishes itself by the existence of a 'surplus of capital', for which there are no profitable investment opportunities in the capitalist country itself. To remedy the decreasing level of profit, the capitalists turn abroad and export their capital to 'backward' countries. The world is divided among the big monopolist enterprises, working together in international cartels. It is further assumed that the state apparatuses of the capitalist countries support the capitalist enterprises and begin to wage a struggle for spheres of influences.

Imperialism is interpreted by Lenin as 'a special stage of capitalism': it is 'the monopoly stage of capitalism'. Lenin's definition of imperialism is as follows:

> Imperialism is capitalism at that stage of development at which the dominance of monopolies and finance capital is established; in which the export of capital has acquired pronounced importance; in which the division of the world among the international trusts has begun, in which the division of all territories of the globe among the biggest capitalist powers has been completed. (1964, pp. 266-7)

Imperialism is not just a special stage of capitalism, it is the *final* stage as well. The decay of capitalism is caused by the 'parasitic' character of imperialism. Because of the monopolies existing in the imperialist stage, the economic flexibility of capitalism is greatly reduced. Moreover, the number of *rentiers* becomes very large and the growing awareness of this fact fosters the resistance against capitalism of the oppressed groups in capitalist society and in the colonized areas. The revolt of the oppressed groups will supposedly bring an end to capitalism.

III NEO-MARXIST THEORIES OF IMPERIALISM

In the preceding section the most important scholars representing the traditional economic approach to imperialism have been dealt with. It is far more difficult, if not outright impossible, to give a similar, equally authoritative line-up of neo-Marxists. First, the number of these writers is far greater. (Cf. Griffin and Gurley 1985, pp. 1099 ff.) Second, 'history' has not yet judged the lasting value of the works of recent writers as it has the traditional economic theories. For these reasons, several neo-Marxist scholars who seem sufficiently important will be considered in this section. These are: Maurice Dobb, Paul A. Baran, Paul M. Sweezy, Michael Barratt Brown, Harry Magdoff, and Arghiri Emmanuel.[4]

Maurice Dobb, a British economist, offers an economic interpretation of imperialism along the lines set out by Lenin and Hilferding. (1937, pp.

226-72) In Dobb's view, imperialism is the expression of highly developed capitalism, in which the rate of profit on invested capital shows a tendency to decline. The main causes for this tendency are, according to Dobb: first, the accumulation and concentration of capital, which leads to a reduction of the opportunities to invest in the capitalist countries, and, second, the shortage of labour, leading to an increase of wages. The attempt to counter the tendency of the rate of profit to fall leads to imperialism, in which 'the export of capital comes to play a dominant rôle, and with it the export of capital goods and the hypertrophy of the industries producing the latter'. (1937, p. 233)

For the underdeveloped regions the main effect of imperialism is 'an accentuated inequality of development between different countries and different areas'. (1937, p. 252) According to Dobb, capitalism is not likely to have an equally progressive impact on the underdeveloped countries as it has had on the presently capitalist ones. For political reasons the capitalist states often support reactionary social and political forms, and the capitalists force the underdeveloped countries to perpetuate their relatively primitive forms of production for fear of competition. As a consequence, foreign investments have mainly gone into 'mining and plantations and raw material processing, or into the development of export industries as a kind of "enclave" of the imperial metropolis'. (1963, p. 18)

Paul A. Baran and *Paul M. Sweezy*, two well-known neo-Marxist economists, have published several works on the development of capitalism and on imperialism, both together and separately.

In 1942 Sweezy published *The theory of capitalist development*, which, according to Brewer (1980, p. 132), can be seen as 'an important bridge' between traditional Marxist writings and recent work. Sweezy's argument focuses on the crises in the capitalist economy. The central element in his analysis of capitalism is underconsumption, which is interpreted as the result of the capitalists' actions to reduce the wage level. (1946, pp. 162-89) Imperialism is seen as a corollary of capital becoming monopolistic. Since the objective of monopoly is interpreted as 'the reaping of extra profits through raising price and limiting supply', Sweezy (1946, p. 299) argues that monopoly capital requires the erection of tariff barriers. This restriction of trade, which subsequently becomes characteristic for all capitalist countries, leads to higher average production costs and to attempts to find alternative outlets for products. For this reason, the capitalist states begin to expand their territory. In order to avoid the competition of other enterprises and to ensure the monopoly's exclusive access to raw materials, the foreign regions are put under the political control of the capitalist states. (1946, pp. 299-302)

According to Sweezy, the consequences of the imperialist expansion for the 'backward areas' are not positive: 'The interests of both native bourgeoisie and native masses are sacrificed to the needs of capital in the advanced countries.' (1946, p. 305) Imperialism has not stimulated the industrialization of the dominated areas, nor has it benefited the development of these areas. On the contrary, as Sweezy (1946, pp. 305-6 and 326-7) has concluded, the capital export of the developed countries has led to a one-sided development of the economies of the receiving countries: the handicraft industry is destroyed as a result of the import of cheap manufactures and agriculture experiences an ever-mounting crisis, partly as a consequence of the inflow of unemployed handicraft workers.

In *The political economy of growth*, published in 1957, Paul A. Baran paid considerable attention to the effects of external domination on the economies of the developing countries. In his view, 'economic development in underdeveloped countries is profoundly inimical to the dominant interests in the advanced capitalist countries'. (1957, p. 12)

Baran argues that the monopolization of capitalism and the resulting excess of capital are the main causes of imperialism. In the aforementioned book, as well as in *Monopoly capital*, which Baran published together with Sweezy, it is asserted that capitalism in its monopoly phase is characterized by a tendency of rising surplus value. (Baran 1957, pp. 44-133; Baran and Sweezy 1966) The main cause for this development is assumed to be the insignificance of price competition under monopoly capitalism. Since the lack of competition leads to higher prices than would be feasible under competitive capitalism, the surplus obtained by monopolistic enterprises will eventually increase to such an extent that it can no longer be absorbed by reinvestment in the firms, nor by investment in other parts of the economy. The economic surplus is then used in other ways. The state in capitalist countries, which, according to Baran, is nothing more than an instrument in the hands of the bourgeoisie, provides an outlet by spending the surplus on 'unproductive purposes of all kinds', most notably on military activities. (Baran 1957, pp. 108-9 and 118-9; Baran and Sweezy 1966, pp. 178-217) The export of capital is also an important instrument for the spending of economic surplus. (Baran 1957, pp. 109-33; cf. Baran and Sweezy 1972; Sweezy and Magdoff 1972)

The main negative effect of the ties between the capitalist and the underdeveloped countries is that the latter are unable to establish a capitalist order. As a result of the 'unilateral transfers' of wealth from the non-European countries to the European colonizers, 'the accumulation of capital in the hands of the more or less steadily expanding and rising class of merchants and wealthy peasants', which according to Baran is the 'strategic precondition for the emergence of capitalism', did not take place in the countries that later turned out to be underdeveloped. (1957, pp. 137-8)

The main reason for the economic backwardness of the underdeveloped countries is to be found in the way in which the economic surplus is used. This surplus, the main part of which is produced in agriculture, is appropriated by landowners, moneylenders, merchants, the state bureaucracy of the underdeveloped countries, and, to a large extent, foreign capitalists. The foreign capitalists 'take home' the surplus as the returns on their investment, while the others tend to spend their part of the surplus in an unproductive way, for instance on 'excess consumption'. In Baran's view (1957, chapters 6 and 7), all groups engaged in the exploitation of the underdeveloped countries share one interest, namely, the maintenance of the subordinate position of the agricultural and working classes in the developed countries.

In a short article published in 1967, Sweezy has formulated the idea that trade and investment relations between advanced and underdeveloped countries do not stimulate, but rather frustrate the development of the latter. In his words,

> the first and most important obstacle to the economic development of the underdeveloped countries is their relationship to the advanced capitalist countries which dominate and exploit them. Until this relationship is either completely ruptured or totally transformed - and of the latter there seems to be absolutely no prospect in the foreseeable future - talk about overcoming the many other obstacles to economic development is at best naive and at worst deliberately deceptive. (1967, p. 197)

Michael Barratt Brown (1970, p. 14), an English neo-Marxist economist, has investigated to what extent the gap between the rich and poor countries of the world is due to the political and economic dependence of the poor upon the rich, in other words, to imperialist relations. According to Barratt Brown, the main reason for imperialism and the colonization of the non-Western world is to be found in needs emanating from capital accumulation and industrialization in the Western countries. The manufacturing, or capitalist, classes in the European countries succeeded in inducing their governments to pursue imperialist policies, aimed at securing the import of raw materials for the newly created industries and at providing outlets for expanding European manufacture. (Barratt Brown 1970, pp. 25-48; cf. 1972)

The imperialist relationship with the colonies turned out to be beneficial for the European countries: their terms of trade between industrial and primary products changed for the better, they were provided with capital needed to finance their industrialization, and capital owners obtained ample opportunities for investment. The effects on the dependent countries, as analysed by Barratt Brown, proved to be negative: no entrepreneurial class managed to develop there, since 'the whole purpose of the operation, i.e. to provide raw materials for British and European industry, worked against the development of industries in the primary producing countries'. (1970, p. 59; cf. pp. 158-86)

Barratt Brown (1970, pp. 253-90; 1972, pp. 64-7) argues that the disappearance of the large colonial empires after World War II does not imply that the fundamental inequality and subordination of states has been terminated. The main agents of 'new style' imperialism are transnational companies, investing in the non-Western countries and as a result extracting large amounts of profit from their economies. As Barratt Brown has written, '[t]he world-wide "synergy" of the trans-national company is, on this view, the logical conclusion of a long historical process of capital accumulation and territorial assimilation'. (1974, p. 228)

Harry Magdoff is also an important and prolific neo-Marxist scholar writing on modern imperialism. He interprets imperialism as 'the competitive struggle among the industrial nations for dominant positions with respect to the *world* market and raw material sources'. (1969, p. 15) According to Magdoff, this description of imperialism can be applied to the 'new' imperialism arising in the late nineteenth century, as well as to more recent forms of 'imperialism without colonies':

> The desire and need to operate on a world scale is built into the economics of capitalism. Competitive pressures, technical advances, and recurring imbalances between productive capacity and effective demand create continuous pressures for the expansion of markets. (1972, p. 148; cf. 1978, pp. 17-113)

The development of imperialism is accompanied by an increase of the economic power of an ever-smaller number of large integrated industrial and financial companies. (Magdoff 1969, pp. 27-66)

According to Magdoff the presently developed countries have obtained a higher standard of living and a great amount of capital by the exploitation of non-Western countries, both during the colonialist and the neo-colonialist phases of history. The imperialist dominance is often reflected in the control over the sources of raw materials, the conquest of foreign markets and foreign investment.

The 'financial sector' occupies an important place in Magdoff's explanation of imperialism. Magdoff argues that the emergence of the United States as the world's major imperialist power has been accompanied by a heightened foreign activity of its banks and by the dollar's rise to prominence as the international reserve currency. As a consequence of its financial power, the United States is considered to be in a position to sustain and enhance control over other countries by private investment, governmental foreign aid and military expenditures. (Magdoff 1969, pp. 117-65; 1978, pp. 198-212)

Arghiri Emmanuel has analysed *trade relations* as the central elements of imperialism. His central assumption is that the value of commodities on the international market is not formed in the same way as on national markets, since labour - in contrast to capital - is not mobile across national borders. As a consequence of this, according to Emmanuel (1972, p. ix), there is no equalization of wages among countries comparable to the equalization of the rates of profit. The wage differences persisting as a result of these characteristics of the capitalist world economy are detrimental to the prosperity of the peripheral countries.

In Emmanuel's theory of unequal exchange it is the disproportionate inequality of wages, as compared to the value of labour power embodied in commodities - which is assumed to be roughly equal in all countries -, that leads to the transfer of surplus from the underdeveloped to the developed countries. In his view, the belief that trade is, or can be, beneficial to all participants - as is argued in the liberal theory of international trade (see section IV) - indicates that theorists have lost sight of the exploitative nature of trade between developed and underdeveloped countries.

Emmanuel's analysis (1972, pp. 189-93) is based on the idea that wages are the *independent* variable in the process of price formation. If the workers of a country are able to demand higher wages - as in the developed countries where there are strong labour unions - the rate of surplus value and the rate of profit in the country concerned will decrease in favour of the wages.

The relative rise of wage levels in developed countries, according to Emmanuel, leads to a worsening of the terms of trade of the underdeveloped countries. An increase of wages in the developed countries will lead to a rise of the production prices of their commodities. Since the workers in the developing countries cannot influence their wages in the same way, the prices of the developed countries' products will exhibit a relative rise. As a consequence, the rate of exchange between developed and underdeveloped countries will alter to the benefit of the former: they will be able to buy more commodities abroad with the proceeds from the sale of the same quantity of export goods as before. (Emmanuel 1972, pp. 202-5)

IV LIBERAL THEORIES OF INTERNATIONAL TRADE

The Western liberal theory of free trade is one of the most important theoretical traditions upon which the dependency theorists have reacted. This tradition, which was started by David Ricardo, and has been elaborated upon by many liberal economists in the nineteenth and twentieth centuries, has had a crucial influence on contemporary economic theorizing about international trade. In this section, attention will be paid to the writings of 'classical' free trade theorists, such as David Ricardo and Richard Cobden, and to the work of more modern economists such as Paul A. Samuelson and W.M. Corden.

In his classic book on the principles of political economy, the British economist *David Ricardo* laid the foundations of what came to be known as the liberal theory of international trade. (1971, pp. 147-67, 269-77, 301-18 and 334-41) Basically, Ricardo adheres to the labour theory of value, meaning that in his theory '[t]he value of a commodity, or the quantity for any other commodity for which it will exchange, depends on the relative quantity of labour which is necessary for its production, and not on the greater or less compensation which is paid for that labour'. (1971, p. 55)

Under a system of perfectly free trade, Ricardo argues, each country will use its labour and capital for the production of commodities for which the country has a 'relative advantage' and which therefore is most beneficial to it. Trade is basically seen as a means of obtaining commodities in other countries where they are produced more efficiently than in the country itself. Without such free trade, all countries would be worse off, as Ricardo shows by describing Portugal's situation:

> If Portugal had no commercial connexion with other countries, instead of employing a great part of her capital and industry in the production of wines, with which she purchases for her own use the cloth and hardware of other countries, she would be obliged to devote a part of that capital to the manufacture of those commodities, which she would thus obtain probably inferior in quality as well as quantity. (1971, p. 153)

The *rationale* for trade is to be found in the differences of labour hours that have to be used in order to produce a given quantity of goods.

According to Ricardo, trade would be beneficial for countries, even if one country were in a position to produce *all* commodities with less labour than other countries. In this case, the *principle of comparative advantages* would make trade interesting for all partners. This means that all countries would benefit from trade if all were to specialize in the production of those commodities requiring the least amount of labour.

Inspired by this logic, Ricardo protested against the levying of duties on imports and the subsidizing of exports. In his view, such measures lead to inefficient production: they would 'divert a portion of capital to an employment, which it would not naturally seek'. (1971, pp. 312-3) These measures would inspire manufacturers to continue or even begin the production of commodities which, judged from the perspective of given labour productivity, could better be taken over by foreign producers. Seen from a macro-national perspective, this situation would reduce overall economic wealth. (Hartwell 1971, p. 27)

The British liberal *Richard Cobden* followed in Ricardo's footsteps by taking up the latter's plea for the repeal of import duties. In Cobden's view, all peoples of the world have one common interest: the avoidance of armed conflicts. The creation of a mutual dependence among different economies by free trade would stimulate politicians to retain peaceful relations in order not to disturb the economic contacts. (See Cobden 1878, pp. 181-7; Cain 1979a, pp. 229-47; Hout 1987)

As a political activist in nineteenth century England, Cobden also indicated what would be the advantages for the English if free trade would be accepted as the principle for conducting international economic relations. According to Cobden, as a consequence of the *Corn Laws,* which put duties on the importation of foreign corn, the British economy suffered a loss of wealth. The repeal of the Corn Laws would bring an end to this unhealthy situation: the wages of the labourers could be reduced, thereby improving the ability of British firms to compete with foreign producers, especially those from the United States. According to Cobden (1868), the nation as a whole would benefit from the increased economic activity that would result. (Cf. Read 1967, pp. 209-18)

The Swedish economists *Eli Heckscher* and *Bertil Ohlin* have put forward ideas about the effect of international trade on the rewards of factors of production, or factor prices. The original Heckscher-Ohlin model has been extended by *Paul A. Samuelson.*

The basic idea presented by Heckscher and Ohlin is that a country tends to specialize in the production of those commodities which uses that country's most abundant factor of production. As a result of this specialization and the ensuing trade, the factor prices in the trading countries tend to become more equal: in all countries specialization will lead to an increase in the production of certain goods and, as a consequence, the demand for the factors used in this production process will grow and the reward for the factors will go up. (Samuelson 1948, pp. 163-9)

Samuelson's extension is concerned with factor-price equalization. In his view, in a situation of perfectly free trade there is no reason to assume that the equalization of factor prices will halt at a certain point. As Samuelson writes: 'not only is factor-price equalisation possible and probable, but in a wide variety of circumstances it is inevitable'. (1948, p. 169)

The modern formulation of the liberal free trade theory starts from the proposition 'that there are gains from trade and, more specifically, that given certain assumptions, not only is free trade Pareto-superior to autarky but it is also Pareto-efficient, being superior to various degrees of trade restriction'. (Corden 1984, p. 69) *Paul A. Samuelson, Murray C. Kemp* and *W.M. Corden* are but three, yet very important, modern authors representing this theoretical approach.

In several articles, Samuelson and Kemp have demonstrated theoretically that countries gain by engaging in free trade or some kind of restricted trade if, previously, they did not have any trade at all. In 1939, Samuelson formulated the following theorem:

> [T]he introduction of outside (relative) prices differing from those which would be established in our economy in isolation will result in some trade, and as a result every individual will be better off than he would be at the prices which prevailed in the isolated state. (1950, pp. 245-6)

Samuelson limited himself to the so-called small country case, in which a country engaging in trade is not large enough to influence its terms of trade.

An extension of Samuelson's theorem has been offered by Murray C. Kemp, who argued that it is not necessary to limit the argumentation about the gains from international trade to the small country case: regardless of the size of the trading countries, trade will be advantageous. Kemp acknowledges, however, that a large country, which can exert influence over the prices of traded commodities, might actually gain by introducing an 'optimal tariff'. Samuelson, in his 1962 article, reaches the same conclusion as Kemp. Notwithstanding some qualifications to the general validity of his conclusions, he emphatically writes:

> Only at a point reachable by free trade would an international individualistic social welfare function be at its *maximum maximorum*. [...] For a given country, autarky cannot be optimal if ideal transfers are possible. Some trade is better than no trade in the sense of making the nation better off, with a farther out consumption-possibility frontier and farther out utility-possibility frontier. (1962, p. 829)

W.M. Corden has begun to break 'the link between the case for free trade and the case for laissez-faire'. (1974, p. 4) In his approach the concept of domestic distortions is a central one. This concept points out that most arguments in favour of trade restrictions focus on distortions in the domestic economy, or 'market failures' (Corden 1984, p. 86), and not on problems in trade relations with other countries. According to the theory of domestic distortions, reactions to these distortions in the form of trade restrictions are bound to be second-best solutions since they do not get to the bottom of the original problem. (Corden 1974, pp. 31-3) In these cases it is optimal to adhere to free trade and try to solve the domestic divergences with direct measures, such as the subsidizing of labour costs or production.

V THE E.C.L.A. APPROACH

The ideas initiated by the Economic Commission for Latin America (E.C.L.A.), a United Nations organization instituted to further the development of Latin America, are closely linked with the work of *Raúl Prebisch*, E.C.L.A.'s first executive secretary. In this section, therefore, much attention will be paid to Prebisch's writings.

In the works of E.C.L.A. the position of the Latin American countries is analysed in terms of their role in the international division of labour; according to the authors, the experience of Latin America can be generalized to the Third World at large. The integration of Latin America in the international division of labour leads to a structurally adverse situation: the Latin American countries are largely dependent on the production of food and raw materials for the industrial countries. Prebisch has summed up the consequences of this situation as follows:

> The enormous benefits that derive from increased productivity have not reached the periphery in a measure comparable to that obtained by the peoples of the great industrial countries. Hence, the outstanding differences between the standards of living of the masses of the former and the latter and the manifest discrepancies between their respective abilities to accumulate capital, since the margin of saving depends primarily on increased productivity. (1950, p. 1)

The principal problem hindering Latin American development is defined as the lack of capital needed for successful industrialization. Industrialization is necessary for the countries to absorb the surplus of labour that is the result of increased productivity in the agricultural sector of the economy. (Economic Commission for Latin America 1951, pp. 4-5) Since, however, the income of the people in Latin America is generally low, the level of savings is too low to be able to finance investment with internal means. It is argued that exports do not offer a way out, either: to a large extent the Latin American countries depend on the production of primary products (raw materials and agricultural products) and the elasticity of demand for these kinds of products is so low that attempts to increase the exports are self-defeating.

This way of reasoning has led Prebisch, among others, to reject the liberal theory of free trade. In reaction to this theory, Prebisch formulated his ideas on the steady worsening of the terms of trade. According to Prebisch, the industrialized countries of the centre are able to retain most of the fruits of technological progress in industrial production, whereas the countries of the periphery have to share their gains:

> The center is in a better position to retain the fruits of its general increase in productivity because the increment in manpower does not need, as in the periphery, to press on occupations with a lower productivity ratio to the detriment of the wage level. In other words, general improvements in productivity tend to be fully reflected in the increment of the wage level at the center, while at the periphery a part of the fruits of these improvements is transferred through the fall of export prices and the corresponding deterioration in the terms of trade. (1959, p. 262; cf. Singer 1950)

When a country's terms of trade deteriorate, it is argued, the value of its production in terms of foreign products decreases. This means that for a given amount of agricultural products or raw materials an ever-decreasing amount of industrial products can be obtained. By implication, the relative wealth of the country declines.

It is exactly because of this supposedly structural element of international relations that Prebisch and E.C.L.A. have formulated an alternative development strategy for developing countries. This strategy has become known under the name of 'import substitution' or 'import-substituting industrialization'. Import substitution is seen as an instrument for reducing the differences in income elasticities of demand for imports and exports. The strategy can thereby correct the structural imbalances in international economic relations. (Prebisch 1959, p. 254; cf. Hirschman 1969) The aim of the strategy is to reduce, in the initial phase, the imports of finished consumer goods and, if this reduction proves to be successful, the imports of intermediate and capital goods. At the same time, industries in the developing countries must take over the production of the previously imported goods, so that the countries are able to reduce their dependence on foreign markets. Under a policy of import substitution the means that previously were employed to produce export goods would be available for the production of goods for the internal market. (Prebisch 1950, pp. 44-5)

VI MODERNIZATION THEORIES

Under the heading of modernization theory many different approaches to the phenomenon of modernization can be subsumed. Authors from economics, sociology, anthropology and political science have contributed to modernization theory. In this section the attention will be focused on the contributions of scholars such as Rostow, Hoselitz, Lerner, Almond, Coleman, Apter, Pye and Huntington.

W.W. Rostow, in *The stages of economic growth*, has presented an economic interpretation of modernization. In this book, five successive stages have been distinguished in the process of modernization. It is perhaps because of the simplicity of the approach that Rostow's work has become archetypal for modernization theory.

The 'analytic bone-structure' of the stages of the modernization process is to be found in production relations, specifically in 'the distribution of income between consumption, saving, and investment [...] the composition of investment and [...] developments within particular sectors of the economy'. (Rostow 1960, p. 13) The *traditional stage* is characterized by a society in which the attainable output per capita is limited, partly because production is predominantly agricultural. The *preconditions for take-off* develop under the influence of scientific progress; scientific innovations are applied in, for instance, agriculture, thereby increasing the funds available for investment. The actual *take-off stage* is usually triggered off by a particular stimulus, often from outside the national society. The prior development of the society and its economy leads to self-sustained growth: investment levels are higher than before - especially in transport, which has a stimulating effect on the whole economy - and important manufacturing sectors experience high rates of growth. For this to happen, an entrepreneurial elite must have developed. The *drive to maturity* is characterized by the growth of new economic sectors, supplanting the leading sectors of the take-off stage; in Europe, new activity was mainly concentrated in heavy industry which took the place of agriculture as an important part of the economy. In the *age of high mass-consumption*, consumption instead of production occupies a central place in society. Rostow (1960, pp. 17-92) sees three possible developments in this phase: the pursuit of power in the form of investment in military strength, the emphasis on the welfare state and the expansion of consumption.

According to Rostow, economic modernization is complemented by *political development*, which is to be perceived as 'the elaboration of new and more complex forms of politics and government as societies restructure themselves so as to absorb progressively the stock and flow of modern technology which is, essentially, uniform'. (1971, p. 3) The process of economic growth places several issues on the political agenda, most notably: welfare, constitutional, and security issues.

Bert F. Hoselitz is considered to be one of the most important scholars who has written about the sociological aspects of modernization. His contribution to modernization theory started as a critique of dominant theories of economic growth. (1960, p. 24)

Since economic development in Hoselitz' view is associated with a more complex division of labour, more developed societies are characterized by an increased specificity of productive tasks. Along with this, the economic process becomes universalized, jobs are distributed by means of competition or ascription and the orientation of the elites becomes more collectivity-focused. With respect to the development of presently underdeveloped countries, Hoselitz stresses that '[t]he very needs of economic advancement must bring about a gradual replacement of ascription as a standard by achievement, and associated with this a replacement of functional diffuseness by functional specificity and particularism by universalism'. (1960, p. 47)

With respect to actual development, Hoselitz has written that:

> apparently one of the primary conditions for increasing industrial development on a world-wide scale, particularly in the economically less advanced countries, is the change in certain social and consequently general psychological conditions still standing in the way of more rapid and effective industrial development. (1965, p. 93)

In the process of development, the so-called entrepreneur plays a crucial role. Industrial development is often seen as a process depending on the activities of such a person. The social environment has to be conducive for entrepreneurs to function: society has to accept that a person, who to a certain extent is 'deviant', plays such an important role. (Hoselitz 1960, pp. 61-8)

Daniel Lerner has also stressed the sociological and psychological components of modernization. Lerner defines modernity as:

> primarily a *state of mind* - expectation of progress, propensity to growth, readiness to adapt oneself to change. The nations of the North Atlantic area first developed the social processes - secularization, urbanization, industrialization, popular participation - by which this state of mind came to prevail. The 'Western Model' is only historically Western; sociologically it is global. (1964, p. iix)

Rationality is a key concept in Lerner's theory of modernization. It implies that people see their future as manipulable, not as given; as a consequence, *mobility* and *change* have become central elements of society. During the process of modernization, people learn to adapt themselves to new demands, imposed on them by society and their natural environment. Modern society, in Lerner's view, is also a participant society: people want to take part in decision-making, they keep in touch with, and have opinions on, public matters. Mass media, therefore, are an indispensable element of modernity: they help to enhance people's experiences of phenomena that do not take place in their direct environment. (Lerner 1964, p. 52)

Modernization is perceived as the process by which participant societies develop. The evolution of such societies involves at least three stages, which have been summed up by Lerner as urbanization, literacy and mass communication. This is seen as a general sequence of stages: 'the model of modernization follows an autonomous historical logic - [...] each phase tends to generate the next phase by some mechanism which operates independently of cultural or doctrinal variations'. (1964, p. 61)

Gabriel A. Almond and *James S. Coleman* have laid the foundations of a political scientific theory of modernization with their co-edited *The politics of the developing areas*. The book adopts a 'functional' approach: the analysis of the political system is cast in terms of the functions performed.

The core of the functional approach to politics is based on the assumptions that all political systems have a political structure, that the same functions are performed in all political systems, that every political structure is multifunctional, and that all political systems contain elements of rationality and traditionality. (Almond 1960, pp. 11-25) The functions that are distinguished on the input side of the political system, are: political socialization and recruitment, interest articulation, interest aggregation and political communication. On the output side, the functions are: rule-making, rule application and rule adjudication. All of these functions can be performed by various political structures. According to Almond, the functions are general ones and 'political systems may be compared with one another in terms of the frequency and style of the performance of political *functions* by *political* structures'. (1960, p. 61)

According to Coleman,

> [t]he most general characteristic of [a modern political system] is the relatively high degree of differentiation, explicitness, and functional distinctiveness of political and governmental structures, each of which tends to perform, for the political system as a whole, a regulatory role for the respective political and authoritative functions. (1960, p. 532)

Judged by these criteria, 'Anglo-American polities most closely approximate the model of a modern political system'; this judgment is made not simply because these polities are competitive, but because their so-called secondary structures - structures performing formal political and legal tasks - are far more differentiated and tend to penetrate and modernize the informal, diffuse and particularistic primary structures. (Coleman 1960, p. 533)

The two most important conclusions drawn by Coleman appear to be that most developing countries are far removed from modernity and that there is a positive correlation between economic development and political competitiveness, which is seen as 'an essential attribute of democracy'.

In a later work, Almond has further specified the views laid out above. Political development is defined as the acquisition of new capabilities. In the course of history several problems have arisen for which political systems had to develop new capabilities. According to Almond, a more developed political system has been more successful in:

> the acquisition of a new capability, in the sense of a specialized role structure and differentiated orientations which together give a political system the possibility of responding effectively, and more or less autonomously, to a new range of problems. (1970, p. 172)

David E. Apter has also analysed modernization in structural-functionalist terms. He emphasizes *authority* as a central element for the theory of modernization. The risks involved in modernizing non-industrialized societies are to be found in the lack of integration of these societies. Political roles change as a result of the modernization process: roles become less 'ritualized' and less dependent upon 'ascription'. The role of the party politician is crucial in the context of political modernization, because political parties have to be the main instruments of modernization. (Apter 1967, p. 179)

Lucian W. Pye has placed more emphasis upon non-formal political aspects of the modernization process. In his view, modernization has too often been equated with the development of administrative and legal structures. In the modernization process, which, in Pye's view, also has to be a process of nation-building, the spread of political capacities among the population is a crucial element. (1966, p. 16)

Samuel P. Huntington, in his famous *Political order in changing societies*, focuses on political stability or political order as a goal during processes of modernization. Huntington identifies a 'political gap' between developed and developing societies in the same vein as there is an economic gap. The political violence and instability characterizing societies with such a political gap 'was in large part the product of rapid social change and the rapid mobilization of new groups into politics coupled with the slow development of political institutions'. (1968, p. 4)

Modernization, according to Huntington, implies social modernization, 'a change in the attitudes, values and expectations of people from those associated with the traditional world to those common to the modern world', and economic development, 'the growth in the total economic activity and output of a society'. (1968, pp. 33-4) As a result of this social mobilization, people will obtain higher levels of wants and aspirations, yet in developing countries the level of economic development is usually such that these cannot be fully satisfied. The resulting social frustration is then likely to lead to demands on the political system and to increasing political participation to enforce those demands. Whether political stability or instability will be the result depends on the political institutions: in situations where political systems show successful development in handling the increased level of participation, stability will be reached; if political institutionalization does not keep pace with participation, instability will result. (Huntington 1968, pp. 78-92)

Under the auspices of the Social Science Research Council's Committee on Comparative Politics between 1963 and 1971 seven books were published which dealt with political modernization and development. It is impossible to summarize the central theses of these books, since they are collections of contributions by several dozens of authors. Moreover, as one reputed commentator on the field has indicated, '[a]n obligatory opening footnote citing the Committee's work would be encountered in many monographs and articles, but there would be little evidence that it made a contribution to method of substance'. (Migdal 1983, p. 310) Problems that have been dealt with in the series include: communication, bureaucracy, education, political culture, political parties and political crises.

VII THE PROBLEM-SOLVING CAPACITY OF DEPENDENCY THEORY

In the first chapter, the concept of scientific progress has been introduced in order to set up a framework with the help of which the value of theories can be judged. According to Larry Laudan, who has developed the so-called problem-solving approach, theories and research traditions must be judged primarily on their problem-solving capacity. The characterizations of, respectively, the traditional economic theories of imperialism, the neo-Marxist theories of imperialism, the liberal theories of international trade, the E.C.L.A. approach and the modernization theories, have been given in the previous sections so that in this section the problem-solving capacity of dependency theory can be judged. In the following chapters an attempt will be made to assess the empirical value of three variants of dependency theory.

A Dependency Theory and the Traditional Economic Theories of Imperialism

Many authors have stressed the resemblance of the dependency approach and traditional economic theories of imperialism. However, since there are important differences separating both approaches, the relationship between them should mainly be interpreted as one of inspiration and orientation. (Palma 1978 and 1979; Griffin and Gurley 1985)

Hoogvelt, for instance, has argued that dependency theory should be seen as the product of the application of Marxist theories of imperialism, to the extent that they address the effects of imperialism on the subordinate nations. (1982, p. 165) According to Warren, the traditional Marxist theories of imperialism, and Lenin's version in particular, have resulted in the conviction that capitalism and imperialism are negative and even 'reactionary' forces in developing countries. As Warren (1980, p. 50) has argued, this way of looking at capitalism and imperialism has wrongly influenced later writers, such as neo-Marxists and dependency theorists. Mommsen (1980, pp. 101 ff.) sees the parallel between the theories mainly in the traditional 'key concept' of monopoly capitalism, which, according to him, experienced a 'renaissance' in dependency and world system theories. (Cf. Chilcote 1974)

Brewer has qualified the supposedly negative judgment about imperialism made by the traditional Marxist theorists. According to him, the latter 'did not anticipate a growing gulf between advanced and underdeveloped areas'. On the contrary, they 'expected the development of capitalism to lead to a growing uniformity in methods of production and in the standard of living of the bulk of the population throughout the world'. (1980, p. 158) Moreover, Brewer (1980, p. 159) has pointed out that the dependency theorists have defined capitalism as a 'system of monopolistic exchange', an interpretation of capitalism fundamentally different from the Marxist one, which stresses the relations of production.

Walleri has indicated the problemshift that can be witnessed in dependency theory: whereas the traditional economic theories stressed the causes of imperialism originating in the contradictions of capitalism, dependency theory has paid more attention to the consequences of imperialist relations for the Third World. Moreover, the traditional theories studied 'formal' imperialism, whereas dependency theory has mainly been concerned with 'informal' neocolonialism. (Walleri 1978b, pp. 604-5)

Since this is not the place to elaborate on the problem which of the interpretations of the traditional economic theories of imperialism is the correct one, only a brief conclusion will be drawn here; a general conclusion about the traditional economic and neo-Marxist theories of imperialism will be presented at the end of subsection B. The dependency approach has certainly been inspired by the traditional theories of imperialism. The most important influence has been one of inspiration and orientation. Concepts such as 'imperialism', 'finance capital', 'monopoly capitalism', 'accumulation' and 'exploitation' have been used by dependency theorists to explain the underdevelopment of the Third World countries. They applied thoughts from the traditional economic theories of imperialism without taking over the whole line of reasoning, if only because the international environment has changed to a great extent. Another reason why the dependency theorists have not followed their traditional predecessors to the full is to be found in the problemshift of the new theories, that is, from an explanation of the causes of the imperialist policy of the capitalist countries to an interpretation of the consequences of this policy for the underdeveloped countries.

B Dependency Theory and the Neo-Marxist Theories of Imperialism

Some authors writing about neo-Marxist theories of imperialism and dependency theory assume both types of theories to be different members of one species. The works of Barone (1985, pp. 85-143), Brewer (1980, pp. 15-24), Edelstein (1982, pp. 103-7) and Foster-Carter (1980) are but four examples of this line of reasoning. Other authors, such as Laclau (1971), have stressed the contrast between neo-Marxist and dependency theories.

Barone simply considers dependency theory to be a new variant of the neo-Marxist theorizing on imperialism. According to Barone, it 'represents a major advance in the Marxist theory of imperialism. [...] It has provided an analytic structure that has furthered our understanding of contemporary imperialism and the history of underdevelopment in the Third World'. (1985, p. 101)

Brewer has also argued that dependency theory is part of the Marxist tradition, and that it has contributed to the development of this tradition by filling the gap left open in (neo-) Marxist theories of imperialism: the explanation of underdevelopment. The application of a definition of capitalism that differs from the standard Marxist one - capitalism as a mode of exchange instead of a mode of production - and the focus on another unit of analysis is not enough reason for Brewer to consider dependency theory as a separate approach to the study of international relations.

Edelstein and Foster-Carter assume standpoints similar to Brewer's.

Both consider dependency theory to be closely related to (neo-) Marxism. Edelstein argues that the former is essentially a specification of the latter, in that it has focused on the problem of why Third World countries have not undergone a capitalist development such as that of the presently developed countries. Foster-Carter stresses that both types of theorizing are alike with respect to the theoretical objects under study, the concepts that are used in analysing the objects and the 'conditions of existence' of the problem that is studied.

Laclau's criticism of dependency and world system theories, and his main argument for separating these from (neo-) Marxism, is based on the idea that capitalism is to be interpreted as a 'mode of production' and not as a 'mode of exchange', which is in effect the common approach of dependency theorists. In Laclau's view, these theorists have left the correct Marxist path since their analysis does not place enough emphasis upon the economic basis of the capitalist class structure and upon the relations among classes.

Since the present analysis of dependency theory is not intended to go into intra-Marxist rivalries, it may be concluded that there is a clear resemblance between the neo-Marxist theories of imperialism and dependency theory. This resemblance is reflected in the terminology used, the way of reasoning and the theoretical insights that have been produced. Nevertheless, there are important differences. The most important and obvious difference is to be found in the concept of the 'capitalist world system', which can be interpreted as the most significant innovation of dependency theory. From this concept, nearly all theoretical statements of the latter have been derived: whether it is the relation between development and underdevelopment, the economic position of specific states, or the conditions and behaviour of social classes, all is related to the influence of the capitalist world system.

Related to this, the analysis of capitalism in dependency theory is clearly different from that in the neo-Marxist theories. While the latter stress the property relations dominating capitalist production and view capitalism as production with privately owned means, the former accentuates relations of exchange and defines capitalism as production for the market. As a consequence of this difference, dependency theory locates the rise of capitalism around 1500, whereas neo-Marxist theories generally date it in the eighteenth century.

The general conclusion with respect to the traditional economic and neo-Marxist theories can be that the dependency theory offers an alternative interpretation of the concepts of imperialism, exploitation, and capitalism. The worldwide relations among states of different levels of development are not just interpreted as the subjugation of non-Western by

Western countries, but as part of an international division of labour, in which the Western countries possess the main industrial productive capacity and the non-Western countries are forced to produce mainly primary commodities (agricultural products and raw materials).[5] By means of unequal exchange the non-Western countries are exploited, that is, their surplus value is taken away from them. Finally, as indicated in the previous paragraph, dependency theory uses an altogether different concept of capitalism, stressing exchange instead of possession of the means of production. As a result of this, the dependency theorists do not divide the world into a capitalist and a non-capitalist part. The capitalist world system is analysed in its entirety, dominated as it is by commercial exchange relations. Whereas in some of the traditional theories imperialism was seen as a potentially progressive force for the subjugated countries, dependency theorists have emphasized the negative consequences of imperialism and dependency for the latter countries. (Cf. Warren 1980) Moreover, the dependency theorists have reinterpreted the relations between the dominant and the dominated countries in terms other than the imperialism of investment and trade.

In sum, then, the dependency approach has offered solutions to important theoretical problems left open by the traditional economic and neo-Marxist theories of imperialism. The first problem, overlooked by the theories of imperialism because of their Eurocentric orientation, has been how to explain the survival of capitalism in a situation where Third World opposition to imperialist relations has increased. The second problem has been how to account for the lack of development in the Third World despite the supposedly progressive nature of capitalism.

C Dependency Theory and the Liberal Theories of International Trade

The differences between the liberal free trade and dependency approaches are very clear. The basic assumptions about international economic reality diverge to such an extent that virtually no common ground can be detected. Free trade theorists stress the positive effects of trade for all trading partners, whereas the dependency theorists emphasize the detrimental consequences of trade, especially for the developing countries. The dependency theory does not believe in genuine free trade *within* the capitalist world system. The laws that govern the capitalist world system make trade 'unfree'; even when the epithet free is attached to trade, this, in the view of the dependency theorists, serves as camouflage for *unequal exchange* as long as capitalist relations predominate. Trade is interpreted as one of the main instruments in the capitalist world system for the transfer of surplus from the periphery to the centre, making the periphery worse and the centre better off. Unequal trade relations are interpreted as fostering underdevelopment in the periphery and development in the centre.

The free trade theorists advocate the opening up of countries as a strategy for growth and development. This development policy is based on the assumption of mutually beneficial trade; those countries having abundant labour would, in this kind of reasoning, benefit from the production and export of commodities for which labour is the main factor of production. Dependency theorists see this as a defective argument, since such policies would only serve to prolong exploitative relations of unequal exchange. For this reason the dependency theorists recommend 'dissociation' of Third World countries from the international capitalist economic system in order to counter exploitation and underdevelopment.

Various authors from the dependency school, such as Andre Gunder Frank and Samir Amin, have attacked the liberal theory of international trade with the arguments presented above. Some theorists have pursued the argument even further and have analysed the theory as an ideological instrument working mainly in favour of the interests of the developed countries and their bourgeoisies. (Frank 1979a, pp. 94-101; Amin 1974, pp. 37-136 and 1976, pp. 133-97; cf. Smith and Toye 1979) For these reasons it is probably no exaggeration to conclude that the liberal free trade theory, which is one of the main products of Western economic thinking, is a central target of dependency theory.

The differences between dependency theory and the liberal theories of international trade can, rather easily, be interpreted as a matter of different emphases. On the one hand, liberal free trade theorists have studied the way in which trade could be beneficial to all participants and have introduced the concept of comparative advantage. They have also argued that the distribution of factors of production need not be harmful to the non-Western countries that do not possess the amount of capital goods present in the Western world, since a gradual equalization of factor prices will result from the relative scarcity of some factors of production. On the other hand, the dependency theorists have studied the consequences of this so-called free trade for developing countries that were less well-off, and they ascribed these countries' lack of development to the fact that trade can only be free in theory. The dependency theorists have also stressed the negative effects of the opening up of developing countries to foreign capital as long as they are still part of the capitalist world system. What appears to be at issue, then, is the different evaluation of the concept of development and its relation to international trade. The liberal free trade theorists have paid attention to those cases in which free trade seems to enhance development, while the dependency theorists look at cases where this does not happen.

The problem-solving capacity of the dependency approach is perhaps best illustrated in the explanation offered for some clear anomalies in the liberal theories: the fact that the increase of world trade has not benefited the majority of underdeveloped countries, and the fact that Third World countries possessing evident comparative advantages (a cheap and abundant labour force, extensive sources of raw materials) have not been able to achieve a significantly higher level of wealth than others.

D Dependency Theory and the E.C.L.A. Approach

The differences between the E.C.L.A. approach and dependency theory are not as great as some authors, particularly those adhering to the dependency perspective, have suggested. (E.g. Frank 1972b, pp. 138-45) Here, several of the most striking differences and similarities between the two branches of theory will be discussed.

The first important similarity between the two theories can be found in the assumption that two groups of states can be distinguished, namely, centre and periphery states; the dependency approach has, additionally, argued that centres and peripheries also exist *within* these states. Furthermore, the unequal relationship that is said to exist between the centre and the periphery, is a common element of the E.C.L.A. approach and dependency theory. The unequal relationship finds its expression in the exploitation of the periphery by the centre and in the negative influence on the level of wealth in the periphery. This implies that the lack of development in the countries of the periphery is mainly attributed to factors external to these countries.

The division of states in a centre and a periphery implies, in both the E.C.L.A. approach and dependency theory, a difference in levels of development, with the centre being developed and the periphery being underdeveloped. The centre is the part of the world that is characterized by the use of technologically highly developed production processes, whereas in the periphery the use of relatively simple technologies is dominant. The main economic activity of the centre is its industrial production, whereas agriculture dominates in the periphery. (Blomström and Hettne 1984, pp. 38-44; Love 1980; Rodríguez 1977; Smith and Toye 1979)

Both the E.C.L.A. approach and dependency theory focus on the relationship of inequality between the centre and the periphery. (Blomström and Hettne 1984; Love 1980; Rodríguez 1977; Smith and Toye 1979; Cardoso 1977; Griffin and Gurley 1985, pp. 1113 ff.) Although dependency theory goes further than the E.C.L.A. approach, both stress that the centre exploits the periphery. The E.C.L.A. approach focuses mainly on the worsening of the terms of trade for the developing countries; dependency theory stresses the structurally exploitative ties between the centre and the periphery, and their expression in trade, investments, monetary and financial relations, et cetera. The exploitative nature of these relations has a negative effect on the wealth of the periphery: as a consequence of the unequal position of the centre and the periphery, the former takes away a substantial part of the wealth of the latter. The final characteristic of the unequal relationship is that it is a cause of underdevelopment *external* to the developing countries. The problems of the developing countries are interpreted as a corollary of their ties to the centre, not as a consequence of internal factors distorting the development of the periphery.

The differences between the E.C.L.A. approach and dependency theory are mainly to be found in the ideas about the existence of a world system, the analyses of the causes of development and underdevelopment, and the advocated development policy.

In the first place, the E.C.L.A. approach and dependency theory differ in their ideas about the world system. The systemic nature of dependency theory is reflected in the idea that a state's situation cannot be analysed without paying attention to its place within the larger whole of the world system. In other words, characteristics of the capitalist world system enter the explanation of processes on the level of distinct states. The E.C.L.A. approach is not systemic in the same vein; in this theory, states are still the objects of analysis and, at its most, relations with other states are introduced to account for the situations of states under study.

In the second place, the E.C.L.A. approach and dependency theory contain differing interpretations of the causes of development and underdevelopment. In the central writings of the E.C.L.A. approach, the international system of free trade is interpreted as the main cause of the underdevelopment of the periphery. (Cardoso 1977, p. 12; Blomström and Hettne 1984, p. 40) In contrast to this view, dependency theory tends to see the free trade system as just one of the elements of the capitalist world system, in which the 'rules of the game' have been unilaterally formulated by the countries of the centre. Therefore it is not just free trade that is responsible for underdevelopment, but rather the entire reality of the existing world system.

In the third place, the development policies resulting from the two theories differ considerably. The E.C.L.A. has supported a policy of import substitution that was supposed to make the developing countries less dependent on capital and production from the developed countries. The developing countries would, however, remain part of the capitalist world system. Dependency theorists have argued that the peripheral countries would have to escape from the laws of the capitalist world system in order to attain self-sustained development. To stay within the capitalist world system would mean, in their view, remaining dependent and, consequently, being exploited and underdeveloped. (E.g. Frank 1969b, pp. 371-409; Blomström and Hettne 1984, pp. 42-4 and 56-69; Cardoso 1977, pp. 25-9)

The contrasts between dependency theory and E.C.L.A. thinking can be traced to the different interpretations of the centre-periphery distinction and to the development strategies that have been brought forward. First of all, the distinction between centre and periphery has quite different meanings in the two theories. In the E.C.L.A. approach, the concepts of centre and periphery are used to denote the contrasting roles played by countries in the world economy. In particular, the place of countries in the worldwide production of commodities and their ensuing trade patterns are stressed. In the dependency theory, the concepts of centre and periphery are used in the context of another theoretical construction, i.e., the capitalist world system. In this view, not only the productive and trade relations are important, but also the 'operating laws' characterizing the world system. This means that the centre and periphery have opposite functions in the world system, and that the benefits obtained in the world system are distributed following the lines of these functions. Related to, and partly emanating from, these analyses, the development strategies advocated by E.C.L.A. and dependency theorists are entirely different. In the 1950s and 1960s the E.C.L.A. encouraged countries to opt for a strategy of import substitution. The development strategy recommended by the dependency theorists has centred on dissociation from the international economic order.

Dependency theory appears to have solved some serious problems left open by the E.C.L.A. approach. First, the former has addressed the problem of why an industrialization strategy such as import substitution cannot succeed within the contemporary economic order. Secondly, the dependency approach has presented a theoretical solution to the problem of why a change in the international trade structure is no panacea for Third World development.

E Dependency Theory and the Modernization Theories

In the discussions about the relationship between modernization and dependency theory, the differences between both branches of theory have received much more attention than possible similarities. In this section, the supposed dissimilarities will be dealt with first. Then, a discussion of points of resemblance will follow.

In the literature on modernization and dependency theory several points of contention have been identified; these can be summed up under the following headings: modernization versus the development of underdevelopment, the emphasis on internal versus external factors in the explanation of development, and integration into versus withdrawal from the international capitalist economy.

The first and undoubtedly most important difference between modernization and dependency theories concerns development and underdevelopment. (Bodenheimer 1970; Foster-Carter 1976; Fitzgerald 1983; Smith 1985a and 1985b; Brown 1985; Dube 1988) Modernization theory analyses the lack of development of the developing countries mainly in terms of the absence of certain characteristics, in particular modern or 'non-traditional' social, political and economic structures and cultural patterns. The path to development is considered to be a natural one, resulting, more or less automatically, from the modernization of the developing countries. According to the dependency theorists, this line of reasoning overlooks the effects which the development of the Western countries has had on the position of the Third World. In their view, the low level of development of the developing countries is not the result of the *absence* of certain attributes, but of the *presence* of the so-called capitalist world system. It is the integration of the non-Western countries in this world system that has *created* the situation in which they now find themselves. Instead of being *un*developed, these countries have become *under*developed, which means that their society and economy have been distorted by the policies of the Western countries, the aim of which was to use the developing countries' economic potential to increase their own wealth.

The second main difference between modernization and dependency theory is to be found in the respective units of analysis. (E.g. Sunkel 1979; Valenzuela and Valenzuela 1979; Fitzgerald 1983; Higgott 1983; Smith 1985a and 1985b; Bauzon and Abel 1986) Modernization theory has chosen the nation-state, and often the individuals living in the nation-state, as its primary unit of analysis. As a consequence of this, the explanation of the Third World countries' lack of development is often focused at the nation-state or individual level; according to some authors, this way of analysing has led the modernization theorists to neglect other important (international) influences. (Esp. Fitzgerald 1983; Higgott 1983; Smith 1985a and 1985b) According to Tony Smith, the failure to take account of factors other than national ones has even been interpreted by the dependency theorists as 'nothing more than an ideological smokescreen behind which North American imperialism freely operated'. (Smith 1985b, p. 552) The reaction of the dependency theorists has been to emphasize the operation of the capitalist world system. This world system is seen as the central unit of analysis, the effects of which on individual countries have to be studied. In sharp contrast to the approach favoured by the supporters of modernization theory, structural factors (such as mode of production, international trade patterns and class structure) take a central place in the dependency analysis. The effects of the capitalist world system, which is said to have spread ever since the sixteenth century, have been found to be especially detrimental to the position of the Third World countries.

The third difference between modernization and dependency theory is connected to the previous one. (E.g. Bodenheimer 1970; Foster-Carter 1976; Sunkel 1979; Wiarda 1985; Brown 1985; Bauzon and Abel 1986; Dube 1988) Modernization theorists have advocated the integration of Third World countries in the world economy, so that they could benefit from the diffusion of modernity and, consequently, wealth. These ideas have come under heavy fire from the dependency theorists. The latter argue that such integration would lead to the prolongation of existing unequal relationships. The partaking in the international economy has been assumed identical to free submission of one's economy and society to exploitation, since the fundamental laws of capitalism would not allow the developing countries to benefit from its fruits. The only development strategy that is considered viable by the dependency theorists is the resolute dissociation or delinking of the economy from the international system. By this act, a barrier would be put up against external influences.

Apart from the three differences mentioned here, some authors have concluded that modernization and dependency theory also have some elements in common. Gavin Williams, in an article in *World Development*, has discussed the so-called 'common ideology of development', which 'identifies progress, circumspectly redefined as development, with the development of capitalist relations of production'. (1978, p. 930) According to this author, several theories of development, including those presently discussed, stress that capitalism is necessary, either as the ultimate aim, or as a prerequisite for a successful transition to socialism.

Richard A. Higgott (1983, pp. 74-5) has emphasized the 'unilinear determinism' that can be found in modernization and dependency theory. Both branches of theory have indicated that some universal processes were responsible for the circumstances in the developing countries. Modernization theorists have stressed the lack of modernity and the consequent low level of development, while dependency theorists have emphasized exploitation in the capitalist world system and the resulting underdevelopment as an underlying process. Common to both approaches is the belief that some factor or factors unilinearly determine the fate of the Third World countries.

The crucial distinction between modernization and dependency theories is to be found in the conceptualization of development. The modernization theorists analyse development as the opposite of traditionalism. As a result of this conceptualization, the main causes for the lack of development in the countries of the Third World are found in the absence of factors pertaining to modernity. Often becoming modern is equated with becoming more like the countries of the West. Further integration of the less developed, and traditional, countries into the world order is seen as potentially conducive to this kind of modernity and development. The dependency theorists have interpreted the focus of modernization theory on tradition and modernity as a way of obscuring the real divergence, that is, between domination and dependence, and, concomitantly, between development and underdevelopment. Dependency theory's focus on the world system has led it to stress the relations between the West and Third World countries. As a consequence, the search for explanations of development and underdevelopment only partially involves factors internal to the countries under study. In particular, the exploitation by the Western countries and the resulting underdevelopment of the Third World is highlighted.

In sum, then, the dependency theorists can be credited with providing a solution to the problem of why there is no direct association between traditional order and lack of development, and between modernity and development. Moreover, the dependency approach has addressed the problem why Third World countries with differing internal characteristics and/or policies nevertheless show similar levels of development. Concerning the latter problem, it is probably best to see dependency theory as a supplement, rather than a fully developed alternative to the modernization approach.

F An Assessment of the Problem-Solving Capacity of Dependency Theory

The foregoing five sections have served to discuss the main differences and similarities between dependency theory and, respectively, traditional economic theories of imperialism, neo-Marxist theories of imperialism, liberal theories of international trade, the E.C.L.A. approach and modernization theory. The analyses presented in these sections have made clear that many ideas which are considered typical for dependency theory can be found in one or more of the theories discussed above. This final section will serve to indicate whether and, if so, to what extent the dependency approach exhibits theoretical progress, compared to the theories discussed in sections II through VI and subsections A through E.

The central elements - the Lakatosian 'hard core' (Lakatos 1970, pp.

133-4) - of most variants of dependency theory can be summed up in the following three points: (Elguea 1984, pp. 82-5)

1) the development of a capitalist world system and, concomitantly, of an international division of labour;
2) the existence of relations of dependence and exploitation within the world system and the resulting division of the world into developed and underdeveloped areas;
3) the derivative nature of political units (the nation-states, the features of which are influenced by or, according to some authors, dependent on economic realities) and the pre-eminence of capital movements across the world. (Cf. Rupert 1990, pp. 429-30)

Certainly not all three elements are based on new empirical insights. Seen from a meta-theoretical point of view, dependency theory has pointed out empirical and conceptual problems that were unsolved by its theoretical predecessors. In its attempts to solve these problems, novel theoretical *concepts* have been introduced, such as 'capitalist world system', 'dependence', 'development of underdevelopment', et cetera.

As many critics of dependency theory have made clear, the approach has generated 'anomalies and conceptual problems' (Laudan 1977, p. 68) of its own. Of these, the two most important ones will be mentioned here. In the first place, the dependency approach can be criticized for placing too much emphasis upon the identical influence of the international capitalist system on Third World countries. It has been argued above that the approach has to be credited with explaining why apparently different countries nevertheless show similar levels of development. This insight has not prevented the dependency theorists from developing their own 'blind spot'. They have not realized that, despite the fact that the international system may have a comparable influence on most Third World countries, policies pursued by individual countries may cause important differences in the situation of those countries. As a consequence of this new blind spot, dependency theory did not recognize the development of the Newly Industrializing Countries (NICs) as genuine; auxiliary hypotheses, such as those of 'dependent development', had to be introduced to account for the experiences of the NICs. (E.g. Frank 1984a, pp. 208-29; Evans 1979)

A second important theoretical problem created by the dependency approach is its overemphasis on the economic world order and its consequent neglect of political factors. The stress on economic phenomena, in particular exchange and accumulation, has led scholars to 'assume away' the political domain. Two anomalies have been the result of this. In the first place, conclusions about economic situations have been translated into political effects too quickly. For instance, the supposedly exploitative nature of the capitalist world system has led some dependency theorists to assume that the oppressed groups in the centre and the periphery would cooperate and together create a 'world revolution'; the differences in interests have clearly been overlooked. (E.g. Wallerstein 1979 and the critique in Gülalp 1987) In the second place, the neglect of political considerations has brought some theorists to explain political situations in exclusively economic terms, even where this has not been warranted. Especially in some of the writing about the position of elites in Third World countries, such as in the case of 'bureaucratic authoritarianism', this anomaly of the dependency approach is very clear. (E.g. O'Donnell 1972; Collier 1979)

The conclusion of this chapter must be that, on the whole, the dependency approach represents theoretical progress. The comparison with its main predecessors and competitors has shown that the approach has solved several important theoretical problems. Nevertheless, the approach itself has produced some theoretical anomalies, two of which have been mentioned in this conclusion. The complexity of social reality renders all attempts at comprehensive explanation *a priori* impossible. Therefore, all progress - interpreted as the solving of certain problems - has to be welcomed. The results of the dependency approach can offer a stepping-stone towards more fruitful theorizing about international inequality and unequal development.

NOTES

1. In this study, terms such as 'developing countries', 'underdeveloped countries', 'less developed countries' and 'Third World' are used interchangeably for reasons of style.
2. Translation W.H. The original version is: 'Der Imperialismus ist der politische Ausdruck des Prozesses der Kapitalakkumulation in ihrem Konkurrenzkampf um die Reste des noch nicht mit Beschlag belegten nichtkapitalistischen Weltmilieus.'
3. Translation W.H. In the original version the quotation is: 'Die kapitalistische Produktion ist von Anbeginn in ihren Bewegungsformen und -gesetzen auf die gesamte Erde als Schatzkammer der Produktivkräfte berechnet. In seinem Drange nach Aneignung der Produktivkräfte zu zwecken der Ausbeutung durchstöbert das Kapital die ganze Welt, verschafft sich Produktionsmittel aus allen Winkeln der Erde, errafft oder erwirbt sie von allen Kulturstufen und Gesellschaftsformen.'
4. A notable exception in the neo-Marxist tradition is Bill Warren. In his view, developing countries gain by letting the developed countries pursue an imperialist policy, that is, having the developed countries invest in and trade with them. (See Warren 1973 and 1980) Since Warren's work cannot be considered to belong to the mainstream of neo-Marxist theorizing on imperialism, his writings are not discussed in this chapter.
5. As Junne, among others, has argued, the theories of imperialism do not focus exclusively on relations between Western and Third World countries. An important element of the theories is their orientation on inter-capitalist rivalries. The latter element is beyond the scope of this book. (See: Junne 1987, pp. 80-1)

3. Andre Gunder Frank: The Development of Underdevelopment

I INTRODUCTION

In this chapter and in the following ones, the writings of several prominent dependency theorists will be examined. The aim of this activity is to distil from these writings the 'hard core' of (variants of) dependency theory, and to build models that can be used in the subsequent empirical analysis. The models will thus be the starting point for the assessment of the adequacy of dependency theory's 'statement of the problem'.

In this chapter, the work of Andre Gunder Frank will be focused upon.[1] Frank, who laid the foundations and initially formulated the central tenets of dependency theory, can be considered as one of the 'grand old men' of this alternative approach to international relations. His book *Capitalism and underdevelopment in Latin America*, first published in 1967, still stands as one of the landmarks of dependency theory. In this book, three foci characterizing all of Andre Gunder Frank's *oeuvre* are already present: the idea of the 'development of underdevelopment', the conception of the historical development, in different guises, of the capitalist world system, and the theory of recurring crises of accumulation under capitalism.

This chapter will be organized along these three foci. First, some attention will be given to Frank's methodological and theoretical assumptions (section II). Section III will focus on the concept of underdevelopment and on the mechanisms operating in the capitalist world system. Section IV will deal with the historical analysis of the present world system as it has been undertaken by Frank. Section V will go into Frank's crisis theory, which is a crucial element of his ideas about the development of the capitalist world system. Finally, in section VI, a theoretical model containing the central elements of Frank's dependency theory will be constructed.

II METHODOLOGICAL AND THEORETICAL ASSUMPTIONS

In order to understand properly the specifics of Andre Gunder Frank's theorizing, it must be clear that Frank has based his work on several methodological and theoretical assumptions which diverge from those present in the 'mainstream' of the social sciences. In this section, first Frank's methodological assumptions will be analysed and, subsequently, attention will be paid to his theoretical assumptions. By doing this, the approach will be different from the one chosen by Simon and Ruccio in their methodological analysis of Frank's theory. They have not differentiated between methodological and theoretical assumptions and have therefore subsumed part of the theoretical under the methodological analysis. (Simon and Ruccio 1986) For reasons of analytical clarity, in the following subsections a distinction will be made between the two kinds of assumptions.

A Methodological Assumptions

In a classical contribution to the philosophy of science, Carl G. Hempel in 1962 outlined the essentials of a model of explanation that might be considered ideal-typical for the modern empirical social sciences: the deductive-nomological model. The structure of this way of explaining 'consists in the deduction of whatever is being explained or predicted from general laws in conjunction with information about particular facts'. (Hempel 1962, p. 98)

Although Andre Gunder Frank has tried to live up to the requirements of the deductive-nomological explanatory model in some of his writings, the greater part of his work is typified by other principles of explanation. The best characterization of Frank's methodology is probably 'functional explanation', a term used by G.A. Cohen (1982), among others. As he has indicated, functional explanation can best be understood as:

> an explanation in which an event, or whatever else, if there is anything else which can have an effect, is explained in terms of its effect. [...] Suppose we have a cause, *e*, and its effect *f*. Then the form of the explanation is not: *e* occurred because *f* occurred [...] Nor should we say that the form of the explanation is '*e* occurred because it caused *f* '. [...] The only remaining candidate, which I therefore elect, is: *e* occurred because it *would* cause *f*, or, less tersely but more properly: *e* occurred because the situation was such that an event of type *E* would cause an event of type *F*. (1982, p. 30)

The essence of functional explanation is that a certain event is said to occur because its effect is assumed to have a function in the context of a certain theory. A good example of functional explanation can be found in Marxist theory, which interprets the exploitation of the labour force as a necessary requirement for the accumulation of capital. Both the repression of labour and the introduction of welfare arrangements can be explained by defining these as a function of the exploitation of labour. Repression might contribute to exploitation because a less rebellious labour force makes possible the extraction of a larger quantity of surplus value. The introduction of welfare arrangements might enhance exploitation because it renders the labour force quiescent and leads to an increase of production, and thereby of profit.

In the work of Andre Gunder Frank, functional explanation takes the form of relating events and processes occurring in the capitalist world system, or in parts thereof, to the interests of the dominant part of the system, the metropolis, and of its ruling classes. Specifically, occurrences are related to the accumulation of capital in the metropolis. These are considered to take place because of their contribution to the accumulation of capital.

Simon and Ruccio have distinguished among 'structural', 'functional' and 'intentional' explanations in the work of Andre Gunder Frank. Structural and intentional explanations, as they define them, do not, however, differ from functional explanations in a fundamental way. Functional explanation, as described in the quotation of Cohen, means that explanations are given in terms of effects and functions. What Simon and Ruccio (1986, pp. 197, 202) seem to mean is that structural explanations are explanations referring to the world capitalist system and that intentional explanations involve the economic interests of classes. This distinction does not clarify, but rather obfuscates the methodological analysis, since Andre Gunder Frank's explanations of processes in (parts of) the world system are basically cast in terms of the positive function they have for the system's metropolis and its dominant classes. Simon and Ruccio appear to have confounded methodological with theoretical assumptions: the fact that Frank uses the capitalist world system and metropolitan class interests as elements of the explanations he offers, can be traced back to the theoretical assumptions, which will be discussed in subsection B.

B Theoretical Assumptions

In his *Answer to critics* Andre Gunder Frank has written that 'I have *never* had the temerity myself to *claim to be* a Marxist nor the desire to deny it; and nowhere in my published - or unpublished - writings can or will anyone find such a personal claim'. (1984a, p. 258) Although Frank clearly refuses to take a stand on the reputedly Marxist orientation of his writings, his basic assumptions are quite similar to those of Marxist authors. (See Booth 1975, pp. 64-9; cf. Leaver 1983a, p. 58) Three theoretical assumptions will be mentioned in this section, since exactly these are fundamental to Frank's theory of dependence.

First of all, economic relations are assumed to dominate all other possible ones. Some authors, such as Tony Smith (1979, pp. 257-9 and 1981, pp. 77 ff.), have even gone as far as labelling Frank's theory as economically reductionist or determinist. The theory's emphasis on economic phenomena, such as the international division of labour, the profit motive and the accumulation of capital, and the central position of these factors in the explanation of international relations, mean that Smith's characterization is largely correct. This assumption conforms to the Marxist emphasis on material factors, which are considered basic to all social and political processes. A striking example of the kind of reasoning caused by economic reductionism in Frank's work is the following:

> The Crusades, of course, are often interpreted as religious events propelled by the desire of Christians to conquer the Holy Land for Christ. If we look a bit more closely, we can find that in fact, at least in substantial part, the Crusades were commercial ventures related to the commercial expansion of Western Europe into the Middle East, which was part of the period of expansion in the 12th and 13th centuries, and which led to a serious crisis in the 14th century. (1983b, p. 17)

The second theoretical assumption present in Andre Gunder Frank's writings concerns the existence, and even the primacy as an explanatory factor, of the capitalist world system. This system is seen as an entity that came into existence in the fifteenth century and expanded ever since, until it comprised all nations of the world during the twentieth century. Frank assumes that within this world system capitalist relations, implying the predominance of production for the (increasingly international) market, have taken precedence over all other relations. (Cf. Brewer 1980, pp. 160-1)

This leads to the third theoretical assumption, which deals with the nature of relations in the capitalist world system. The fundamental characteristic of these relations is that they are exploitative. This means that the dominant groups within the world system - the countries belonging to the so-called metropolis and within these countries the respective bourgeoisies - take away part of the economic fruits produced by other groups in the system without providing these latter groups with adequate compensation. According to Frank, the exploitative nature of relations within the capitalist world system has resulted in an extreme polarization between the dominant and dominated parts of the system, which is unmistakably reflected in the inequality of wealth of the respective parts.

III UNDERDEVELOPMENT AND THE CAPITALIST WORLD SYSTEM

Without any doubt, the theory of underdevelopment is the most obvious result of Andre Gunder Frank's work. In devising the concept of underdevelopment, Frank has leaned heavily on the neo-Marxist work of Paul Baran, as Frank has stressed in the preface to *Capitalism and underdevelopment in Latin America.* (1969a, pp. xi-xviii) Underdevelopment, as Frank understands it, is fundamentally different from 'undevelopment' or the simple lack of development. Frank has criticized 'the received theory and analysis of economic development and cultural change' for exactly:

> the assumption that underdevelopment is an original state which may be characterized by indices of traditionalism, and that, therefore, development consists of abandoning these characteristics and adopting those of the developed countries. (1969b, p. 24)

The main difference between Frank's variant of dependency theory and mainstream economic, sociological and political theories of development is to be found in the former's essential thesis that '[t]he now developed countries were never *under*developed, though they may have been *un*developed'. (1969b, p. 4) Instead, development and underdevelopment are interpreted as the twin results of the history of capitalism and its most pervasive manifestation, the capitalist world system. A lengthy quotation of Frank's original formulation clarifies this point:

> Economic development and underdevelopment are the opposite faces of the same coin. Both are the necessary result and contemporary manifestation of internal contradictions in the world capitalist system. Economic development and underdevelopment are not just relative and quantitative, in that one represents more economic development than the other; economic development and underdevelopment are relational and qualitative, in that each is structurally different from, yet caused by its relation with, the other. Yet development and underdevelopment are the same in that they are the product of a single, but dialectically contradictory, economic structure and process of capitalism. Thus they cannot be viewed as the products of supposedly different economic structures or systems, or of supposed differences in stages of economic growth achieved within the same system. One and the same historical process of the expansion and development of capitalism throughout the world has simultaneously generated - and continues to generate - both economic development and structural underdevelopment. (1969a, p. 9)

The relations in the capitalist world system have thus resulted in the creation of developed and underdeveloped parts. The developed parts are subsumed under the term 'metropolis'; the underdeveloped ones form the 'satellite'. Although the distinction is primarily a worldwide one, Frank argues that relations within countries can be analysed with the same theoretical framework. There, too, metropolises and satellites can be distinguished, and the relations between these are equally (and sometimes even more) exploitative. (1969a, p. 10) Systemic relations are clearly of overriding importance to Frank, as he makes clear in his characterization of the 'lumpenbourgeoisie', the bourgeoisie in the underdeveloped satellites. (1972b, pp. 5, 13-14) According to Frank, this bourgeoisie has some autonomy to pursue its own interests, but only in so far as it also serves the interests of the metropolis.

The background to the relation between development and underdevelopment in different parts of the world system is to be found in exploitation, which is the result of one of different possible forms of colonization. Colonization, in its turn, is interpreted as the imposition of capitalist relations on previously autonomous areas. (1975, pp. 2-9 and 43-5) As Frank has written: 'In short, "colonial", "imperial", and "capitalist" all refer to a set of relationships, and more importantly as a *system* of relations, in which domination, super-subordination, exploitation, and of course, development and underdevelopment, play a central part.' (1975, pp. 2-3) According to Frank, only those countries which have not been integrated into the capitalist world system at some point in their history have been able to escape dependence on and subordination to the capitalist metropolis.

The example of Japan plays a central role in Frank's argumentation. Since Japan never was a colony, or, in Frank's words, 'did not get caught in the imperialist system', the capitalist countries of Europe and North America have not been able to impose the same exploitative conditions on Japan as on other, presently underdeveloped, countries. (1975, pp. 6) Since the capital that was accumulated in the country has not been appropriated by the metropolitan capitalists, Japan has been able to pursue economic development policies answering its own needs, instead of adapting these to the interests of the metropolis.

The same argumentation is applied to the so-called Newly Industrializing Countries (NICs), the development and apparent wealth of which have often been mentioned as counterexamples of the dependency approach. According to Frank, the experience of the NICs is atypical: their growth has only been possible because of the state of the capitalist world system. Frank has argued that:

> this development or ascent has been misperceived as taking place in particular countries, when it has really been one of the processes *of* the world system itself. The recent export-led growth of the NICs also is part and parcel of the process of capital accumulation on a world scale (to cite the appropriate title of Samir Amin): to reduce costs of production and to make room for more technologically advanced development elsewhere, a part of the labor- (and some capital-) intensive production is relocated in the NICs and the 'socialist' countries. (1984a, p. 217)

Because of this, the growth in the NICs is not, and cannot be, *real* development in Frank's conception. The fruits of the new economic activity do not reach all social groups to the same extent and the society is disrupted by the forced pattern of industrialization. Moreover, the NICs 'are simply increasing their dependent integration into a worldwide division of labor and technological development in which they are allocated the least remunerative and technologically obsolete contributions and the corresponding meager benefits'. (1984a, p. 219)

In Andre Gunder Frank's theory, the position of individual states and groups within states is analysed in the context of the capitalist world system. In this respect, the theory can be characterized as an explicitly *holist* one. The clearest formulation in Frank's work of this holist starting point is perhaps the following:

> The *central fact* is that the worldwide historical expansion of mercantile, industrial, and monopoly capitalism brought all humanity on this particular globe into a *single* social system. This system has always functioned, and still functions, so as to generate socioeconomic development for the few while simultaneously causing degenerative change without development for the many. (1984a, p. 45, first italics added)

The world system which, according to Frank, has expanded since the fifteenth century and now comprises the entire globe is of a capitalist nature. In Frank's conception, capitalism means the production for a market; this implies that market relations form the central elements of the system.[2] The accumulation of capital is seen as the main objective of economic relations in the world system.

During the last several centuries the satellites have been made economically dependent by the metropolitan countries in order to enable exploitation of the former. The central element in Frank's analysis of this situation of dependence is the deliberate and successful attempt of the metropolitan countries to render the satellites incapable of becoming economically self-reliant. The main instrument applied by the metropolis is found in the institution of 'monocultures', implying the reorganization of satellite economies in order to have these produce only one or a limited number of mainly agricultural products and raw materials. Since the production of intermediate goods and manufactured products was monopolized by metropolitan industries, the satellite economies grew more and more dependent on exporting their primary products to and importing other goods from the metropolis. This situation forged an unbreakable economic link between the developed and underdeveloped parts of the capitalist world system:

> Thus, nineteenth-century and even earlier specialisation in the production of raw materials for export and their exchange for imported manufactures severely handicapped capital accumulation and productive consumption among the producers of primary compared to those of manufactured products, even disregarding the capital drain from the former to the latter through unequal exchange. (1979a, p. 117)

Free trade, which has been applauded by liberal groups in the developed and the underdeveloped countries alike, is seen as an instrument to prolong the relations of dependence and exploitation in the context of the world system. The concept of comparative advantage, which stresses the benefits of specialization, is considered to be a mere ideological tool in the hands of the metropolitan bourgeoisie. (1979a, pp. 94-101)

Exploitation, which stands apart from but is closely linked to dependence, is a central concept in Andre Gunder Frank's theory of the development of the capitalist world system. Frank uses the concept of exploitation to indicate that, in his view, part of the 'surplus' produced by the satellite economies is expropriated by the metropolitan countries, which use it to stimulate their own development. Frank refers to Paul Baran's distinction between 'actual' and 'potential' surplus (see chapter 2, section III) and argues that the unavailability of the potential economic surplus for the satellite economy is caused by the 'monopoly structure' of the capitalist world system. Frank is not entirely clear when he writes about the consequences of exploitation, however. The original formulation in *Capitalism and underdevelopment* may lead to the conclusion that the inability to realize the potential surplus is the main factor in causing underdevelopment. In the remainder of this as well as in subsequent books, Frank emphasizes the expropriation of the actual economic surplus as the central element of exploitation. (E.g. 1969a, pp. 6-8; 1978b, pp. 239-48; 1971, pp. 237-42; cf. Gülalp 1983, pp. 115-20 and Brewer 1980, pp. 174-7)

Frank has mentioned several mechanisms of exploitation, which can be grouped into the broad categories of exploitation by means of trade and exploitation by means of investment. The first category has already been referred to above: it concerns the exchange of manufactured goods from the metropolis for agricultural products and raw materials from the satellites. According to Andre Gunder Frank, this exchange is unequal because the prices of the satellites' products show a tendency to fall relative to those of the metropolitan products. This tendency is reflected in the deterioration of the terms of trade of the developing countries. (1979a, pp. 103-10)

The second category of exploitation is connected with the metropolitan investments in the satellite economies. According to Andre Gunder Frank, the exploitative element of these investments is to be found in the use of their returns. Unlike the situation in which capital owners invest for productive purposes - a situation usually characterized by the reinvestment of the returns from the original investment -, the metropolis-satellite relationship causes the use of profits in a way that is detrimental to the developing countries. Profits made on investments in developing countries will usually not be reinvested there. In the case of domestic capital, the profits will normally be spent on luxury consumption. When the profits are the result of foreign investments, a substantial part will as a rule be repatriated by the firm responsible for the project. In either case, the developing country as a whole does not benefit from the investments. (E.g. 1969a, pp. 281-318; 1969b, pp. 162-74; 1979a, pp. 189-99)

The upshot of the exploitation of the satellites is that they possess insufficient means to accumulate capital. The expropriation of the surplus produced in the satellites brings these countries in a situation which, according to Frank, 'denies the laborer even the minimum necessary for subsistence by any definition and which, at some times and places, prohibits even the reproduction of labor power'. (1978b, p. 240) Since not even the basic needs of the masses can be satisfied, the satellite countries certainly do not have the means to pursue development strategies. The countries are caught in a vicious circle: in order to be able to develop, they have to become less dependent on the metropolitan states, and the dependence can only be reduced when they take in other positions in the capitalist world system. Frank's solution for the underdeveloped countries is a radical one: they have to withdraw or, in other words, dissociate, from the existing world system and follow a non-exploitative development strategy, which enables the underdeveloped countries to accumulate the capital they need for their own purposes. (E.g. 1984a, pp. 215-29; 1978a, pp. 346-7; cf. 1990)

One of the most important obstacles to the adoption of such development strategies, according to Frank, is the existence of the 'lumpenbourgeoisie'. This local bourgeoisie is thought to work together with the metropolis because it reaps (part of) the benefits from the exploitation of its own country. It has been stressed above that Frank sees the 'lumpenbourgeoisie' as the dependent collaborator of the metropolitan bourgeoisie. As he has phrased it with respect to Latin America:

> The dominant bourgeoisie in Latin America accepts dependence consciously and willingly but is nevertheless molded by it. If dependence were purely 'external', it could be argued that objective conditions exist which would permit the 'national' bourgeoisie to propose a 'nationalist' or 'autonomous' solution to the problem of underdevelopment. But in our view, such a solution does not exist - precisely because dependence is indivisible and makes the bourgeoisie itself dependent. (1972b, pp. 3-4; cf. 1972b, pp. 88-91 and 1972a, pp. 20-4, 39-45)

This quotation clearly illustrates that Andre Gunder Frank's explanations of situations and processes in the underdeveloped countries are based to a considerable extent on what might be called a *double determinism*. First, the dependence on the metropolis is seen as a factor influencing and conditioning the political, social and economic situation in the satellite countries. Secondly, the economic requirements connected with the position of the satellite bourgeoisies are interpreted as dominating the political and social circumstances of the underdeveloped countries. As a result, politics and social relations are extremely polarized; there is hardly any common ground on the basis of which cooperation between political and social groups would be possible. Since the function of the satellite 'lumpenbourgeoisie', in the framework of the capitalist world system, is to contribute to the overall exploitation of the underdeveloped countries, they try to keep the 'lumpenproletariat' under control. In Frank's view, this sometimes results in oppression - for instance by military governments - and at other moments leads to pacification by, mainly populist, bourgeoisie-controlled political movements. (Cf. the different explanations in: 1977; 1981a, pp. 6-27 and 230-79; 1969b, pp. 192-200 and 340-9; 1981b, pp. 53-65)

According to Frank, the interference of the metropolitan countries with the satellites depends on the overall situation of the world economy. In periods of relative stagnation or recession, the developed countries will be less able to pay attention to developments within the underdeveloped ones, since then the state of their own economies requires that reconstructive policies be enacted. In those periods, satellite governments will be able to reduce the dependence of their countries and introduce policies aiming at industrialization and more autonomy. Then, the traditional emphasis on the production of commodities meant to be traded with the developed countries can also be reduced. The worldwide recession of the 1930s is one of Frank's favourite examples to illustrate this point: in that period, many underdeveloped countries in Latin America and Asia proved able to adopt so-called import-substituting policies, aimed at producing the articles that previously were imported. (E.g. 1969a, pp. 174-81; 1969b, pp. 302-6; 1972b, pp. 75-91; 1981b, pp. 53-65)

By way of conclusion, the main elements of Frank's 'underdevelopment syndrome' may be summed up. As Frank has written, the 'major structural factors in the capitalist development of underdevelopment' are:

> the development of an export economy with an excessively unequal distribution of income, the drain of economic surplus to the metropolis, the transformation of the national and local economic and class structure as a function of world capitalist development and metropolitan developmental needs, the natural alliance between the metropolitan colonial power and the local reactionary interests and their underdevelopment policy, the close connection between the length and intensity of capitalist colonialisation and ultra-underdevelopment. (1979a, pp. 148-9)

IV THE HISTORICAL ANALYSIS OF THE CAPITALIST WORLD SYSTEM

Andre Gunder Frank's analysis of the history of the capitalist world system is linked directly to his thoughts about the development of underdevelopment. The analysis originates from the idea that there is a 'single historical process of capitalist development'. (1969b, p. 5) According to Frank, this historical process can best be described as one of 'continuity in change'. (1969a, pp. 12-4) This means that, in his view, the visible characteristics of the system have changed continually, while the underlying mechanisms of exploitation and underdevelopment have remained essentially the same throughout the past centuries.

In Frank's words, the development of the capitalist world economy has been 'unequal' and 'uneven'. According to Frank, this means that:

> its structure and development have always been and still remain very unequal over space and uneven over time. This inequality is reflected in the conflicts between developed and underdeveloped, rich and poor, powerful and oppressed, etc. The uneven development is expressed through long cycles of accelerated and retarded growth and recurrent world economic crises, of which the present one is one of a long historical series. (1983b, p. 2)

Throughout his work, Frank presents several periodizations of the history of the capitalist world system. Since Frank's historical analysis is not the central focus of this study, the stages adopted in *Dependent accumulation and underdevelopment* will be used here. In this book, he distinguishes three main stages: the mercantilist (1500-1770), industrial capitalist (1770-1870) and imperialist (1870-1930). (1979a, p. xi) Elsewhere, Frank has written about the period since 1930 (or better 1945) as the stage of neoimperialism and neodependence. (1972b, pp. 92-137)

The *mercantilist*, or *mercantile capitalist* (1979b, p. 1), period is the phase in the history of the capitalist world system during which the original expansion of the (European) metropolises took place. This first stage in the development of so-called world capital accumulation is seen as 'dominated by a marked and irreversible increase of European commercial or mercantile activity and the growth of colonial production for export, which was in turn stimulated, controlled and exploited by European metropolitan commerce'. (1979a, p. 13) Frank's functional mode of explanation is reflected in his interpretation of the objective of European expansion: in his view 'the colonial economy [...] was a by-product of - and contributed to - the world-wide expansion and development of the mercantile capitalist system'. (1979b, p. 2)

The way in which the non-European parts of the world became incorporated into the capitalist world system, according to Frank, has primarily been trade-induced. In the sixteenth century there were two major 'trade triangles', one connecting Europe with Asia, the other linking Europe to the Americas. The Asian trade triangle, which had existed for centuries before Europe started to expand, centred on the importation to Europe of spices and manufactures, paid for by European, and later American, bullion. The second, Atlantic, trade triangle involved fisheries, gold and silver, sugar and rum; later, it became linked to Africa by the slave trade. European commerce connected the trade triangles and became the basis of the international division of labour. This division of labour 'generated an important flow of capital from the productive colonies to the metropolis which accumulated this capital and channelled it into its own development'. (1979a, p. 17)

According to Andre Gunder Frank, the effect of the internationalization of the division of labour on the indigenous modes of production in the non-European areas was not the same in all parts of the world. The Spanish colonies in Latin America were the first to experience its influence: the conditions under which agriculture and mining operated there were adapted to the needs and interests of the metropolitan economies. (1978b, pp. 44-50; 1979a, pp. 21-3; 1979b, pp. 8-36) This meant that production became increasingly commercialized and oriented toward Europe.

During the seventeenth and eighteenth centuries, Africa also became part of 'the historical process of world capitalist development' as a consequence of the creation of plantation economies in the Americas that were dependent on imported slave labour. (1979a, p. 19; 1978b, pp. 90-1, 120-34) The European economic impact on Asia remained comparatively slight until the end of the eighteenth century, because 'Europe had little else [than gold and silver] to offer civilised Asians and still lacked or could not finance sufficient military power to enforce trade or production on them'. (1979a, pp. 17-18)

According to Frank, the second phase in the history of the capitalist world system is the so-called *industrial capitalist* period, spanning the latter decades of the eighteenth and the greater part of the nineteenth century. This phase was introduced during and induced by the depression lasting from 1762 until 1789. This depression is to be interpreted as a 'crisis of accumulation', caused by, among other things, a reduction in the production of gold and a stagnation in the production of silver. (1978b, pp. 167-73) The crisis of the eighteenth century led 'not only to the invention of the technology that underlay the new textile economy and the industrial revolution but also directly to the French and American revolutions'. (1983b, p. 34)

The industrial capitalist phase was characterized by a shift of emphasis in international trade, away from the search for foreign products and towards the exportation of manufactured goods, at first mainly textiles, in exchange for tropical and semitropical products. (1979a, p. 77) This development has been of crucial importance, Frank argues, since:

> [t]his international trade and the high profits derived from it made an important contribution to the process of capital accumulation in northwestern Europe, particularly England, and northeastern America; and the rapid growth of manufacturing exports significantly facilitated and furthered the development of industry and the Industrial Revolution. (1978b, p. 214)

From the above it can be concluded that Andre Gunder Frank sees the industrial revolution primarily as a reaction to the accumulation problems faced by the metropolitan countries of the capitalist world system at the end of the eighteenth century. The policies enacted by the countries of the metropolis have had different effects for different parts of the underdeveloped world.

North America became part of the capitalist metropolis, with the southern part of the United States becoming a regional satellite; in Frank's interpretation, 'the development of the North at the expense of the underdevelopment of the South itself generated a growing crisis as a result of the development of northern productive forces: the Civil War'. (1979a, p. 81)

In Latin America, a similar polarization of the economy and society took place after the Independence, although there the conflict of interests was between the agricultural and mining producers and exporters on the one hand, and the industrialists on the other. The former group allied with the metropolitan bourgeoisie in order to create free trade and to increase the dependence on the metropolis, while the latter group was economically nationalist and preferred the adoption of protectionist policies.

(1972b, pp. 51-62; 1979a, pp. 82-7) The free trade advocates were the winners in this struggle for power; their policy of underdevelopment, in Frank's words, 'concentrated income in a few hands, limited the internal market, discouraged domestic industry, and thus increased dependence still further'. (1972b, p. 62)

In Asia, it was especially India that experienced important changes in its relation to the developed countries. According to Frank, the development of industry in the metropolis required 'the destruction of industry and of the socio-economic nexus between manufacturing and agriculture in the countryside'. (1979a, p. 88) As a consequence of British protectionism, India's textile, iron and steel industries were destroyed.

The industrial capitalist phase thus had important consequences for the subsequent development of the capitalist world system. Frank mentions the 'technological gap', which came into being between the metropolitan and satellite countries, as the most significant result of this phase. This technological gap 'between the manufacture or really machinefacture of consumer goods, particularly cotton textiles, in the North and the de-manufacturalization or de-industrialization of important parts of the Third World', later enhanced by the monopolization of capital goods production in the developed countries, 'has never to this day been closed again by the South'. (1983b, pp. 36, 37-8)

The third stage that has been distinguished by Andre Gunder Frank is *imperialism* (1870-1930). Frank sees this period as one characterized by the prolongation of the trade-dominated exploitative mechanisms, which in the earlier stages of world capitalist development gave rise to the 'development of underdevelopment'. A new element distinguishing this period from earlier ones, according to Frank, was the increase of investments by the developed, metropolitan countries in the United States, other white settler colonies and the underdeveloped countries. These investments were directly and indirectly financed by 'the underdeveloped countries' export surplus to Europe' (1979a, p. 194; cf. 1984a, pp. 77-81) and they contributed to furthering the underdevelopment of those countries.

The main change in the period of imperialism concerned Africa. In the earlier phases of the history of the capitalist world system, this continent was hardly incorporated into the trade streams that developed from the fifteenth century onward. Africa's most important contribution was not the exchange of commodities, but the provision of slaves. The abolition of slave trade led to the replacement of the trading of slaves by the exportation of products from agriculture and mining. According to Frank, the main instrument used by the metropolis to force the Africans into the production for export was found in 'depriv[ing] the indigenous population of their land'. (1979a, p. 160) The result of all this was an increase of the dependence of the African satellites and an enhancement of underdevelopment.

Latin America, according to Frank, also suffered from increased dependence, despite its formal political independence. On the one hand, mining and large-scale *latifundia* agriculture for the purpose of exportation became more important. On the other hand, the metropolitan countries started to invest in projects, mainly railroads, meant to facilitate the exports of minerals and agricultural produce. (1972b, pp. 67-74; 1979a, pp. 164-71)

In the parts of Asia that were not or only barely incorporated into the capitalist system before 1870, roughly the same thing occurred as in Africa: the destruction of 'developed agricultural and handicraft systems' and the replacement of these by export-oriented ones. In the areas that had already become part of the capitalist system, such as India and Indonesia, existing forms of exploitation were perfected and new ones, such as the investment in railroads, were added. (1979a, pp. 146-51)

According to Andre Gunder Frank, the most recent phase in the development of the capitalist world system started after World War II and might be labelled *neoimperialism* or *neodependence*. Despite the political independence of most of the Third World countries at some point during this period, the fundamental mechanisms of the world capitalist system as they developed in the centuries past are still present. For this reason, Frank describes the 'postwar boom' as 'boon for the West, bust for the South'. (1980a, pp. 1-19)

The exploitation of the Third World, which, of course, after the Second World War is as much the *raison d'être* of the capitalist world system as it has been during all of its history, has changed in form, but not in essence. Although Frank still sees (unequal) trade as an important instrument for the transfer of economic surplus from the Third World to the capitalist countries, this instrument has been complemented by foreign investments, mainly by multinational firms, and financial transactions, such as aid or loans.

Where trade is concerned, *unequal exchange* has remained a crucial mechanism for the transfer of surplus. According to Frank, the monopoly character of the developed economies causes the prices of the, mainly agricultural, products of the Third World to fall relatively to the prices of the developed countries' industrial products. This leads to the deterioration of the terms of trade of the underdeveloped countries, meaning that, in a situation in which the proceeds from their export remain stable, these countries have to pay increasingly more for the products they import from the developed world. (1979a, pp. 101-10)

The activities of so-called trans- or multinational firms have become far more important after World War II. The reason for their interest in the underdeveloped countries is mainly to be found in the level of wages in these countries. Since the costs of producing in the underdeveloped countries are much lower, a number of multinational companies have chosen to invest there in production processes set up for exportation to the developed countries. The resulting profits are much higher than they would be if the production had taken place in the developed countries themselves. Frank has mentioned the Newly Industrializing Countries as a prime example in this respect. (See section III above)

Andre Gunder Frank has mentioned another way in which the activities of the multinationals can turn out to be harmful to the underdeveloped countries. Some multinational companies raise part or most of the capital needed for investments on the national markets of underdeveloped countries. By drawing large quantities of capital from the national capital markets, other investors are 'crowded out'. Since national investors are more likely than multinational companies to use the capital for increasing the domestic productive capacity, the crowding-out of investments is detrimental to Third World countries. (1983b, pp. 41-2; 1969a, pp. 298-303)

Finally, the financial transactions, or 'invisible services', are interpreted as extremely harmful to the developing countries. According to Frank, the creation of so-called agri-business for the export of agricultural commodities has been a 'process of debt financed re-location of industry and change in the international division of labour between the North and the South'. (1983b, p. 44) This means that, in order to produce for the international market - under the pretext of pursuing 'export-oriented growth', which is particularly favourable to parts of the bourgeoisie -, the underdeveloped countries run into debt.

The direct consequence of the build-up of debt by the underdeveloped countries is that they have to pay back the original amount, with interest, in the years to come. Since, according to Frank, foreign finance is hardly ever used to reduce the dependence on foreign capital goods, the repayment is a real economic burden. This burden is reflected in the balance of payments deficits of many Third World countries and, ultimately, in a reduction of the value of their currencies. In turn, this stimulates firms from the developed countries to take over companies in the Third World. (1969b, pp. 181-91; 1972b, pp. 106-12; 1981a, pp. 132-56) Further international consequences for the underdeveloped countries are summed up by Andre Gunder Frank:

> The desperate need of Third World countries to borrow from Peter to pay Paul exposes them to pressures so intense they amount to blackmail by the International Monetary Fund and the big Western banks to adopt policies that further export promotion. These policies are the standard IMF package: currency devaluation, reductions in public spending and in subsidies for social purposes and reduced wages, all of which increase the exploitation of the poor and often lead to 'IMF riots'. Therefore, the imposition of these measures usually requires an increase in political repression, which the IMF sometimes calls for by demanding the replacement of one economies minister or even a whole government by another. (1981a, p. 132)

V THE THEORY OF RECURRING CRISES OF CAPITAL ACCUMULATION

Above it has already been noted that Andre Gunder Frank considers the development of the capitalist world system as uneven. The fluctuation is expressed through 'long cycles of accelerated and retarded growth and recurrent world economic crises'. The mechanism that is held responsible for the cycles of growth and crises is capital accumulation itself. Capital accumulation can be considered the motive force of the capitalist world system, and since it is dependent upon the rate of profit of economic transactions - this itself being dependent upon exploitation - the tendency of the rate of profit to fall causes periodic crises. According to Frank, these crises generate a 'pressure for new inventions' and also engender 'an accelerated change or transformation in the international division of labour'. Frank concludes that 'it is in the periods of economic crises that the unequal structure of the world economy undergoes its most rapid transformation'. (1983b, p. 16) It is also during those crises that 'the "rise" from the periphery and [...] the "decline" at the center' takes place and leads to the 'development of intermediate, semiperipheral economies and powers'. (1981a, p. 3)

The major crises in the capitalist world system, in Frank's view, took place during the seventeenth century, from 1762 until 1790, from 1873 until 1895, in the 1930s (the Great Depression) and between 1967 and the mid-1980s. The main reactions to those crises were, respectively, the commercial revolution of the eighteenth century, the Industrial Revolution, the metropolitan expansion by means of imperialism, the creation of neoimperialism and monopoly capitalism, and the rise of neo-conservatism in the West and the transfer of (parts of) production processes to the Third World. Since the empirical part of this study will focus on the post-World War II period, most attention will be devoted to Andre Gunder Frank's interpretation of the most recent crisis in the capitalist world system.

The main cause of the crisis of the 1960s, 1970s and 1980s is sought by Andre Gunder Frank not in deficient demand but in overproduction, originating in the developed industrial countries. (1980b, p. 675) He has analysed the cause in the following terms:

> The increase in the organic composition of capital (that is, an increase in the capital/labor ratio) and the partly associated increase in workers' bargaining power and militancy have, since the mid-sixties, led to a decline in the rate of profit and rate of growth and, in some instances, to an absolute reduction in the demand for industrial commodities, particularly of capital or investment goods. (1981c, p. 499)

For the industrial countries the crisis is clearly functional, since it drives 'capital into bankruptcy to clean up the capitalist house' and breaks 'the back of labor organization and militancy'. (1981c, p. 502) Together with the curtailment of the social security programs, which has taken place in most developed nations, and the 'deliberate unemployment policies', this should lead to a reduction of the costs of production. (1982, pp. 126-33; 1980a, pp. 102-77) 'Reaganomics' and 'Thatcherism' are interpreted by Frank as the clearest reflection of the neo-conservative reaction in the developed countries, although he also stresses the fact that 'these austerity policies have been implemented in most parts of the West by social democratic governments, and often with the support of communist parties'. (1981c, p. 505; cf. 1984a, pp. 189-207) An international instrument contributing to the reduction of these costs has been found in the relocation of labour-intensive industry to countries of the Third World and, increasingly, of the socialist world. (1980a, pp. 178-93; cf. 1986 and 1987a) According to Frank, the tensions among the capitalist countries are enhanced, because to a certain extent they are one another's competitors in achieving solutions to the problems they face. (Cf. 1983a)

The consequences of the crisis for the Third World have been much graver than they have been for the developed capitalist countries. Many underdeveloped countries had introduced strategies of export promotion during the 1960s and 1970s, hoping thereby to stimulate their economic growth. The demand of the developed countries was reduced, however, because of the economic crisis. Another setback for the developing countries was the increase of the general price level, which was, according to Frank, 'not so much the result of the increase in the price of oil, but the result of the increase of the price of everything else they had to import, or in other words, the reflection of the price inflation in the West'. (1984c, p. 801)

The resulting balance of payments deficits were predominantly financed with loans from Western banks; this, in turn, stimulated the accumulation of debts and led to the debt crisis in the Third World as some countries eventually were unable to pay back their debt. (1984b, pp. 1036-7 and 1039-40) Some Third World countries tried to repay their debts, albeit at the cost of political repression by military and otherwise authoritarian governments: the repayment of the debt implied that these countries had to accumulate an export surplus, which, in its turn, required a reduction of the proportion of domestic production that was being consumed at home. (1981a, pp. 188-279; 1982, pp. 138-42; 1984b, p. 1040) This situation has led Andre Gunder Frank to speak of circumstances of 'debt where credit is due'. (1987b; cf. 1988)

VI MODELLING ANDRE GUNDER FRANK'S DEPENDENCY THEORY

In this section, a testable model will be constructed on the basis of the discussion of Andre Gunder Frank's dependency theory in this chapter. This model, as well as the models that will be constructed in the next chapters, will serve as a reference point in establishing the empirical value of dependency theory. The model is pictured in figure 3.1 on page 72.

Obviously, as with all models, the model presented in this section is a reduction of the originally formulated theory. A model, by its very nature, is unable to capture all the nuances of a theory. The object of the model is to represent the 'hard core' of Andre Gunder Frank's theory of dependency, i.e., to outline the variables and relations among these which are central to the theory. Not all variables that have been introduced by Andre Gunder Frank will necessarily be found in the model; the *important* variables will all be there, though.

It has become clear above that Andre Gunder Frank's theory establishes relations among economic, social and political variables. It is obvious, though, that his theory is focused on the relationship between *dependence* and *development*. The degree of dependence determines, in Frank's view, the position of a country in the capitalist world system and, thereby, also this country's ability to exploit other countries: those countries experiencing the most intense dependence have the least opportunities to exploit others; the so-called semi-peripheral countries have an important function in the context of worldwide exploitation, and they in their turn are exploited by the developed, capitalist countries.

The situation of the capitalist world system in this theory is a very important factor in determining the circumstances of individual countries. In periods of expansion, the developed nations exert more pressure on the underdeveloped ones; thereby, dependence is enhanced. In periods of crisis, however, the metropolitan countries have to find ways to deal with their own problems and it is in those periods that the satellites are more or less able to pursue their own development. According to Frank, the satellites have been able to introduce import-substituting policies in stages of world capitalist development characterized by crisis.

The state of the capitalist world system also influences the internal polarization in the satellites. In periods of crisis, the already existing polarization between socio-economic groups is enhanced even further. Also, and partly because of this, the political regime becomes more autocratic: in order to keep potentially, or actually, rebellious groups under control, the level of repression has to be increased. In Frank's view, the military coups in many Third World countries are to be explained in the context of the periodic crises pervading the world capitalist system.

The internal polarization of the satellite countries is an important variable in the dependency-development nexus. On the one hand, the degree of dependence determines the rise to power of certain socio-economic groups that are to play a role in worldwide exploitation and accumulation. On the other hand, the internal polarization contributes to the underdevelopment of the satellite countries, because then some groups have an interest in exploiting and, thereby, underdeveloping parts of their own countries.

The concentration of production, meaning the reliance on the production of a small number of commodities, is influenced by the degree of dependence and by the situation in the capitalist world system. The more dependent countries will be driven to a situation of (near-) monoculture, which in itself is seen as an impediment to achieving more development. The situation in the capitalist world system also influences the concentration of production. It has already been indicated above that a situation of world economic crisis enables the satellite countries to change something about their own situation. During periods of crisis, the satellite countries will therefore try to diversify their economy by producing more types of commodities than before. This is thought to curtail the possibilities of exploitation by the metropolitan countries and to reduce the level of underdevelopment.

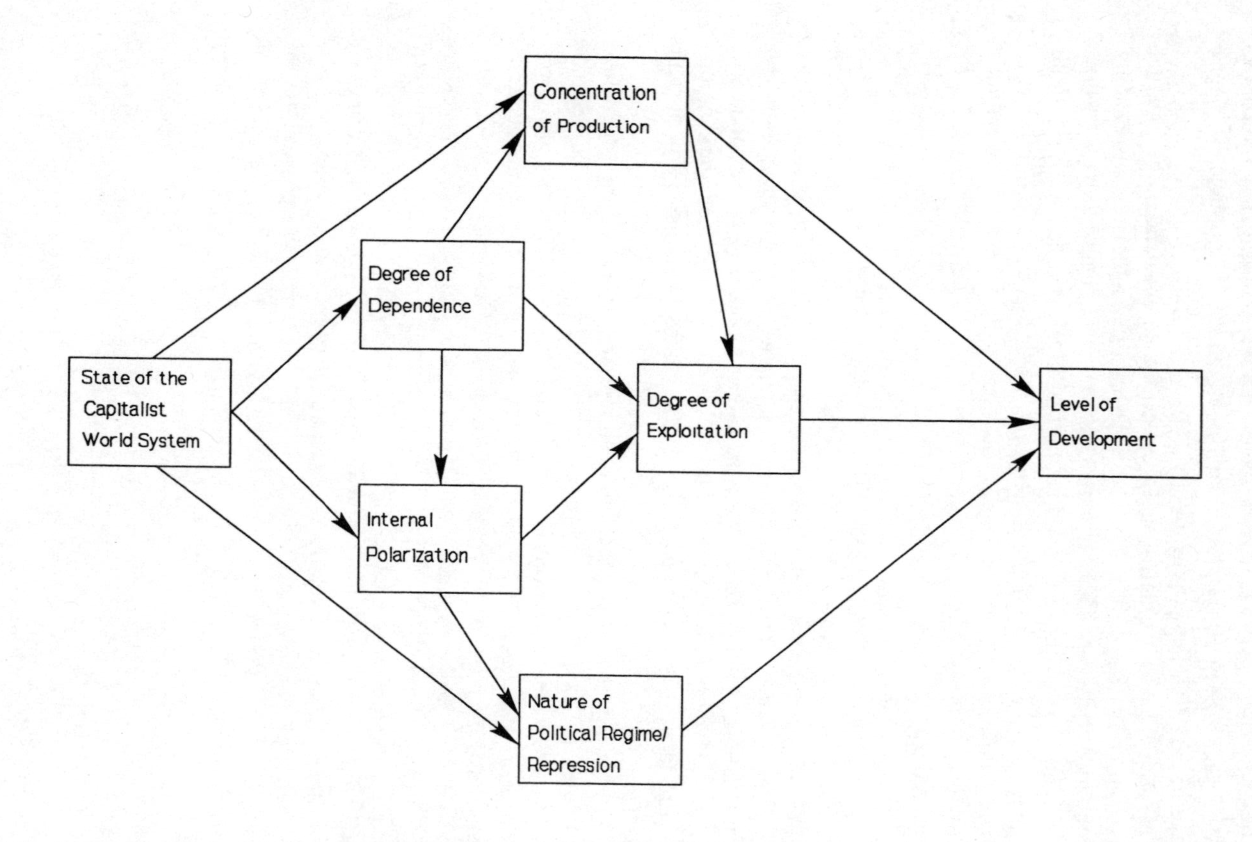

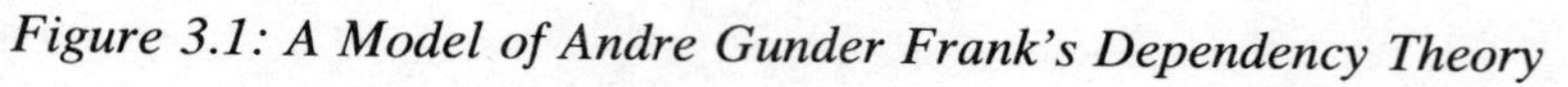
Figure 3.1: A Model of Andre Gunder Frank's Dependency Theory

NOTES

1. Where 'the work' of Andre Gunder Frank is referred to in this chapter, only his writings on dependency are meant. Until about 1964 Frank was a 'mainstream' economist, writing on problems of productivity and capital formation. The work published in this period will not be considered in this study. Frank's articles have sometimes been published in several journals and finally have been collected in books. Apart from Frank's books, his articles will be discussed only when they have not been re-published in book form.
2. See e.g. Frank (1978b, p. 250): 'Insofar as relations of production - in relation to exchange and realization - are the significant criterion, it is the *transformation* of the relations of production, circulation, and realization through their incorporation into the process of capital accumulation that is, in principle, *the relevant criterion of the existence of capitalism.*' (Latter italics added) Cf. on this issue: Laclau (1971) and Banaji (1983, pp. 98-100).

4. Samir Amin: Accumulation on a World Scale

I INTRODUCTION

In this chapter, the outline of which follows that of the previous one, the work of Samir Amin will be analysed. To an important extent, Amin's theorizing is focused on the process of so-called accumulation in the world capitalist system, which, in his view, is characterized by unequal development. In Amin's work, three central elements can be discerned: the ideas about value and unequal exchange in the context of the world system, which might be interpreted as the foundations of his accumulation theory; the theory of the development of the world capitalist system; and the theory of 'delinking', that is, the development strategy for the Third World supported by Samir Amin.

This chapter will successively deal with these three elements. First, the methodological and theoretical assumptions in Amin's work will be scrutinized in section II. Section III will discuss the theory of value, accumulation and unequal exchange. In section IV the focus will be on Samir Amin's theory of the development of the capitalist world system. Section V will go into Amin's ideas about a viable development strategy to be adopted by the countries of the Third World. The final section of this chapter, VI, will contain a model featuring the central elements of Amin's dependency theory.

II METHODOLOGICAL AND THEORETICAL ASSUMPTIONS

Samir Amin's theorizing may be characterized as 'historical materialist'. However, as he himself has argued, his assumptions differ from those in both mainstream and Marxist thinking about development and international relations. (E.g. 1984b and 1983) In this section, Amin's methodological assumptions will be identified and, subsequently, his theoretical assumptions will be analysed.

A Methodological Assumptions

On pages 53-4 above, so-called functional explanation has been discussed. What has been true of Frank's theorizing, is also true of Amin's: Amin explains events that occur in the capitalist world system by relating these to the 'functions' they are supposed to have for the capitalist system, and especially for the accumulation of capital by the bourgeoisie of the centre. Examples of this type of explanation abound in Amin's writings. One of the most striking and explicit examples is Amin's explanation of the rise of imperialism during the final decades of the nineteenth century:

> Throughout the nineteenth century, until the 1880s, because real wages at the center did not increase sufficiently, a form of expansionism was necessary that conferred certain functions upon the periphery. Since the last decades of the nineteenth century, however, real wages at the centre have increased at a faster rate, and this has caused the expansionism of the capitalist mode to assume new forms (imperialism and the export of capital) and has also given the periphery new functions to perform. (1976, p. 76)

A second crucial methodological assumption is to be found in Amin's *holism*. In his view, individual actions have no significance whatsoever in the historical development of society and politics. It is the abstract development of modes of productions that dictates the course of history. In his *Criticism of microeconomics*, Amin has argued, for instance, that the economic behaviour of people, dictated by the mode of production they find themselves in, cannot be separated from their behaviour 'in connection with the family, as regards the number of children they want, the organization of marriage and inheritance, etc.'. (1977b, p. 21)

B Theoretical Assumptions

Samir Amin's theorizing not only resembles Frank's with respect to methodological assumptions; there are also striking similarities concerning theoretical assumptions. This is something that could be expected, since both theories are branches of the same tree of dependency. The difference between them is that Frank has not taken a stand on the reputedly Marxist character of his writings, while Amin has declared himself to be a Marxist at several places in his work. With respect to Amin's theory there are at least five theoretical assumptions that have to be mentioned and analysed in order to come fully to grips with it.

The first theoretical assumption in Amin's work concerns the status of 'historical materialism' and the role of economic factors in the explanation of social and political processes. The relation that people have to the means of production is evidently the central factor in Samir Amin's explanation of international relations. In his view, it is this relation that determines class positions. Class positions, in turn, are responsible for people's interests and political and social behaviour, expressed in the class struggle: 'history is, in the final analysis, the history of class struggle'. (1980a, p. 2)

Samir Amin's second theoretical assumption concerns the capitalist world system. (Cf. Smith 1980, pp. 11-12) This system has come into existence as a result of the worldwide expansion of the capitalist mode of production since the sixteenth century. The power of the capitalist mode of production has been, according to Amin, so devastating that all other non-capitalist modes have been subjected to it. This has led Amin to conclude that '[o]ur world no longer consists of juxtaposed national systems carrying on ''external'' relations with each other (even if these are important), as was the case until quite recently. Rather it constitutes a unity, a whole - the world capitalist system.' (1977b, p. 181) To Amin, the world system is a reality, and it causes capital accumulation, the ultimate aim of capitalism, to take place on a worldwide, instead of a national, basis.

The third assumption to be found in Amin's writings concerns the concept of *value*. As Amin repeatedly stresses, value is not synonymous with the price of commodities. The idea that there is a relation between the two is an invention of 'bourgeois economics' designed for 'eluding the question'. (1983, p. 381; cf. Brewer 1980, pp. 247-8 and Smith 1980, pp. 16-18) Amin assumes that value is determined and determinable, even apart from market relations; he adheres to the 'law of value', which amounts to the following:

> [P]roducts, when they are commodities, possess value; [...] this value is measurable; [...] the yardstick for measuring it is the quantity of abstract labor socially necessary to produce them; and, finally, [...] this quantity is the sum of the quantities of labor, direct and indirect (transferred), which are used in the process of production. The concept of the commodity and the existence of the law of value, formulated in this way, are inseparably interconnected. (1978b, p. 9; cf. Leaver 1983b, pp. 64-5)

Connected with the third assumption is a fourth one, implying that the relations between countries of the centre and of the periphery in the capitalist world system are by their very nature exploitative. Since the capitalist centre countries have the power to impose unequal and inequitable conditions of exchange upon the peripheral countries, the international market works at the detriment of the latter. Values and prices differ to such an extent that the centre gains and the periphery loses. (1974, pp. 53-9, 64-90; 1976, pp. 138-54; 1977b, pp. 183-223; cf. Schiffer 1981, p.

517)

The fifth theoretical assumption in Samir Amin's work concerns economic development. According to Amin, a development policy can only be successful when it is really *autocentred*, implying that economic activities are required to conform to the needs of the country concerned. Development on a so-called *extroverted* basis is not possible, because in that situation the interests of other countries will predominate. The latter is the case in export economies, in which no viable economic structure can develop because national production is oriented towards exportation and imports mainly consist of luxury goods. Autocentred development requires the production of both mass consumption goods and capital goods. (E.g. 1971 and 1972a)

III VALUE, ACCUMULATION AND UNEQUAL EXCHANGE

Starting from the 'law of value', which stresses that the value of commodities is measurable by the quantity of labour needed for producing them, Samir Amin has built a theory of accumulation and unequal exchange in the capitalist world system. According to Amin, the accumulation of capital 'is an essential inner law of the capitalist mode of production, and doubtless also of the socialist mode of production, but it is not an inner law of the functioning of precapitalist modes of production'. (1974, p. 2)

Although Amin has defined capitalism in terms of the mode of production, he nevertheless brings elements into his clarification of the concept resembling those stressed by Andre Gunder Frank; this means that, in Amin's work, capitalism can be understood as a system of production for a market. (E.g. 1977b, pp. 37-40; cf. Barone 1982, p. 11) The fundamental difference between the capitalist and precapitalist modes of production is to be found, in Amin's view, in the relative importance of economic and political factors. Since the precapitalist modes of production were not characterized by production for a market, political forces were allowed to determine the productive process and the ensuing distribution of the economic product. Under capitalism, the dominant economic actors, that is, the owners of capital, are assumed to have subordinated the political system to their interests and thereby to have substituted political with economic considerations with respect to production and distribution. (1989, pp. 216-17; 1985)

At present, according to Amin, all societies form part of the so-called capitalist world system, which has expanded gradually over the last few centuries. As a consequence of this development, '[n]ot a single concrete socioeconomic formation of our time can be understood except as part of this world system'. (1974, p. 3) It is not simply the integration that is important to Amin; the concomitant subjection of previously autonomous countries to the rule of the capitalist system implies that a theory of 'accumulation on a world scale' has to be used to explain the present-day relationship between developed and developing countries. Amin even goes as far as writing that:

> the [capitalist world] system is defined in the abstract by the great mobility of goods and capital and by a relative immobility of labor. This means [...] that commodities are primarily worldwide. This implies that, throughout the system, social labor is crystallized in goods which have an international character. The result is that an hour of simple labor in the Congo and in Germany are as comparable as an hour of labor in a Detroit factory and in a New York barbershop, since both generate the same value; that is, the labor of both the Congolese and the German producer culminates in worldwide commodities destined for the same world capitalist market. (1977b, p. 181; see also pp. 216-18; cf. Chandra 1986, p. PE 80)

Amin's explanation for the expansionary inclination of capitalism is based upon the purported tendency of the centre's rate of profit to fall. Amin here follows the ideas developed by some Marxist authors, who assumed that the exploitative nature of capitalism, and the consequent drive to intensify the rate of exploitation, would eventually reduce the purchasing power of the workers and thereby cause the rate of profit to decline. The integration of the periphery into the capitalist world system would have as its main objective the countering of this negative tendency '(1) by enlarging markets and exploiting new regions where the rate of surplus value was higher than at the center; and (2) by reducing the cost of labor power and of constant capital'. (1976, p. 185; cf. 1977b, pp. 206-8)

Amin's theory of accumulation on a world scale starts from the idea that the centre and periphery play different, unequal roles in the capitalist world system. The centre is the dominant part of the world system and is therefore able to impose its will upon the countries of the periphery with respect to the relations of exchange. The exchange of commodities between the centre and the periphery turns out to be *unequal*, i.e., favourable for the centre and unfavourable for the periphery.

The fundamental mechanism of 'unequal exchange' is to be found in the structure of remuneration of labour:

> Analysis of exchanges between advanced countries and underdeveloped ones leads to the observation that exchange is unequal as soon as labor of the same productivity is rewarded at a lower rate in the periphery, as is the case today. This *fact* cannot be

explained without bringing in the policy (economic policy, and policy in general) followed by the capital that dominates in the periphery, as regards organization of the surplus of labor power. (1974, pp. 62-3)

According to Amin, the 'superabundance' of labour power in the peripheral countries is not a 'natural law', but, instead, an act of policy. The ruling classes of the periphery, often allied to those of the centre and thereby benefiting from the exploitation of their own country, stimulate the creation of an unemployed proletariat, so that the wages can be reduced and, given a certain level of productivity, the surplus rate can be increased.[1] When wages are reduced, the prices of commodities can be lower. Under the assumption of equal productivity of workers in the centre and the periphery, a given quantity of value (i.e., the embodiment of a certain number of labour hours) can be obtained by the centre with less money than would be needed when the value was to be realized by investments at home.

The central mechanism contributing to the process of 'accumulation on a world scale' is, according to Samir Amin, the transfer of value from the periphery to the centre. This value is accumulated in the form of capital goods, the acquisition of which in itself contributes to the widening of the gap between the opposite parts of the world system. As a corollary to the process of accumulation, technological progress in the capitalist world system for the larger part takes place in the centre.

The ruling classes in the centre and the periphery are not the only actors who benefit from exploitation through unequal exchange. In Amin's view, the working class in the centre is 'bribed' with full employment, social services and higher wages in order to ally with the bourgeoisie against the interests of the periphery's proletariat. The 'monopoly capital' in the centre 'consents to these concessions only because it can raise its overall rate of profit by extracting surplus profits from the exploitation of labor in the periphery'. (1977a, p. 28)

The main loser in the capitalist world system is the periphery, and especially its least privileged part, the proletariat. Amin's view is perfectly summarized by the following quotation:

The imports that the advanced countries of the West receive from the Third World represent, it is true, only 2 or 3 percent of their gross internal product [...] But these exports from the underdeveloped countries represent 20 percent of *their* product [...] The hidden transfer of value due to unequal exchange is thus of the order of 15 percent of this product, which is far from being negligible in relative terms, and is alone sufficient to account for the blocking of the growth of the periphery, and the increasing gap between it and the center. The contribution that this transfer makes is not negligible, either, when seen from the standpoint of the center, which benefits from it, since it comes to about 1.5 percent of the center's product. But this transfer

> is especially important for the giant firms that are its direct beneficiaries. (1976, p. 144)

The ever-continuing tapping of resources from the periphery causes a situation of *underdevelopment.* In Amin's view, underdevelopment is first and foremost a situation of unbalance. Underdevelopment is not so much a *quantitative* as it is a *qualitative* characteristic. (Cf. 1991, p. 312) Underdevelopment does not in the first place manifest itself in the level of production per head, but in structural features, of which Amin mentions three crucial ones. (1974, pp. 262-99; 1976, pp. 201-2)

The first feature is the extreme unevenness in the 'distribution of productivities' across economic sectors in the periphery; Amin argues that the differences are much larger there than is the case in the centre. The spread of capital goods to all or most economic sectors has tended to equalize productivity in the centre. Moreover, the price structure of the centre is transmitted to the periphery, because the periphery and the centre belong to the same world system; the resulting application of a system of rewards alien to the periphery enhances the differences even further.

As a second characteristic of underdevelopment, Amin mentions the 'disarticulation', or lack of linkages, between different productive sectors, due to the periphery's orientation to the centre's needs. (See figure 4.1 on page 81.) This fact limits the transmission of economic benefits throughout the economy of the periphery.

The third feature of underdevelopment is the economic domination of the periphery by the centre, expressed in international specialization and the dependence on foreign capital.

In an attempt to elucidate the crucial differences between peripheral and central 'social formations', Samir Amin has used the scheme that is reproduced in figure 4.1. (1972a, p. 704) In Amin's view, the determinant link in an economy belonging to the centre of the capitalist world system is the one between sector 2, the production of mass consumption goods, and sector 4, the production of capital goods. The principal link in peripheral dependent economies is the one between sector 1, the export sector, and sector 3, the consumption of luxury goods. The difference between both types of economies is also expressed by the use of the adjectives 'autocentred' and 'extroverted', implying that the centre economies are well-integrated, autonomous units with their own dynamics, while the peripheral economies are dependent, oriented toward the centre and incapable of functioning on their own.

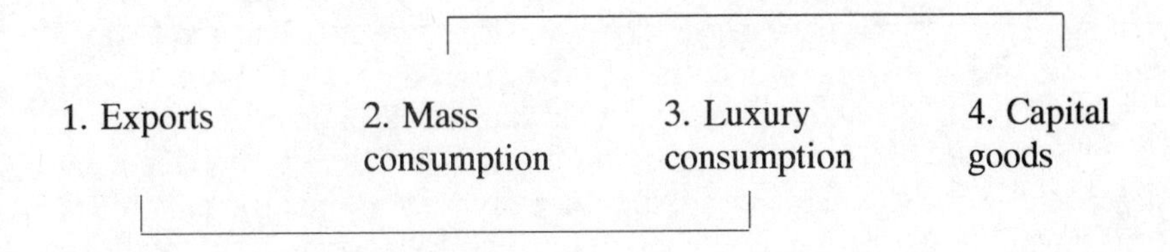

(principal peripheral dependent link)

Figure 4.1: The Links between Economic Sectors in Peripheral and Central Social Formations

In Amin's view, the periphery is condemned to play the role of exporter of raw materials and agricultural produce. Because of this 'unequal specialization' (1976, p. 191), the periphery is extremely dependent upon the centre. Amin provides the following, typically functional, explanation for this state of affairs:

> The *reason* for the creation of such an export sector has been the possibility to obtain from the periphery those products which are necessary for the formation of constant capital (raw materials) or variable capital (foodstuffs) at production prices which are lower than they would have been at the centre for analogous products (or for evident substitutes in the case of specific products such as coffee or tea). (1972a, p. 708)[2]

Since the periphery is outward-oriented it does not obtain the means necessary for the pursuit of an autocentred development policy. The surplus that is realized on the production in the periphery cannot be used for investment, since the better part is tapped by the centre; the remainder of the surplus is collected by large landowners who tend to use it for luxury consumption. This is also the reason why, according to Amin, the so-called multiplier mechanism does not apply to underdeveloped countries. As he writes, the multiplier effect is present 'only if demand creates its own supply through the intermediary of *production*. This intermediary, overlooked by Keynes, is essential. In a country where there are no free productive forces, the extra demand is lost in a price increase.' (1974, p. 226)

In Samir Amin's view, the domination of the centre over the periphery is not a direct consequence of the fact that the latter's exports consist mainly of primary products. In any case, countries such as Australia, New

Zealand and Canada once were also mono-product exporters. The determining aspect of the periphery's dependence is 'the fact that the peripheral economies are *only* producers of basic products - in other words, that this production is not integrated into an autocentric industrial structure'. (1976, pp. 246-7) The dependence on exports is enhanced by financial dependence: for the larger part, the capital used to finance productive investments in the periphery comes from abroad. Eventually, this leads to an outflow of profits; this money cannot be used for local development programmes.

According to Amin, '[a]ll peripheral formations have four main characteristics in common'. (1976, p. 333; cf. 1977d) The first of these characteristics is the predominance of agrarian capitalism, implying that there usually is an extensive class of large landowners, using their land for the production of agricultural goods for the world market. The second feature is the existence of a *comprador* (literally: trading) bourgeoisie; this class is directly tied to the bourgeoisie in the centre and is not in a position to develop independently from the latter. For this reason, the development policy initiated by the comprador bourgeoisie during the Great Depression of the 1930s was bound to fail. The third element is the tendency in the peripheral countries towards the origination of a dominant bureaucracy, either of civil or, very often, military origin, which tries to take over the role of the bourgeoisie in developing the country. The fourth characteristic of peripheral formations is the extreme inequality in the distribution of income, caused by the spread of unemployment and underemployment. (1976, pp. 333-64; cf. 1984a)

The processes sketched here lead to the 'marginalization of the masses'. (1976, p. 194) This entails, among other things:

> [the] proletarianizing of the small agricultural and craft producers, rural semiproletarianization, and impoverishment without proletarianization of the peasants organized in village communities, urbanization, and massive growth in both open unemployment and underemployment in the towns, etc. (1976, p. 194)

These developments are not accompanied by industrialization, since, as it has been pointed out above, the extroverted economy of the periphery is not able to generate enough surpluses to support such industrialization. From this Amin concludes that '[t]his lack of a way forward through autocentric industrialization accounts for the increased "pressure on the land" that is so frequently to be observed in the Third World'. (1976, p. 205) This means that many Third World countries experience 'urbanization without industrialization'. This situation is crucially different from the experience of the presently developed countries during their history, since these have been able to pursue autocentric development strategies.

IV THE THEORY OF THE HISTORICAL DEVELOPMENT OF THE CAPITALIST WORLD SYSTEM

Samir Amin's theory of the development of the capitalist world system fits in with his ideas about value, accumulation and unequal exchange that have been expounded in the previous section. The history of this world system cannot, in Amin's view, be analysed separately from what he considers to be the immanent and permanent features of capitalism.

As has already been emphasized above, the expansion of the capitalist world system is analysed by Amin as the most significant process in the history of the past several centuries. No social group, or 'formation', as Amin calls it, has been untouched by this expansion, and especially the areas where the periphery came into being have suffered considerably.

Throughout his work, Samir Amin has provided elements for a theory of the historical development of the capitalist world system. In various places, Amin has distinguished four phases in the history of this world system. The first one (before 1600) invariably is the pre-mercantilist period. The second phase (1600-1800) is alternately called the phase of mercantilist expansionism or the mercantilist period of primitive accumulation. The third phase (1800-80) is named the period of integration or the classical period of mature premonopoly capitalism. The most recent phase (1880-present) is either called the period of colonization, the imperialist or the imperialist-monopoly period. (1972b; 1974, pp. 39-40; 1977b, pp. 103-4; cf. 1965, 1966, 1970 and 1973) Amin has paid more attention to Africa and the Arab world than to the other parts of the periphery, but he contends that his interpretation of the historical development of the capitalist world system has general validity.

According to Amin's interpretation, during the long *pre-mercantilist period* in the history of the regions that, at present, form the periphery of the world capitalist system, there were few links between these regions and the rest of the world. Although long-distance trade existed between Europe on the one hand, and Africa, Asia and the Middle East on the other, this did not have much impact on the economies of the respective countries.

In Amin's view the frequently used typology of slavery, feudalism and capitalism as the historical phases toward the development of capitalism is invalid. This sequence he considers 'to be West-centered in its overgeneralization of the specific characteristics of the history of the West and its rejection of the history of other peoples in all its peculiarities'. (1980a, p. 250) Instead of this typology, Amin has distinguished four modes of production existing in the non-European areas before the commercial expansion of Europe began. (1976, pp. 13-16) The first one of these is the 'primitive-communal' mode, historically anterior to all the other modes of production, in which commodity trade does not exist and the social product is distributed in accordance with rules based on kinship organization. The second mode of production is the 'tribute-paying' one, and it is based on the exploitation of the peasantry by a ruling class. The third mode is the 'slave-owning' one, in which the worker, as a slave, is turned into the central means of production. The fourth non-capitalist mode of production is the 'simple petty-commodity' one, implying the production of commodities by free and equal petty producers. According to Amin, there is no historical sequence to be detected in these four modes of production. During the expansion of capitalism across the world, the four non-capitalist modes of production are subordinated to the capitalist one, in which all products, including labour, are turned into commodities. The capitalist mode of production, in Amin's view, becomes exclusive: 'It constitutes a world system in which all the formations, central and peripheral alike, are arranged in a single system, organized and hierarchical.' (1976, p. 22)

Amin does not pay much attention to the pre-mercantilist period. His judgment with respect to Africa during this period is typical for his attitude toward the time before the capitalist expansion started; Amin stresses that 'Black Africa was not on the whole more backward than the rest of the world'. (1972b, p. 506) The long-distance trade between Africa and the rest of the world meant that Africa exported gold, ivory and gum and imported other luxury goods. The influence of this trade remained fairly limited, because it involved 'rare' products, with no domestic equivalents, and consequently the costs of production of these were unknown in the importing countries. (E.g. 1980a, pp. 50-4)

The *mercantilist period* introduced a major change for the Third World. The development of mercantile capitalism in the countries of Europe led to the expansion of European influence on economic activities across the world. In this period, according to Amin, capital was still in a 'prehistoric form', with the bourgeoisie accumulating it on the basis of slave-based export agriculture in America. In Europe, furthermore, feudalism disintegrated and agriculture was proletarianized and commercialized. Linked with this, capitalist production relations and wage labour started to develop. (1977b, pp. 50-3)

This is not to say that Amin does not pay attention to the centre-periphery relations during this period. On the contrary, Amin considers these relations as crucial for the development of capitalism. As he has written, '[t]he commercial relations of this period were quantitatively and qualitatively a fundamental element in the capitalist system being formed'. (1974, p. 40) The centre imported mainly luxury goods and primary products from the periphery, mainly from the Americas and Asia, but had not much to offer in return. During the first phase of European expansion, plunder was one of the most important means to obtain goods. After a while, a 'slave-owning mode of production' was founded in America in order to produce the goods for the centre. (1974, pp. 40-1)

Amin is very clear about the purported consequences of all this for Africa: 'Reduced to the function of supplying slave labour for the plantations of America, Africa lost its autonomy. It began to be shaped according to foreign requirements, those of mercantilism.' (1972b, p. 511) Because of this, the integration of regional African communities came to a standstill and the African peoples were fragmented and isolated - this, according to Samir Amin, is one of the most important causes of the resulting problems in Africa.

The *period of integration* of the periphery into the capitalist world system started with the industrial revolution in the capitalist countries. The importance of this period is underlined by Amin when he writes that '[i]t was in this period that the international specialization between industrial and agricultural countries was decided'. (1974, p. 41) Industrial production became the new focus of economic activity in the countries of the centre. The function of the periphery, in Amin's view, changed into 'provid[ing] *products* which would tend to reduce the value of both constant and variable capital used at the centre: raw materials and agricultural products'. (1972b, p. 516) Moreover, the peripheral American, Asian and Arab-Ottoman areas became important outlets for the products manufactured in the centre. (1977b, pp. 103-4) The principal instrument for the centre to keep the periphery under control has been the creation of alliances with landowning and merchant, *comprador*, bourgeoisies. (1976, pp. 295-305)

According to Amin, there are several instances when the centre directly rendered the periphery more dependent. Amin mentions, among others, the following examples: India, where the British destroyed Indian textile industry and imposed agricultural specialization; Indonesia, Malaya, Indochina and the Philippines, where industrial plantations were created for export purposes; and Egypt, where the industrial renaissance was repressed in the 1840s and the country returned to cotton growing. (1976, p. 299 and 1978a, p. 30)

Integration into the full capitalist system was not, according to Amin, completed until the *imperialist period*. By this time, capital at the centre had reached the 'monopoly stage' and proved to be able to 'organise production on the spot'. (1972b, p. 518) The exportation of capital from the centre to the periphery becomes the defining characteristic of this phase. The situation of dependence is perpetuated: because of the extroverted nature of the peripheral economies, the internal market is primarily oriented towards luxury goods, at the expense of mass consumption goods. (1980a, pp. 134-7)

The situation sketched here lasted until about 1914, when World War I introduced a 'crisis' in the world system. At different places in the periphery, national liberation movements emerged under bourgeois leadership. Attempts at industrialization were made by introducing the so-called strategy of import substituting industrialization. Amin is rather adamant in his conclusion about this attempt at development:

> This second phase of imperialism is in no way a stage toward the establishment of an autocentered economy. It is not the reproduction of an earlier phase of central development but, on the contrary, an extension of the first extraverted phase. In fact three points can be made. The agricultural revolution has still not taken place. [...] The dominant class alliances are still international: the bourgeoisie replaced old feudal and comprador elements as the subordinate ally of imperialism. [...] The development process continues to depend on exports, which consist of raw materials. This primary means of financing necessary imports of equipment in the last instance determines the pace of growth, which in this sense remains extraverted. (1980a, pp. 139-40)

The most recent stage in the development of imperialism is the post-World War II period. According to Amin, this stage ' "recuperated" the limited anti-imperialist victories of the previous crisis'. (1977b, p. 115) Although light industries have been established in countries of the periphery, this has not meant a break with the capitalist world system. On the contrary, the relocation of certain branches of previously central industries has offered the centre new opportunities to further the accumulation of capital. (E.g. 1982a, pp. 442-4)

The international division of labour in this period differed considerably from that in the directly preceding one. In the period from the end of the nineteenth century until the First World War there were, in Amin's view, class alliances between:

> the nascent monopoly capital of the imperialist centers and a combination of local ruling classes, as, for example, between the latifundia oligarchy (typical of Latin America, the Ottoman Empire, Egypt, and India), the feudals or semi-feudals, and the comprador bourgeoisie. (1981, pp. 34-5)

The 'second age of imperialism', after the Second World War, was characterized by a class alliance 'between monopoly capital and the local industrial state bourgeoisies: the private and state-created bourgeoisies that were linked to the neocolonial system and the import-substitution policies of industrialization'. (1981, p. 35)

These developments in the post-war period have not led to the disappearance of crises. In Amin's view, the growth phase, lasting from 1944 until the second half of the 1960s, came to an end because 'increasing contradictions' grew to dominate in the capitalist world system. In the first place, the economic position of the United States, which until then was the hegemonic power in the world system, was weakened by the increasing strength of Western Europe and Japan. As a consequence, the United States developed a chronic deficit in its balance of payments; this deficit has had a decisive influence on the monetary level, leading to a collapse of the post-war, U.S. dominated, monetary system. Secondly, the Soviet Union became a second superpower, thereby challenging the United States' dominant position in the political and military realm. Thirdly, 'the crucial aspect of the present crisis' (1982b, p. 189) was the emergence of a crisis in the relationship between North and South. The policy of development chosen by most Third World countries was that of import-substituting industrialization. According to Amin, this policy inevitably limited the growth of the internal market to the provision of, mainly luxury, goods for the upper strata in the peripheral countries; the wages of the masses have stayed very low, resulting in 'superexploitation'. As a consequence of this, total world demand became insufficient to keep the world productive capacity fully employed. (1982b, pp. 180-96; cf. 1981, pp. 34-5 and 1988b, pp. 16-18)

Amin's ideas about crises are an element of his historical theory which deserves separate treatment. Since these ideas do not form a clearly distinct element of his theory of dependency, as was the case in Andre Gunder Frank's theory, they are dealt with in this section, not in a separate one.

Samir Amin distinguishes between so-called A and B phases in the history of the world capitalist system:

> A phases are characterized by long waves of relatively rapid growth that coincide with a fairly well-coordinated system of production, a stable international division of labor, and as a rule a firmly established hierarchy of nations. B phases, on the other hand, are distinguished by long waves of relatively slow growth associated with an increasingly unstable structure of the world capitalist system: the social and class alliances that helped maintain the preceding stability begin to break up; international competition intensifies; the preceding hierarchical arrangement among nations is challenged; and consequently international alliances and the international division of labor are subject to change. (1981, pp. 33-4)

A and B phases are seen as recurring phenomena in each of the previously distinguished stages in the development of the world capitalist system. The B phases are transitory ones that bring a certain dynamic into the world system: it is in response to these phases that the major changes in the world capitalist system take place. In reaction to the crisis of the B phases, for example, the exploitation of the periphery by the centre is altered, so that previously used instruments of exploitation can be replaced by other, more effective ones. In most cases this will mean that the outward-oriented development of the peripheral countries is enhanced even further. Moreover, this will lead to an intensification of underdevelopment.

V THE THEORY OF DELINKING FROM THE CAPITALIST WORLD SYSTEM

Apart from analysing the fundamental structures and processes characterizing the capitalist world system, Samir Amin has also developed a theory of development for the underdeveloped countries of the periphery. It might be called the 'theory of delinking'. Amin's concept of delinking follows directly from his analysis of value, accumulation and unequal exchange, which has been discussed in section III.

The basis of Samir Amin's ideas about delinking is to be found in his fifth theoretical assumption (see section II), stressing that a development policy can only be successful if it is *autocentred* or *autocentric*. This means that economic and social policy decisions should not be subjected to considerations imposed by the interests of other countries - if the latter would be the case, the development policy would be *extroverted*. According to Amin, the presently developed countries are the ones that have followed an autocentred development course *par excellence*. With, and because of, the expansion of capitalism and the creation of the capitalist world system, no country - with the exception of Japan, which had never been integrated in the system (E.g. 1976, pp. 55-6, 369) - has been able to pursue an autocentred capitalist development policy since the rise of modern imperialism. The underdeveloped countries, which have been exposed to extroverted development, have not been able to orient their economies towards the production of mass consumption and capital goods, which is the essential precondition for autocentred development. Their economies have, on the contrary, been export-oriented; the internal markets have not been able to grow and for this reason mass consumption has not developed.

Samir Amin's version of dependency theory does not preclude the possibility of development for the countries belonging to the periphery of the capitalist world system. The central precondition for such development is that peripheral countries 'delink' their economies from the world system. As Amin has phrased it himself:

> Delinking is not synonymous with autocentric development. It indicates another phenomenon: a demand imposed by the system. It is the condition for autocentric development, on the basis of a legacy of peripheral capitalism. [...] In a word, it deals with a principle: that of 'delinking' the criteria of rationality of internal economic choices from those governing the world system. These criteria are only the expression of the law of value governing a socio-economic system. We have argued that the world capitalist system as a whole - centres and peripheries included - was governed by the same law of value that we categorize as 'world capitalist'. [...] We have therefore proposed that one should define the criteria of economic rationality on the basis of constraints and social relations internal to the nation. (1990, pp. 18-19)

According to Amin, more moderate development policies are likely to fail. Amin has frequently mentioned the plea of the so-called Group of 77 for a New International Economic Order as an example of such moderate proposals. (See 1977c; 1979a; 1981, pp. 39-41; 1982a; 1988a) In his judgment, the concept of a New International Economic Order is by its own nature self-defeating, since it 'places the highest ever priority on the objective of intensified links of world economic interdependence, basing it on comparative advantages'. (1979a, p. 65) For Amin, proposals such as the increase of raw materials prices, the reduction of debts and the transfer of technologies might have some positive effects on the Third World countries, but would not, on the whole, lead to a reversal of the transfer of value from these countries to the countries of the core.

The necessity to restrain the flow of surplus from the periphery to the core requires more drastic measures, according to Samir Amin. Peripheral countries should bring the operation of their economies in agreement with their own needs instead of those dictated by the core. Amin makes clear that, in his view, capitalism does not serve the interests of the peripheral countries. He argues that, therefore, any attempt at introducing a development policy conducive to the needs of the presently underdeveloped countries will require a socialist political order: 'we support the view that delinking, whether one likes it or not, is associated with a "transition" - outside capitalism and over a long time - towards socialism'. (1990, p. 55)

The socialist character of Amin's concept of delinking, which he himself has explicitly distinguished from autarky, is to be found in the use of a 'law of value with a national foundation and a popular content'. This means that the government of the country concerned will see to it that 'the net product of society [...] will be shared between rural and urban populations in proportion to their contribution in the quantity of labor'. (1987b, p. 437) In this model, the capitalist law of value, which necessarily operates on an unequal basis, no longer determines the incomes of workers in the Third World. The relative prices of products will have to be adjusted from time to time under the influence of differing rates of productivity growth, but this will not be allowed to influence the income distribution. (1987b, pp. 440-1) As a consequence of this distribution policy, it will be possible to orient production in a way conducive to satisfying the basic needs of the population at large, instead of the luxury demand of a limited elite. (1986, pp. 167-8)

Samir Amin has formulated several conditions which, in his view, are necessary for a policy of delinking to succeed. (1986, pp. 168-70; 1984b, pp. xvi-xx) In the first place, agriculture should be given economic priority to ensure that enough food be obtained for the entire population. Secondly, the interests of industry should be made subservient to the progress of productivity in agriculture; industrial production should therefore be focused on inputs for agriculture (fertilizer, equipment), infrastructural works and preservation and processing of the produce. Thirdly, the production process should be subjected to national and popular control, exercised by the workers and peasants, on the one hand, and the government, on the other. Fourthly, technology should not just be 'bought' in the developed countries, but should be developed or adjusted according to the specific needs of the Third World countries. Fifthly, external relations should be limited and differ fundamentally from those characteristic of the import substitution and export-oriented strategies. Finally, a 'national structure of interdependent pricing and financial instruments' should be developed, in order to bring incomes in accordance with needs and not necessarily with (sectorally unequal) productivity.

According to Amin, a strategy of delinking can only be introduced when the country concerned is characterized by a minimum level of 'real' democracy. The history of the world capitalist system has resulted in a sharp polarization between distinct parts of the system and it is this polarization:

> which is in fact responsible for the appearance of socially and politically unacceptable regimes in the periphery of the system. They are socially unacceptable because they are founded on impoverishment and the exclusion of the great mass of the people. They were politically unacceptable in the past in the sense that the setting up of the system required colonial domination; and they remain unacceptable because the pursuit of a form of local development integrated within the system demands that the new independent state remains despotic. Thus, democracy is not the 'rule', but the exception, produced from time to time by the impasses of capitalist development, but always vulnerable. (1987a, p. 1147)

The kind of democracy accompanying the process of delinking should have, in Amin's view, an explicit 'social dimension'. It is not sufficient for the peripheral countries to have a formal democratic political system, since this does not ensure popular involvement and support. Instead, the democratization following delinking should entail the participation of workers and peasants in economic decisions regarding, for instance, investments, prices and wages.

VI MODELLING SAMIR AMIN'S DEPENDENCY THEORY

As in chapter 3, the final section of this chapter will be used to construct a model of Samir Amin's dependency theory. The analysis of Amin's theoretical work in this chapter serves as the basis for deriving the 'hard core' of central relations. The *caveat* of chapter 3 also applies here: the following will be an attempt at creating a *model*, which by its very nature implies a reduction of the complex relations formulated by Amin.

The central relationship in the case of Andre Gunder Frank's theory appeared to be the one between dependence and development. In Amin's theory this relationship is also central. Peripheral countries are in a more dependent position in the capitalist world system and will be exploited more than the countries that have been able to withdraw from the system's influences. Likewise, more dependent countries will be less able to avoid the situation of outward-directed or extroverted development, which in its turn enhances the countries' degree of underdevelopment.

The degree of dependence of a peripheral country does not only determine the degree of exploitation and the extent of extroversion, but also the extent of social and political inequality. When a peripheral country is more dependent, the countries of the centre will stimulate the creation of alliances with certain 'compradorized' groups in the country concerned. The degree of social and political inequality will consequently be enhanced. This inequality will, on the one hand, lead to an intensification of exploitation and, on the other, stimulate the process of underdevelopment.

The conjunctural situation of the capitalist world system is an important factor in Samir Amin's theory. International upswings - 'A phases' in Amin's terms - will lead to stability in the international division of labour; for the peripheral countries, this implies a tendency toward more outward-directed development. In periods characterized by a negative conjuncture - so-called B phases - the countries of the periphery will have the opportunity to reduce the degree of extroversion of their economy.

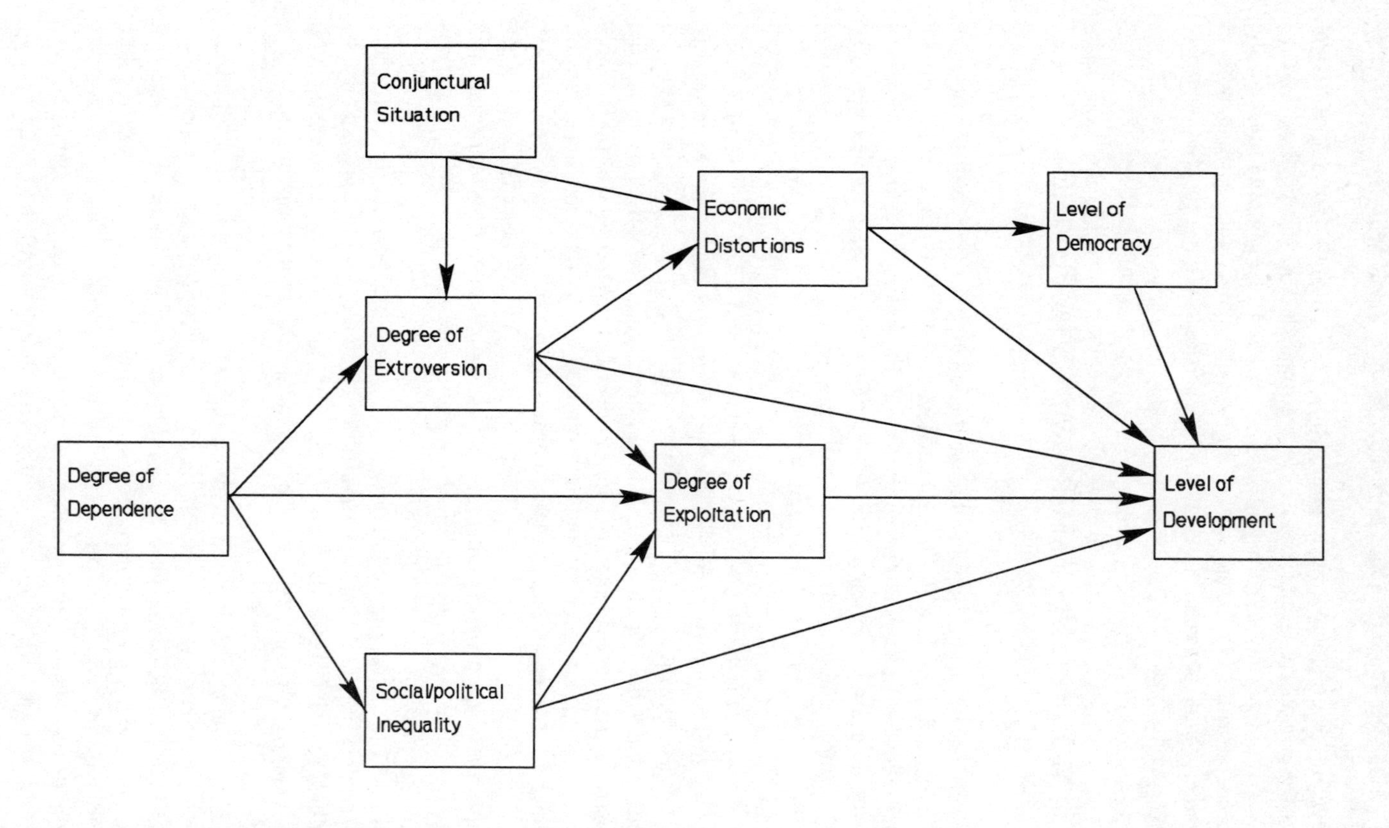

Figure 4.2: A Model of Samir Amin's Dependency Theory

The economic distortions characterizing the Third World countries - for instance, crises of the budget and the balance of payments or lack of public savings - tend to intensify in periods of conjunctural downswing. These distortions also depend on the degree of extroversion of a peripheral economy. The economic distortions themselves exert a certain influence on the level of democracy and the level of development. An intensification of the economic distortions will have an adverse influence on the degree of democracy, because, according to Amin, the only means to fight the economic distortions in most developing countries is to force the working masses to pay for them - for instance, by forced savings, a reduction of wages or an increase of unemployment. Likewise, the intensification of economic distortions negatively influences the level of development. Finally, a worsening of the democratic level of the political system, induced by the economic distortions, will tend to go together with enhancement of the situation of underdevelopment.

NOTES

1. One of the most controversial examples of this strategy is South Africa. According to Amin (1979b, p. 21), 'South African racism [...] is essential to the economic mechanism. The society and economy of South Africa are in no way ''dualistic'' because the ''home lands'' perform an essential function at the service of the ''modern'' sector: that of furnishing labour at a low price.' ['[L]e racisme sud-africain [...] est essentiel au mécanisme de l'économie. La société et l'économie de l'Afrique du Sud ne sont nullement ''dualistes'' car les ''réserves'' ont une fonction essentielle au service du secteur ''moderne'': celle de fournir de la main-d'oeuvre à bon marché.'] Cf. 1987c.
2. Translation W.H. The original version is: 'Obtenir à la périphérie des produits qui constituent des éléments constitutifs du capital constant (matières premières) ou du capital variable (produits alimentaires) à des prix de production inférieurs à ceux qui charactérisaient la production au centre de produits analogues (ou de substituts évidemment quand il s'agit de produits spécifiques comme le café ou le thé), telle est la *raison* de la création de ce secteur exportateur.'

5. Johan Galtung: The Structural Approach to Centre-Periphery Relations

I INTRODUCTION

In this chapter, the writings of Johan Galtung will be focused upon. Johan Galtung has become well-known among social scientists primarily for his work on peace research. Apart from, but clearly linked with, his activities as one of the founders of peace research, he has published widely on centre-periphery relations and on the structure of domination and dependence, which he considers inherent in those relations. His best-known publication in this realm undoubtedly is the 1971 article *A structural theory of imperialism*, originally published in the Journal of Peace Research and re-published in many books and overviews dealing with the relations between developed and developing countries.

Galtung's work essentially deals with two phenomena. In the first place, it provides a view on power and on the resulting structural conflict and domination in international relations. In the second place, Galtung's writings deal with alternative options for the development of Third World countries wanting to end their position of subjugation and exploitation. Galtung elaborates on the theme of self-reliance because it is, in his perspective, a policy option that would enable the developing countries to further their development without having to make too many concessions to the developed countries.

In this chapter, as in the two preceding chapters, first (in section II) some attention will be paid to the methodological and theoretical assumptions. Section III will focus on Galtung's structural views on power, conflict and imperialism. In section IV, Galtung's theory of self-reliance will be analysed. The final section of this chapter (section V) will be used to develop a model representing the basic elements of Johan Galtung's theory of dependency.

II METHODOLOGICAL AND THEORETICAL ASSUMPTIONS

Johan Galtung's theory of dependency may be characterized as a *structural* approach to social science, as the author himself has made clear in several of his books and articles. This distinguishes Galtung's approach from the mainstream of the social sciences and even, as Chris Brown (1981) has argued, from Marxism. Brown has analysed Galtung's opposition to Marxism in the following way:

> Galtung's own account of his relationship to marxism involves both an appropriation of some marxist ideas and literature and a claim that his own work goes beyond the tradition. Galtung sees marxism as concrete, historical, and non-scientific; it is reductionist, seeing imperialism as 'an economic relationship under private capitalism, motivated by the need for expanding markets'. His own work, however, is to be seen as abstract, structural and scientific, viewing imperialism as 'a more general structural relationship between two collectives'. (1981, p. 220)

A Methodological Assumptions

The main methodological assumption in Johan Galtung's theorizing concerns the need for structural explanation. In his book *The true worlds*, Galtung has probably presented his views on this issue most clearly. There he has distinguished two 'basic perspectives' that are used in studying social affairs: the one is an *actor-oriented*, the other a *structure-oriented* perspective. (1980j, p. 41; cf. the critique in Waltz 1979, p. 31)

The actor-oriented perspective appears to be equivalent to methodological individualism, which means that explanations focus on individual actors and their intentions and interests. According to Galtung, such a perspective can be applied at the domestic and the international level. In the first case the actors are persons, whereas in the second case they are states.

In the structure-oriented perspective, it is not the individual actor that is focused upon. Instead, 'structures' become the main object of analysis. As Galtung himself has phrased it, '[t]he structure-oriented view emphasizes structure because it denies the implicit autonomy assumption of actor-oriented perspective'. (1980j, p. 42) The implications of the structural perspective in Galtung's work on centre-periphery relations are clearly exhibited in the following quotation:

> [The structural theory of imperialism] is structural in the sense that *no specific actors* are indicated, and also in the sense that for the concrete actors that happen to be performing rôles in the structure in question *no specific motivation* is necessary. The basic assumption is that the *structure* (of imperialism) is extremely strong and has its

> own internal logic so that once it has started operating it is not necessary for those who are acting within it to desire all the consequences. (1980i, p. 183)

The corollary of Galtung's methodological structuralism is that improvements are sought not in the change of people's motivations but in the change of structures: 'According to the first [actor-oriented] view, evil is caused by evil intentions, particularly when held by the strong and active actor; according to the second [structure-oriented] view, evil is caused by a bad structure.' (1980j, p. 43)

Although Galtung has recognized the need to include dynamic elements into his theory, his analyses have remained fundamentally *static*, as Van Benthem van den Bergh has noted in an early critique of Galtung's structural theory of imperialism. For this reason, Van Benthem van den Bergh (1972, pp. 78-80) argues, the approach can more aptly be interpreted as a *taxonomy* of structures, rather than as a theory.

B Theoretical Assumptions

In the previous two chapters, dealing with the theories of, respectively, Andre Gunder Frank and Samir Amin, it appeared to be necessary to analyse an author's theoretical assumptions in conjunction with his methodological assumptions. In Johan Galtung's theory of dependency at least five theoretical assumptions can be distinguished.

The most fundamental theoretical assumption that can be found in Galtung's work concerns the unequal distribution of power and wealth. Galtung has differentiated between so-called 'resource power' and 'structural power'. Resource power is a result of the possession of different types of resources, be it money, weapons, strength or knowledge. Structural power is linked to the occupation of a certain position in a structure. (1980j, pp. 62-5) The corollary of this is the following:

> For 'power' to be 'power-over-others' it is not enough that somebody be high in innate power or resource power or both. Somebody else has to be low on them; there has to be inequality in the distribution of resources. Along this power gradient, influence - of the ideological, remunerative and punitive kinds - flows down to the poor periphery at the bottom of it all. No wonder the power elite can be small and the masses numerous, if the difference in power potential can be so tremendous and the gradient so steep. (1980j, p. 64)

In Galtung's view, power and differences in power are based on inequality, injustice, exploitation, penetration, fragmentation and marginalization.

Linked to Galtung's assumption about power is a second one. Development, according to Galtung, is 'the opposite of unequal power: *develop-*

ment implies reduction of power differentials'. (1980j, p. 65) Development would therefore only be possible when the six impediments that were mentioned in the previous paragraph are corrected or, in other words, when the unequal power distribution is redressed.

The third theoretical assumption in Johan Galtung's work concerns the place of *conflict* in social relations. Unlike the situation that would exist in the 'preferred world', the currently existing world is characterized by conflicts. Underlying Galtung's *structural theory of imperialism* is the idea that there is a conflict of interests between the countries of the centre and those of the periphery. Galtung has tried to make this concept somewhat more operational by focusing on the notion of 'living conditions' (LC), which summarizes indicators such as income, standard of living, quality of life and autonomy. The conflict of interests is then considered as follows:

> There is *conflict*, or *disharmony of interest*, if the two parties are coupled together in such a way that the LC *gap* between them is *increasing*;
> There is *no conflict*, or *harmony of interest*, if the two parties are coupled together in such a way that the LC *gap* between them is *decreasing down to zero*. (1971, p. 82)

Where Galtung's discussion of the 'preferred world' - as opposed to the 'real world' - is concerned, it is more appropriate to speak of a belief in a natural harmony of interests. Galtung assumes that once a social structure is created in which differences of power and wealth are minimized, people will find themselves in harmony with one another, and will not experience conflicts of interests. (Maley 1985, p. 589)

Johan Galtung's fourth theoretical assumption is one that can also be found in the work of several other dependency theorists. This assumption starts from the supposedly *zero-sum character* of the relationship between dominated and dominating countries. It is assumed that the production of wealth is finite and that, in the short run, a country can only increase its own wealth by taking it from other countries. Galtung has applied this way of reasoning to the dynamics of imperialism:

> [I]mperialism permits Center countries to grow and theoretically even to become increasingly egalitarian because the Periphery needed for capitalistic growth is located outside themselves. But these Periphery countries have no outside peripheries unless they also engage in imperialism, as they sometimes do. If not, then their peripheries are doomed to stagnation, unless they break out of the structure. (1980j, p. 126)

Closely related to this fourth assumption is the fifth, which focuses on *exploitation*. (Brown 1981, pp. 224-5; Maley 1985, p. 581) For reasons that are closely linked with the latter assumption, Galtung assumes that within the capitalist world system centre-periphery relations are doomed to be exploitative. According to Galtung, relations are non-exploitative 'if and only if the total inter- and intra-actor effects that accrue to the parties are equal'. (1971, p. 88)

III THE STRUCTURAL THEORY OF IMPERIALISM

The best-known and probably the clearest formulation of Galtung's structural view of centre-periphery relations is to be found in his 1971 article, *A structural theory of imperialism.* Galtung's later writings on related issues are to be interpreted as amendments, elaborations and specifications of the original themes. For this reason, this section will be started by analysing Galtung's original formulation of the structural theory of imperialism in some detail.

Galtung begins his analysis in the same way as other dependency theorists: by stressing that a centre-periphery opposition exists both on a world scale and within nations. This opposition and the inequality resulting from it are seen as 'one of the major forms of *structural violence*'. (1971, p. 81; cf. 1980b, pp. 145-6)[1] The centre-periphery relation is seen as a typical *dominance relation* and, more specifically, as a *relation of imperialism.* Galtung has defined imperialism in the following way:

> *Imperialism* is a relation between a Center and a Periphery nation so that
> (1) there is *harmony of interest* between the *center in the Center* nation and the *center in the Periphery* nation,
> (2) there is more *disharmony of interest* within the Periphery nation than within the Center nations,
> (3) there is *disharmony of interest* between the *periphery in the Center* nation and the *periphery in the Periphery* nation. (1971, p. 83)

Having these characteristics, imperialism, in Galtung's view, is not merely an international relationship. Rather, it is a combination of *inter-* and *intranational* relations.

In the original formulation of the structural theory of imperialism, Galtung has distinguished two basic mechanisms of imperialism: first, the mechanism of the vertical interaction relation and, secondly, the mechanism of the feudal interaction structure. (Cf. 1980a and 1980e) The importance of these mechanisms is indicated by Galtung in the following way:

> In short, we see vertical interaction as the major source of the inequality of this world, whether it takes the form of looting, of highly unequal exchange, or highly

> differential spin-off effects due to processing gaps. [...] If the first mechanism, the *vertical interaction relation*, is the major factor behind inequality, then the second mechanism, the *feudal interaction structure*, is the factor that maintains and reinforces this inequality by protecting it. There are four rules defining this particular interaction structure:
> (1) interaction between Center and Periphery is *vertical*
> (2) interaction between Periphery and Periphery is *missing*
> (3) multilateral interaction involving all three is *missing*
> (4) interaction with the outside world is *monopolized* by the Center, with two implications:
> (a) Periphery interaction with other Center nations is *missing*
> (b) Center as well as Periphery interaction with Periphery nations belonging to other Center nations is *missing*. (1971, p. 89)

In his later work, Galtung has specified these fundamental mechanisms of imperialism. The mechanisms discussed in other places are: exploitation, penetration, fragmentation and marginalization. (1980j, pp. 113-27)

As has been pointed out above in subsection B, Galtung sees *exploitation* as an integral element of imperialism, existing as long as the inter- and intra-actor effects of relations between the centre and the periphery stay unequal. Galtung has defined exploitation in terms of 'unequal exchange' or 'asymmetric interaction'.[2] In his view, three (quasi-historical) stages or types of exploitation can be defined. The first stage of exploitation is characterized by looting and robbing. In the second stage, the exploiters start to offer something in return for the goods that are taken away; still, '[t]he price paid is ridiculous'. (1971, p. 86) In the third stage of exploitation, 'there may be some balance in the flow between actors, but great differences in the effect the interaction has within them'. (1971, p. 86) The intra-actor effects of (unequal) exchange in the third stage are seen as highly asymmetrical. In general, the centre countries produce goods and services at a higher level of processing than the peripheral countries.

Trade consists mainly of finished products from the centre and primary goods from the periphery. In Galtung's analysis, the production of goods and services at a higher processing level has all kinds of *spin-off effects*, resulting in higher levels of research facilities, a better infrastructure, better education, more highly developed means of communication and, as a corollary, a stronger military potential. (1971, pp. 86-7; 1979a, pp. 8, 15-16) In the original formulation of this idea, Galtung linked the externalities to the nature of the commodities being produced and exported. In a re-analysis of the phenomenon, he has left open the possibility that primary goods-producing countries reap more spin-off benefits than countries producing finished goods. Examples from the former group are countries such as Sweden, Australia and New Zealand; the latter group consists of Third World countries receiving investments of Western companies which produce for external markets. (1980i, p. 189)

The mechanism of *penetration*, which in Galtung's view is the opposite of autonomy, is 'a combination of submissiveness, dependence, and fear'. (1980j, p. 119) In the structural view of imperialism, the centre countries succeed in 'penetrating under the skin' of the peripheral countries by establishing a 'bridgehead' in the form of the periphery's centre. The interests of the peripheral elite are interpreted as running parallel to those of the centre's elite: it is assumed to be in the interest of both elites that the mass of the periphery (the periphery of the periphery) is exploited. The wealth of the peripheral elite is, according to Galtung, founded upon the presence of a huge inequality in the periphery. In the periphery,

> the small elites and the vast masses are well separated. If it were not, then there would not be in the Periphery countries the availability of what the Center is looking for: cheap labor, combined with an elite that can serve as a market for consumer goods. (1980j, p. 120)

The third mechanism of imperialism, *fragmentation*, is based on the principle of *divide et impera*. First of all, this implies that the contacts among peripheral countries are limited to a minimum. Whatever interaction there is, is between the centre and the periphery. The opportunity for peripheral countries to cooperate is thereby minimized. Another aspect of fragmentation is the separation between the masses of the centre and the periphery. In order to keep the masses in the centre under control, the elite shares with them some of the gains of the exploitation of the periphery. Here Galtung appears to refer implicitly to Lenin's ideas about a *labour aristocracy* that is created under capitalism. With respect to this aspect of imperialism, Galtung concludes that 'there is small wonder that anticapitalist revolutions have taken place only in Periphery countries, starting with the Russian Revolution'. (1980j, p. 123)[3]

Closely connected with the previously discussed mechanism of imperialism is the mechanism of *marginalization*. Marginalization 'is a way of constituting an inner and outer circle in the world, leaving no doubt as to where the point of gravity for important decisions concerning the whole world is located - to the point of isolating the Periphery'. (1980j, p. 124) Galtung mentions the position of 'associated states' in the context of the European Community as an example of how the marginalization of the periphery can take place.

Johan Galtung has not limited his discussion of imperialism to the economic aspects. Therefore, he has defined four other types of imperialism: political, military, communication and socio-cultural imperialism.[4] Since the basic mechanisms do not change from one aspect of imperialism to another, all these aspects are characterized by vertical interaction patterns, with the centre occupying the leading position and the periphery being dependent. In general terms, the centre is seen as the producer (of decisions, protection, news, means of communication and values) and the periphery as the consumer. (1971, pp. 91-4) In Galtung's interpretation, there are close links among the five different types of imperialism, and these might even result in a *generalized imperialism*, 'if the five elites defined through these five types of exchange are *coordinated* into generalized upper classes based on a rich network of kinship, friendship, and association (not to mention effective cooperation)'. (1971, p. 98; cf. Van Benthem van den Bergh 1972, p. 80)

According to Galtung, the structure of imperialism does have repercussions for the level of development attained in different parts of the world. It follows from Galtung's assumption about the zero-sum character of the distribution of wealth that any gains made by the centre are seen as detrimental to the periphery. As other dependency theorists have done, Galtung has also formulated a direct relationship between the *overdevelopment* of the centre and the *underdevelopment* of the periphery:

> [T]here is a pattern, a total social formation that drives people towards overconsumption in one way or the other [...] This pattern, or social formation, is what could be referred to as overdevelopment, just like underdevelopment is a pattern that enforces underconsumption upon people. It is obvious from what has been said that these are two sides of the same coin, that they are dialectically related. (Galtung, Preiswerk and Wemegah 1981, pp. 16-17)

Although Galtung's analyses of Western imperialism are the most pertinent ones, he has explicitly left open the possibility that the 'real existing socialist' countries engage in 'social' imperialism. This type of imperialism would be of a more politico-military nature and would result in the copying of the (socialist) centre country's social and political structures, the control by the centre of the internal affairs and the foreign policy of the periphery, and the creation of a buffer zone. (1976a, p. 156)

The main Western imperialist power is, in Galtung's view, the United States. The power of the United States is such that it cannot uphold the imperialist construction on its own: 'however strong the motivation, the US is no longer capable, nor willing, to exercise "policing" activities all around the world, as it has been doing in countries like Guatemala, Cuba, Dominican Republic, Lebanon, Vietnam, Cambodia, Laos and Korea'. (1976a, p. 163) For this reason, the United States has tried to make use of the imperialism of other countries and thus created a structure of *sub-imperialism*. (1976a, pp. 160-4)

Galtung sees the European Community as a potential superpower which might serve as a sub-imperialist unit for the United States and might even, in due course, supplant the United States as the principal Western imperialist force. (See 1973 and 1989a) The European Community has all the characteristics of an imperialist power; Galtung has termed the EC an instrument of 'collective colonialism'. (1973, p. 73) First of all the EC has created and supported a vertical division of labour: the Third World countries, for the greater part former colonies of EC member states, serve as providers of raw materials, labour and markets, while the EC countries supply capital and knowledge in the form of multinational corporations' investments and research. Secondly, EC policy is aimed at fragmenting the Third World: the EC enters into separate trade agreements with different groups of developing countries, such as the so-called ACP countries in the Yaoundé and Lomé treaties and the associated states.[5] Finally, the EC tries to penetrate the Third World by having its 'Eurocentric' formula of development accepted by local elites. (1973, p. 59)

In several recent articles, Galtung has emphasized the potential rise of the countries in East Asia or, in other words, the 'China-Japan-Southeast Asia triangle', which might threaten the dominant position of the 'United States-European Community-Japan triangle'. (1985a, pp. 23-38; 1986; 1989b, pp. 9-16) According to Galtung, this development would change the centre of gravity of the world capitalist system, while the essence of the system would remain intact. Therefore, the basic elements of the structural theory of imperialism as they have been outlined above would not need to be altered. The changes predicted by Galtung would simply mean that the contents, but not the essence, of the terms 'centre' and 'periphery' would change.

IV THE THEORY OF SELF-RELIANCE

Galtung's theory of self-reliance is based partially on ideas that have been identified, in the foregoing sections, as the constituent elements of his structural theory of imperialism. It follows from the latter theory that the countries of the periphery would have to attack the international structures of dominance and inequality in order to change their own economic, political, social and cultural position.

Johan Galtung has constructed his theory of self-reliance on the premise that the strategy of development pursued by the presently developed countries is unsuitable for the countries of the periphery. It has been emphasized above (in subsection B) that Galtung assumes that exploitation has been a *necessary and inevitable* element of the development experienced by the centre countries. Moreover, he argues that the dominant Western strategies of development have been based on a reification of the characteristics of societies that are considered to be developed. Galtung mentions three such reifications: the division of labour is seen as inevitable, inequality in society is seen as necessary, and allocation is seen as a problem of fitting individuals to jobs rather than the other way around. The image of development that is linked to these kinds of ideas is one of increasing differentiation and specialization. (1978c, pp. 316-17)

In this context Galtung has presented a typology of interactions (see figure 5.1, derived from 1978c, p. 320), which is fundamental for understanding his theory of self-reliance. With the help of this typology, Galtung's ideas about a preferred development can be illustrated. In a situation where the self-sufficiency of nations is low and the interaction is vertical (i.e., in a situation where the division of labour leads to different inter- and intra-actor effects), the interaction is characterized by *dependence*. The relation between centre and periphery countries in the capitalist system is of this type. In a situation where the self-sufficiency is low, but the interaction is horizontal (meaning that inter- and intra-actor effects are about equal), the interaction is one of *interdependence*. This is the central feature of relations among centre countries. In a situation where self-sufficiency is high, it is possible to speak of *self-reliance* and *independence*.

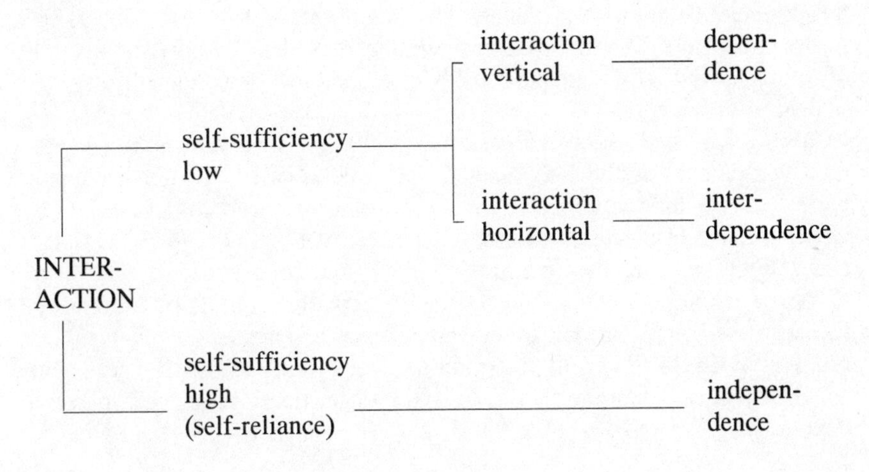

Figure 5.1: A Typology of Interaction Processes

It has been stressed above that there is, in Galtung's view, a necessary link between the existing capitalist world system and phenomena such as the exploitation and dependence of the periphery. For this reason, the only way for the periphery to attain a reasonable level of development is found in its *dissociation* from the capitalist world system and its pursuit of *self-reliance*.

Galtung's concept of self-reliance is not synonymous with the New International Economic Order (NIEO), although the latter might serve as a phase on the way to self-reliance. Galtung has termed the NIEO a form of 'capitalism for everyone'. (1983, p. 26) In his view, the NIEO is a way of re-organizing the international economic system, consisting basically of three elements: the improvement of the terms of trade between the centre and the periphery; the acquisition of control by the periphery over the world economic cycles that affect these countries (for instance, by the nationalization of natural resources, soil, processing facilities, distribution machinery and financial institutions); and the increase and improvement of trade among the periphery countries themselves. (1978b, p. 127; 1979c, p. 455)

In the first part of this section, the focus has been on the *strategic* part of Galtung's views of development. Self-reliance is to be interpreted as a strategy for periphery countries to attain a higher level of development, coping with the structural limitations imposed by the capitalist world system. The strategic view is directly linked to a *substantive* definition of development. Although Galtung has highlighted different aspects of development in different books and articles, it is clear that the satisfaction of human needs is fundamental to his conception of development. (1979a, p. 3)[6]

Galtung has tried to list the basic needs that are involved in the process of development. As the fundamental material needs he mentions: physiological needs, individual environmental needs, the need for group/family environmental protection, health, education, the freedom of expression and impression, and the freedom to move and to be visited. The basic non-material needs concern the following: creativity, identity, autonomy, togetherness, participation, self-fulfilment, and a sense of meaning in life. (1979a, p. 3) In order to have these needs fulfilled in the periphery countries, most attention should be paid to the least privileged in those countries:

> The best strategy of development [...] would be to stimulate those processes that give first priority to the satisfaction of the basic needs of those most in need. This would mean, concretely, giving first priority to the production of food, clothes, housing, etc., for the undernourished, the underclad and the shelterless, and giving first priority to the provision of more opportunities for, say, creative, meaningful work for those who have the most boring, degrading work (not necessarily the same people as those who are undernourished). Thus, what is rejected is [...] the idea that need-

satisfaction will best take place, or can only take place, through a trickle-down process, starting with providing those already well off materially with more material satisfaction, and those well off non-materially (intellectuals, for instance) with even more non-material satisfaction. (1979a, p. 4)

Johan Galtung has formulated several other requirements that must be met in order to guarantee an adequate process of development in the periphery. The first requirement is the decentralization of periphery society, meaning that the dependence on the centre in the periphery is reduced. Decentralization is also meant as an instrument of emancipation for the people of the periphery: people would regain control over their own resources, be it capital, labour or raw materials. (1980j, p. 157; 1980g, pp. 357, 361-4; 1980c, pp. 216-18)

The second requirement mentioned by Galtung is that the 'local parasitic elites' have to be removed from the position of power which they have obtained. It is assumed that the elites will use the resources of the periphery country primarily for their own benefit and that their (economic or political) power has to be broken in order to permit an equitable development of all social groups. (1980c, pp. 215-16; 1980j, p. 157)

Galtung's third and fourth requirements are closely related. According to Galtung, a stronger political mobilization in the periphery and a higher level of consciousness about the functioning of the current structures and the possibilities for building new structures would be essential for the periphery to sustain a viable development strategy. It would be necessary for the periphery countries to reject the models and ideology presented by the West and replace them by their own creations, since these can be expected to better suit their needs. (1980j, pp. 157-8) An important example of a Western model that should not, in Galtung's view, be copied, is Western technology: 'technology is never "politically neutral" [...] it always carries a code which is expressed in the structure, social and/or cultural, accompanying it'. (1979b, p. 283; cf. 1979a, pp. 15-22; 1980f, pp. 225-9; 1980d, pp. 351-7) For this reason, a technology should be developed that is more suitable for Third World countries with their different economic, social, cultural and political systems.

These internal changes in the periphery countries would be needed, according to Johan Galtung, to support a policy of external self-reliance towards the countries of the centre. Galtung has indicated that, in his view, self-reliance is not the same as autarky; self-reliance 'implies a redirection and recomposition of trade and cooperation, not the building of tight walls around all units'. (1980h, p. 27) Self-reliance, understood as the enhanced autonomy of the periphery, can be realized at several levels. Apart from the national level, Galtung has also mentioned the local (i.e., sub-national) and regional (Third World) levels:

> Thus, far from being antithetical to trade, exchange and cooperation a consistent policy of self-reliance may even increase the exchange level in the world because it will engender much more cooperation between neighbours in geographical and social space. The point is not to cut out trade but to *redirect* it and *recompose* it by giving preference to cooperation with those in the same position, preferring the neighbour to the more distant possibility, cooperation to exchange, and intra-sector to inter-sector trade. (1980h, p. 26)

The building of a self-reliant society and, *a fortiori*, of a world system consisting of self-reliant societies could only take place 'from the bottom up': 'One would start with what is available locally and needed locally, and build from there in circles of equitable exchange.' (1980g, p. 360) With respect to the provision of basic material needs, such as food, clothes, shelter, educational and medical equipment and personnel, each unit would have to be self-reliant. Beyond this, patterns of exchange would have to be established on a reciprocal basis. (1980g, pp. 356-7; 1983, pp. 28-30) Regional or Third World self-reliance is perceived as a supplement to the local and national forms of self-reliance. Third World cooperation is seen as necessary because the countries and the regions within these countries are too weak, compared to the West, to achieve self-reliance by themselves. 'Solidarity action' is required in order to avoid the exploitation, penetration, fragmentation and marginalization which are the result of the power of the centre over the periphery.

According to Galtung, one of the prerequisites of a successful policy of self-reliance is the development of a new international technological order. Western technology is, in his view, capital-intensive, research-intensive, organization-intensive and labour-extensive. Moreover, it is dependency-creating and fragmenting in the sense that it does not require contact between producers and consumers. (1979b, pp. 284-6) The transfer of Western technology to the periphery is perceived as a 'structural and cultural invasion, an invasion possibly more insidious than colonialism and neo-colonialism, because such an invasion is not always accompanied by a physical Western presence'. (1979b, p. 288)

In order for self-reliance to be a viable policy, the Western technology (or *alpha-type technology*) has to be supplanted, at least partially, by a non-Western variant (or *beta-type technology*). The alpha-type technology, as a representative of alpha-structures, tends to increase its scale as it has no size limitation, and results in the total manipulation of nature. The beta-type technology has size limitations and is more dependent on nature:

> If people are to have meaningful relations with each other and not be fitted into centre-periphery hierarchies, and in addition are to participate in deciding what happens around them, then there is an upper limit to how many can become

> members of a beta-unit. This is one reason why family-run farms and shops, and villages, have the size they have. Moreover, if the beta-structure is more inward-oriented, more local and decentralized, the economic cycles (not super-cycles, which belong to the alpha-structure) on which it is based materially would be more exposed to the discontinuities of nature in space and time. (1979a, p. 10)

By introducing beta-type technologies, which imply equal exchange, a horizontal division of labour, autonomy, solidarity, participation and integration, the currently underdeveloped countries would be able to escape from the oppression and exploitation of the alpha-type capitalist world system. (1979a, p. 44)

V MODELLING JOHAN GALTUNG'S DEPENDENCY THEORY

In the same way as in the concluding sections of chapters 3 and 4, in this section a model of Johan Galtung's structural theory of dependency will be constructed. This model will be used, in subsequent chapters, to establish the empirical value of dependency theory.

In figure 5.2, a model is presented which contains the most important relations of Johan Galtung's structural interpretation of centre-periphery relations. Central to Galtung's theory - the ultimate independent variable, so to say - is the position taken in by countries in the world structure. Although this variable might be explained by other variables, most notably those related to the history of the countries under study, Galtung has taken the position in the world structure as a given.

In Galtung's structural theory the position of countries in the world structure determines which position they have in the world division of labour. The production of certain types of commodities and the related modes of production are interpreted as results of the position taken in by countries in either the centre or the periphery of the capitalist world system. In Galtung's view, countries can only alter their position in the world division of labour when they succeed in breaking out of the existing world structure and are able to establish economic, social and political self-reliance.

The structure of the division of labour in the capitalist world system determines, according to Galtung, the relative power position of countries and the degree of inequality in the system. The relative power position of countries is of eminent importance in Galtung's theory. This variable explains to what extent the benefits deriving from the relations between countries are distributed in a just way.

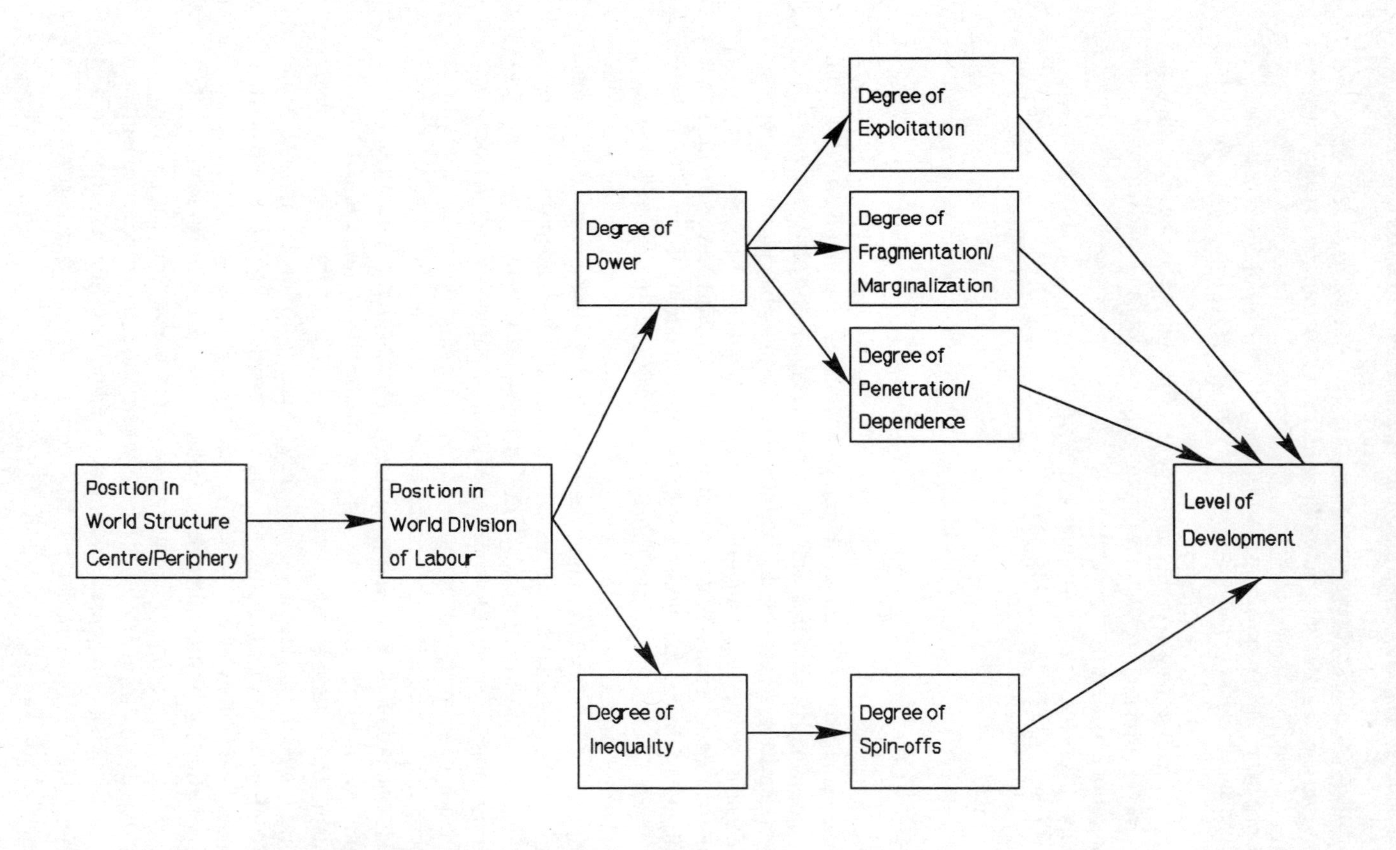

Figure 5.2: A Model of Johan Galtung's Dependency Theory

In Galtung's terms, the power distribution across countries determines the degree of exploitation of one country by another, the degree of fragmentation and marginalization and the degree of penetration and dependence. The relatively powerless countries will be the ones that suffer from exploitation, fragmentation, marginalization and penetration by the relatively powerful.

The relative inequality resulting from the world division of labour also has important effects for the internal situation of the countries participating in the capitalist world system. According to Johan Galtung, to the extent that the level of processing of goods and services is higher, the spin-off benefits for the society and economy become larger. Among other things, research, education and infrastructure will be of a qualitatively higher level in the countries succeeding to monopolize highly developed production processes.

The ultimate dependent variable in the model based on Johan Galtung's dependency theory is the level of development. It is hypothesized that countries that take in a subordinate position in the world division of labour and, consequently, fail to obtain significant spin-off effects, are exploited, marginalized and dependent, and will become underdeveloped. Countries succeeding to escape from the logic of the capitalist world system by adopting policies of self-reliance will tend to achieve a higher level of development.

NOTES

1. According to Galtung, '[s]tructural violence "just happens" without any specific actor behind it. The slum child, brain-damaged for life because of protein deficiency, who will have a self-realization level far below any reasonably defined potential, is not necessarily the "object" of any evil will of any particular "subject" who has committed the violence. The violence is built into the structure, usually derived from some fundamental inequity that then generates, and is reinforced by, inequality and injustice. It is invariant of actor substitution; like a body, it persists even when all persons (atoms) have been exchanged for new ones.' (1980j, p. 68)
2. Galtung (1980i, p. 185) specifies the origin of this definition of exploitation. There he writes that 'the structural theory of imperialism had an approach to exploitation which came out of one particular question: under what conditions would we say that there is no longer exploitation?'
3. Galtung has also formulated the *smoke-screen hypothesis*, meaning that people are made to believe 'that the real problem is to control, even limit, the capabilities in the East-West formation, whereas the basic problem seems to be how to resolve North-South conflicts'. (1985b, p. 9)
4. Galtung (1971) has distinguished five types of imperialism, whereas Galtung (1980j, p. 127) has defined six. Since the social and cultural types are defined in terms of the transmission of values, they are dealt with in one category here.

5. Galtung's conclusion with respect to the first convention of Lomé was unequivocal: 'the essence of the Lomé Convention is the continuation of internationalized capitalism, the continued flow of raw production factors in one direction and processed materials in the other'. (1976b, p. 40)
6. Galtung does not support the claims for a 'basic needs approach', which have sometimes been voiced in the development debate. In his view, a 'basic needs approach' can be and has been used as an instrument to avoid the discussion about the NIEO. See 1978a, pp. 43-7 and 1978b pp. 134-43.

6. Immanuel Wallerstein: The Modern World System

I INTRODUCTION

In many respects, Immanuel Wallerstein's interpretation of the development of the modern capitalist world system[1] can be seen as the culmination of dependency theory. Wallerstein's formulation of the theory of the world system is the most highly developed and probably the most frequently cited variant of dependency theory.

There is one problem connected with Wallerstein's work, which renders it impossible to deal with it in the same way as with the theorizing of Andre Gunder Frank, Samir Amin and Johan Galtung in the previous three chapters. Wallerstein's *oeuvre* has, until now, principally focused on the historical development of the capitalist world economy since, roughly, 1450. The third volume of his *magnum opus*, *The modern world-system*, deals with the period until the 1840s. For purely methodological reasons, attempts at modelling Wallerstein's theory and confronting it with empirical data derived from the most recent history (1965-85) are unsound and would not do justice to its theoretical variety.[2]

Since Wallerstein's work is a very important element of the development of dependency theory, it cannot be left out of a discussion of different variants of this theoretical perspective. For the reasons mentioned above, the present discussion of Wallerstein's theorizing will be limited to expounding its main methodological and theoretical assumptions (section II), and to discussing the theoretical components that are felt to be relevant for the study of international relations. In consecutive order, these elements are: the theory of the hierarchy within the modern world system (section III), the analysis of the historical development of the capitalist world economy since 1450 (section IV) and the theory of capitalist crises and antisystemic movements (section V).

II METHODOLOGICAL AND THEORETICAL ASSUMPTIONS

In the writings of Immanuel Wallerstein, numerous references can be found to Marxism, dialectics and the unity of theory and praxis. Yet, Wallerstein does not consider himself to be a Marxist. At several places in his work, he distinguishes his world system perspective from both Marxism and liberal developmentalism. (Cf. 1979, pp. 50-4) The aim of this section is to analyse, first, the methodological assumptions and, secondly, the theoretical assumptions that can be found in Wallerstein's work.

A Methodological Assumptions

In chapters 3 and 4, Frank's and Amin's explanations have been characterized as functionalist. Immanuel Wallerstein's explicit assumptions about explanation show a remarkable similarity to those found in the work of Frank and Amin. As Wallerstein indicates in *The capitalist world-economy*, his 'dialectical scientific methodology' implies that:

> one asks not what is the formal structure but what is the consequence for both the whole and the parts of maintaining or changing a certain structure at that particular point in time, given the totality of particular positions of that moment in time. (1979, p. 54)

Wallerstein's explanation of processes and events in the capitalist world system amounts to indicating what function they have in the totality of the system, and this clearly is the fundamental characteristic of functionalist explanation as expounded in chapter 3, section II. (Cf. Skocpol 1977, p. 1088; Terlouw 1985, pp. 163-4; Tromp 1988, p. 10) Examples of Wallerstein's functionalist explanations abound in the three volumes of *The modern world-system*. The rise of capitalism in the fifteenth and sixteenth centuries is explained by pointing out the system's need to avoid 'decimation and stagnation'. (1974, p. 24; 1980b, p. 31) The significance of Dutch hegemony in the seventeenth century is explained as a situation sustaining the world system 'over some difficult years of adjustment, until the English (and the French) were ready to take the steps necessary for its definitive consolidation'. (1974, p. 210) The transformation of the English aristocracy into a bourgeoisie, and the opposition of the aristocracy to the bourgeoisie in France are integrated into Wallerstein's theory of the development of the world system by defining the behaviour of the English and French ruling classes as 'essentially a function of their differing relationship to the world-economy'. (1974, p. 284) Wallerstein explains the incorporation of the Americas into the capitalist world economy by pointing out the subsequent economic function of these areas in the world system: they were crucial to the operation of the system because they provided 'a solid currency base for an expanding capitalist system'. (1980b, p. 109; cf. 1989, p. 129) The French Revolution of 1789 is not interpreted as a phenomenon with fundamental domestic roots; rather, it is explained in terms of the world economy as an event that 'broke out, in large part, precisely in response to the structural transformations going on in the world-economy and would, by its dynamic [...] ''accelerate'' the evolutions'. (1989, p. 112)

Connected with Wallerstein's functionalist explanations is the occasional use of *counterfactual reasoning*. In order to arrive at conclusions, Wallerstein compares the existing state of affairs with a situation that would have come about under different conditions. Examples of this way of reasoning can be found in *The modern world-system*. A first example is Wallerstein's 'proof' of the existence of a semiperiphery:

> The world-economy was based precisely on the assumption that there were in fact these three zones [i.e., core, periphery and semiperiphery] and that they did in fact have different modes of labor control. Were this not so, it would not have been possible to assure the kind of flow of the surplus which enabled the capitalist system to come into existence. (1974, p. 87)

A second example of counterfactual reasoning can be found in Wallerstein's attempt to fit the 'contraction' of the seventeenth century into his historical scheme of the development of the capitalist world system. As he has indicated, this contraction should be interpreted as a 'needed change of pace', which proved to be a useful instrument in breaking positions of power and privilege: 'Without such a period, the next qualitative leap forward would not have been possible.' (1980b, p. 33)

The third methodological assumption in Immanuel Wallerstein's work concerns the 'unity of the social sciences' and the role of generalizations about history. (Cf. Bonnell 1980, pp. 163-4, 170-1) As Wallerstein has argued, the different recognized social sciences, such as anthropology, economics, geography, political science and sociology, have become artificially separated. Moreover, in his view, 'history and social science are one subject matter', which he terms *historical social science*. (1979, p. ix) According to Wallerstein, it is impossible to analyse historical occurrences without using general concepts that imply generalizations about recurrent phenomena. He also argues that 'not only is all ''social science'' a set of inductions from ''history'', but there are *no* generalizations which are ahistorical, that is, universal'. (1979, p. ix, cf. pp. 6-7) Furthermore, Wallerstein asserts that there is no such thing as value-free historical social science, since '[e]very choice of conceptual framework is a political option. Every assertion of "truth", even if one qualifies it as transitory truth, or heuristic theory, is an assertion of value.' (1979, p. x) Nevertheless, one critic has argued that 'Wallerstein's epistemological assumptions owe much to the attempt to make historical sociology as rigorous as natural sciences are presumed to be'. (Aronowitz 1981, p. 511) Wallerstein is of the opinion that scientific activities support political action: in his view, the value of scientific endeavour is derivative of the unity of theory and praxis. (1979, p. xi)

B Theoretical Assumptions

Wallerstein has himself declared the systemic focus of his theory to be its foremost characteristic:

> If there is one thing which distinguishes a world-system perspective from any other, it is its insistence that the unit of analysis is a *world*-system defined in terms of *economic* processes and links, and not any units defined in terms of juridical, political, cultural, geological, or other criteria. (Hopkins, Wallerstein et al. 1982b, p. 72)

In Wallerstein's work, five theoretical assumptions stand out. In order of discussion these assumptions concern: the reality of the capitalist world system with its own laws and dynamics; the holistic character of social and political organizations; the materialist foundations of social phenomena; the pervasiveness of exploitation; and the expansive nature of capitalism.

Wallerstein considers the capitalist world economy to be a distinctive reality in world history, which has its own laws and dynamics. The *raison d'être* of this world economy is the accumulation of capital. (1979, pp. 134, 276; 1984b, pp. 14-15, 43-4) This accumulation takes place through the activities of individual and independent entrepreneurs who try to maximize the profits on their sales. Producers tend to increase their production capacities in order to increase profits. The demand for their products is dependent, however, on the distribution of income, which tends to become increasingly unequal. At a certain point in time, demand and supply will grow so far apart that a crisis of production results. According to Wallerstein, the temporal sequence of expansion and contraction is an important feature of the dynamics of the capitalist world economy. (1984b, pp. 98-100)

The second theoretical assumption in Wallerstein's work concerns the holistic view on social and political organizations. (See Aronowitz 1981, pp. 504-5, 510-12; Terlouw 1985, p. 166; Denemark and Thomas 1988, pp. 48-50, 53-5) Wallerstein assumes that all elements of the social and political organization of territorial units, such as states, derive from the position of these units in the world system. (Cf. 1974, pp. 354-5) Wallerstein has himself phrased the relationship in the following manner:

> The development of the capitalist world-economy has involved the creation of all the major institutions of the modern world: classes, ethnic/national groups, households - and the 'states'. All of these structures postdate, not antedate capitalism; all are consequence, not cause. (1984b, p. 29)

Wallerstein's third theoretical assumption, concerning the materialist foundations of social phenomena, is related to his holistic view of the world system. (See Skocpol 1977, pp. 1078-80; Zolberg 1981, pp. 255, 258 ff.; cf. the critique of Skocpol's and Zolberg's positions in Garst 1985) According to Wallerstein, ideological positions cannot really be understood unless they are analysed in terms of social and economic relations. Wallerstein stated his position very clearly in the first volume of *The modern world-system*: 'To dissect the ideological coordinates of a political and social conflict is however never meaningful unless one can root that analysis in the social relations prevailing at the time and thereby comprehend the implication of ideological demands for these relationships.' (1974, p. 283) At other places in his work, Wallerstein has indicated that he prefers to see racial, ethnic and nationalist consciousness in terms of the class structure. In his analysis, racial, ethnic and national divisions are subordinate to class relations: 'Ethno-national consciousness is the constant resort of all those for whom class organization offers the risk of a loss of relative advantage through the normal workings of the market and class dominated political bargaining.' (1979, p. 228; cf. the different interpretation in Brewer 1980, p. 167)

Wallerstein's fourth theoretical assumption pertains to exploitation. According to Wallerstein, all forms of social organization involve the expropriation of surplus value from direct producers by elites dominating the legal and state apparatuses. Wallerstein rules out the possibility of *equal development*: '[t]he so-called "widening gap" is not an anomaly but a continuing basic mechanism of the operation of the world-economy'. (1979, p. 73) In the capitalist world system, exploitation has taken the form of proletarianization in the core, and of unequal exchange in the relation between core and periphery. Wallerstein goes as far as criticizing the integration of the periphery in the world system *per se:* 'the involvement of various parts of the world as peripheral zones of the capitalist world-economy has not been historically beneficial to their populations'. (1991, p. 101)

The fifth theoretical assumption that can be found in Wallerstein's work concerns the expansive nature of capitalism. Since the search for maximum profit is defined as the motor of capitalism, the capitalist world system has been forced to expand continuously, internally by the development of new production processes, externally by the inclusion of new areas into the international division of labour. (1979, p. 134; 1984b, p. 17) The ongoing expansion of the capitalist world economy has, according to Wallerstein, sown the seeds for its ultimate demise: the 'contradictions' of the system increase, while antisystemic forces become more important. This has brought Wallerstein, in two volumes of his essays (1979 and 1984b), to predict that the world system has almost reached its *kairos*, the right time for the transition to a socialist world economy, the completion of which might take 'a good 100-150 years'. (1984b, p. 111; 1979, pp. 281-3) In a more recent essay, Wallerstein is much less adamant about the fate of capitalism; there he writes about the construction of socialism 'as an option, but scarcely as a certainty'. (1991, p. 96)

III THE THEORY OF THE HIERARCHY OF THE MODERN WORLD SYSTEM

The starting point of Immanuel Wallerstein's theory of the hierarchy of the modern world system is the idea that 'social systems' are the only legitimate units of analysis in (historical) social science. In Wallerstein's view, the focus of many social scientists on the concept 'society' clouds the real subject of social theorizing:

> [W]here can we find 'societies' other than in the minds of the analysts, or of the orators? Social science would, in my view, make a great leap forward if it dispensed entirely with the term. [...] My own unit of analysis is based on the measurable social reality of interdependent productive activities, what may be called an 'effective social division of labor' or, in code language, an 'economy'. (1984b, p. 2)

In Wallerstein's 'utilitarianism on a global scale' (Bergesen 1980, pp. 9-11) the division of labour is a crucial variable. The only 'totalities' that have historically existed, according to Wallerstein, are *minisystems* and *world systems*. Minisystems are 'primitive' social systems, characterized by the existence of a single division of labour and cultural unity. Usually, they are highly autonomous, relatively small subsistence economies. World systems are units having a complete division of labour and multiple cultural systems. There are two kinds of world systems: *world empires*, which have a single political structure over most of the system's area, and *world economies*, which contain multiple political structures. (1974, pp. 347-8; 1979, pp. 4-5)

According to Wallerstein's interpretation of world history, world economies have always been unstable until the rise of the modern, capitalist world system. In the long run, world economies either disintegrated or were conquered by one group and were transformed into world empires. Although trade existed in world empires, these systems were nevertheless 'basically redistributive', with a political elite determining the distribution of economic surplus. (1979, p. 6) The modern world system, which is a capitalist world economy, came into being during the long sixteenth century (1450-1600) and caused the gradual decay of allocation mechanisms other than the market. In Wallerstein's view, the capitalist world economy managed to survive over more than 500 years because no one political entity succeeded in controlling the worldwide division of labour. (Cf. 1983c, pp. 57-8) Wallerstein goes as far as considering capitalism and the modern world economy (a single division of labour coupled with multiple polities and cultures) as 'obverse sides of the same coin', implying that the one could not have survived without the other. (1979, p. 6)

The fundamental principle of capitalism, as it has been defined above, is the maximization of capital accumulation. (1983c, pp. 13-8) The main instrument for accumulating capital is the reduction of the costs of production. This is where exploitation enters Wallerstein's argumentation:

> The primary tool in the reduction of costs is force applied to the direct producer, reducing his income to a minimum and allowing someone else to appropriate the remaining 'value' he has produced. The mechanisms of such appropriation are multiple, but they take three main forms. One is forced labor, in which the direct producer receives from the legal 'proprietor' part or all of his income in kind. A second is wage labor, in which the direct producer receives from the legal 'proprietor' part or all of his income in money. A third is petty proprietorship, in which the direct producer is indirectly forced, often through debt mechanisms, to sell his product at below the market value. (1984b, p. 3)

All three modes of exploitation are applied in the capitalist world system; the question of which mode will be used when and where, can only be answered by reference to the specific circumstances existing at a certain place and time. (E.g. 1974, pp. 87-9) According to Wallerstein, the history of the capitalist world system demonstrates that a mode of exploitation will be eliminated when it becomes less economical than other modes. For instance, slavery was abolished when cash-crop production and wage labour proved to be more efficient means of exploiting the work force. (1979, p. 28; 1974, p. 89)

In Wallerstein's view, *households* are 'one of the key institutional structures' of the capitalist world system. (1984a, p. 17) Households occupy a distinct place in the processes of exploitation and capital accumulation in the system at large. Although the 'commodification of everything' (E.g. 1983c) is one of the hallmarks of Wallerstein's interpretation of capitalist accumulation, this does not imply that labour is also fully commodified. Wallerstein argues that the 'mode of remuneration' of a majority of households under capitalism has been 'partial wage labour'. (1984a, p. 19; 1983c, pp. 25-8) The separation of the roles of 'breadwinner' and 'housewife', which has also been referred to as 'institutionalized sexism' (1983c, p. 25), has contributed to accumulation, because it led to a reduction of the costs of production. The circumstance that household members, usually the women, produce real income by working in and around the house without receiving a salary implies, according to Wallerstein, that these services do not have to be bought on the market and, consequently, that the wage of the 'breadwinner' can be less. (1983c, pp. 27-8; 1983a)

Wallerstein has developed his ideas about exploitation in the context of his general analysis of the capitalist world system. The modes of exploitation occupy a place within the worldwide division of labour. In Wallerstein's interpretation, the worldwide exploitative process has three tiers: 'That is to say, there is a middle tier, which shares in the exploitation of the lower tier, but also shares in being exploited by the upper tier.' (1979, p. 223) In the capitalist world economy, the three tiers are the core, the semiperiphery and the periphery. The development of the world economy forges a close link between core and periphery in the sense that '[c]ore-cum-periphery and periphery-cum-core form and develop always and only in relation to one another, by definition'. (Hopkins, Wallerstein et al. 1982b, p. 46)

The *core* of the world economy consists of the countries possessing relatively sophisticated production processes. In these areas, indigenous bourgeoisies have set up autonomous industries producing manufactured commodities for the world market. The predominant modes of labour control have been wage labour and self-employment. (1974, p. 87) The countries of the core are characterized by relatively strong state machineries. Historically, the core of the modern world system has consisted of countries in Northwest Europe. North America (the United States and Canada), Japan, Australia and New Zealand can also be considered as core countries.

The *periphery* of the world economy has historically been dominated by relatively simple production processes. This means that countries in that part of the world tend to specialize in agriculture and raw materials production with badly rewarded labour. The export of peripheral products has contributed to capital accumulation in the core because trade has been subject to unequal exchange. (1984b, p. 82) Labour control has taken place by means of coercion, in the form of outright slavery or of 'feudalism'. (1974, p. 87) The state structures of peripheral countries are relatively weak. Wallerstein describes the 'optimal' state structure of peripheral countries as 'one that (1) was not strong enough to interfere with the flows of commodities, capital, and labor between this zone and the rest of the capitalist world-economy, but (2) *was* strong enough to facilitate these same flows'. (1984b, pp. 80-1)

The capitalist world economy has expanded gradually over the last five centuries; it was not until the twentieth century that all parts of the world were incorporated into this world economy. Before the twentieth century, large parts of the world still belonged to the *external arena* of the world economy. According to Wallerstein, the defining characteristic of the external arena is the fact that production processes can be accounted for by other considerations than the maximization of capital accumulation in the core. (1989, p. 130; cf. 1976) The incorporation of parts of the external arena into the world economy has been described by Wallerstein in the following way:

> Incorporation means fundamentally that at least some significant production processes in a given geographic location become integral to various of the commodity chains that constitute the ongoing divisioning of labor of the capitalist world-economy. (1989, p. 130)

As Hopkins and Wallerstein (1981, p. 239-40) have indicated, there are 'at least four well-known features' of incorporation into the periphery of the world economy: integration of the previously external areas into the 'axial' worldwide division of labour and the interstate system; specialization of production emphasizing produce and commodities that can be sold on the world market; the transformation of previously independent workers into 'labour-in-relation-to-capital'; and the securement of the reproduction of capital.

Apart from the core and periphery, Wallerstein has distinguished a middle stratum, the *semiperiphery*. The semiperiphery takes in a place between the core and the periphery with respect to structural features such as the complexity of economic activities, the mode of labour control, the strength of the state machinery, et cetera. The semiperiphery is 'assigned as it were a specific economic role, but the reason is less economic than political'. (1979, p. 23) The political role of the semiperiphery is that of a buffer between two opposing forces. The semiperiphery is 'both exploited and exploiter' (1979, p. 23); this implies that it 'partially deflect[s] the political pressures which groups primarily located in peripheral areas might otherwise direct against core-states and the groups which operate within and through their state machineries'. (1974, p. 350) The historical form of labour control in the semiperiphery is sharecropping. (1974, p. 87, 103; 1979, p. 38) Historically, the semiperiphery consisted of countries declining and ascending in the worldwide hierarchy. The seventeenth-century periphery included former great powers such as Spain, Portugal, and the 'old dorsal spine of Europe' (Western Flanders, Southern Germany and Northern Italy) as well as rising countries such as Sweden, Brandenburg, Prussia and the British colonies in North America. (1980b, pp. 180-1) Wallerstein has not specified which countries belong to 'the many semiperipheral zones in the world' during the twentieth century. (1984b, p. 110)

One concept which deserves to be mentioned in the context of a discussion of Wallerstein's theory of the hierarchy of the capitalist world system is *hegemony*. According to Wallerstein, hegemony has to be understood as:

> that situation in which the ongoing rivalry between the so-called 'great powers' is so unbalanced that one power is truly *primus inter pares*; that is, one power can largely impose its rules and its wishes (at the very least by effective veto power) in the economic, political, military, diplomatic, and even cultural arenas. The material base of such power lies in the ability of enterprises domiciled in that power to operate more efficiently in all three major economic arenas - agro-industrial production, commerce, and finance. (1984b, pp. 3-39)

Wallerstein has distinguished only three instances of hegemony in the capitalist world economy: the Dutch United Provinces in the seventeenth, the United Kingdom in the nineteenth, and the United States in the twentieth century. (1984b, pp. 39-40)

Because of their overwhelming power, the hegemonic states have traditionally advocated international free trade. The competitive edge of the enterprises originating in the hegemonic countries was such that they tended to dominate the world market, and hence they could only gain from the opening up of foreign markets. (1984b, pp. 5-6) The economic dominance of the hegemonic states is accompanied by political-military power. The hegemons of the modern world system all emerged as the dominant military powers from world wars leading to a reconstruction of the international system: respectively, these were the Thirty Years' War (1618-48) followed by the Peace of Westphalia, the Napoleonic Wars (1792-1815) followed by the Congress of Vienna, and the combined struggle of the First and Second World War (1914-45) followed by the creation of the United Nations and Bretton Woods regimes. (1984b, pp. 41-2)

The decline of United States' hegemony since 1967 has led Wallerstein to speculate about the future political situation of the world system. In his view, Japan and Western Europe are the 'two successor candidates' for hegemony. (1991, p. 44) Wallerstein envisages a reordering of alliances, with a Japanese-U.S. bloc, possibly allied to China, and a pan-European bloc, linked to the former Soviet Union, as a likely outcome. (1991, pp. 44-5, 58-9)

The so-called *interstate system* is interpreted by Wallerstein as the 'political expression' of the capitalist world economy. (1984b, p. 4) As indicated above, Wallerstein sees the division of the world system into separate political units as a precondition for the survival of capitalism. If one state had succeeded in creating a world empire, the forces of competition would no longer have ruled the world system. In such circumstances, decisions would have been taken on political grounds, giving rise to a redistributive instead of a productive economic order. States, in Wallerstein's view, are 'created institutions reflecting the need of class forces operating in the world-economy'. (1984b, p. 33) States are used by the bourgeoisies to increase profits. Competing bourgeoisies try to obtain state power in order to limit the working of market forces in a legitimate way, creating monopolies where possible under the aegis of a state. (1979, pp. 69-70, 149; 1984b, p. 154; 1974, p. 16)

IV THE HISTORICAL ANALYSIS OF THE MODERN WORLD SYSTEM

According to Immanuel Wallerstein, the origins of the modern world system, which is a capitalist world economy, can be dated in the 'long' sixteenth century from 1450 until approximately 1600. In the fifteenth century, Europe suffered from a crisis of feudalism, which was a 'decisive' crisis of accumulation: it proved to be no longer possible to increase productivity by the reinvestment of profits because of 'the inherent limitations of the reward system of feudal social organization'. (1974, p. 23) In order to counter stagnation, it was necessary to expand the system's land area and exploitable population base and to change the methods of labour control. (1974, pp. 24, 38) In the fifteenth century, European countries started their expansion into different parts of the world. Expansion was primarily directed at the Mediterranean and Atlantic islands, North and West Africa, Eastern Europe, Russia and Central Asia.

The expansion of European countries resulted in an increase of the land/labour ratio of the European-dominated world economy, which 'made possible the large-scale accumulation of basic capital which was used to finance the rationalization of agricultural production'. (1974, p. 69) The 'long' sixteenth century was characterized by secular inflation - the so-called 'price revolution' - which stimulated economic growth. Inflation led to forced savings and thus stimulated capital accumulation. (1974, p. 84)

In different parts of the world economy, different modes of labour control were applied. Wage labour and self-employment dominated in Europe. Slavery came to be used as a means of labour control in sugar production on the Atlantic islands and later in the Caribbean and in America. In Hispanic America, coerced cash-crops were also introduced as a means of labour control. According to Wallerstein, the latter form of labour coercion differed from European feudalism - although many scholars have described it as a similar phenomenon - because the function of the two modes of labour control were different. Wallerstein stresses that European medieval feudal landlords produced for the domestic market, while American cash-crop production took place within the context of the capitalist world economy for the purpose of exportation. (1974, p. 91) The inclusion of external areas into the world economy enabled the core countries to specialize in more highly rewarded production, while the periphery was transformed into monocultures.

In the European core, the sixteenth century witnessed the rise of strong states. During the crisis of feudalism in the fifteenth century, the nobility felt threatened by peasant rebellions and turned to the kings for protection. The kings exploited this situation by increasing taxation and strengthening the state apparatus, or 'bureaucracy'. They developed strong standing armies, thereby monopolizing the use of force, and legitimated their position by cultivating the ideology of absolutism, the divine right of the king. (1974, pp. 133-47)

The development of strong states did not, in Wallerstein's view, result in the creation of a world empire by Spain or France, the two main contenders for empire, because the growing financial demands of imperial state machineries and the consequent inflation of public credit produced the bankruptcies of these two states in the mid-sixteenth century. (1974, p. 185) The United Provinces of the Netherlands took over the lead in the European world economy at the turn of the century. The United Provinces gained in importance as a result of their dominance of international trade (especially with the Baltics, the East Indies, the Mediterranean, the Western Hemisphere and West Africa), their position as a centre of shipbuilding, their productive efficiency in fishing and agriculture (industrial crops and livestock), and the development of Amsterdam as the prime capital market. (1974, pp. 210-12; 1980b, pp. 39-57) The rise of the United Provinces and the collapse of Spain and France marked the beginning of a new phase, the 'second' sixteenth century, which was 'oriented to the creation of coherent nation-states obtaining politico-commercial advantages within the framework of a nonimperial world-economy'. (1974, p. 265)

Whereas the sixteenth century, in Wallerstein's interpretation, was a phase of expansion and growth in the development of the capitalist world economy (a so-called A phase), the seventeenth century was a period of contraction and crisis (a B phase). The seventeenth century, roughly from 1600 until 1750, was characterized by, among other things: unfavourable terms of trade for cereals; agricultural shifts such as a decrease of land reclamation and a reduction of the average yield of cereals; a degradation of the peasant class; a shift of industrial activity (mainly textiles) to the rural areas; a decrease of the price of cereals and an increase of real wages; a shortage of credit; and a lack of trade growth. (1980b, pp. 13-18) Wallerstein interprets the seventeenth-century contraction as functional; it is this contraction that paved the way for the spurt of the industrial revolution, economically, politically, intellectually and socially. (1980b, p. 27)

The seventeenth century saw the rise of *mercantilism*, which is a form of economic nationalism. The Dutch state, however, professed *mare liberum*. Its hegemonic position in the world economy, lasting from, roughly, 1625 until 1675, meant that it would gain most from free trade. (1980b, p. 60) England provided state assistance to its own merchants and imposed constraints on foreign merchants, in order to strengthen its commercial position *vis-à-vis* the Netherlands. Dutch involvement in wars with England and, later, France, caused its hegemonic position to crumble. Holland appeared to be too small to carry the burden of military and naval defence and had to give up its hegemonic position as a consequence of changed power relations. (1980b, p. 80) The period between 1672 and 1763 was dominated by the struggle between France and England. Both countries tried to protect their own industries through mercantilist policies, and Dutch textile industry ran into trouble. Wallerstein perceives a more general tendency in French and British policies: 'This struggle of core powers to export unemployment to each other is a recurrent phenomenon of the capitalist world-economy in its moments of stagnation.' (1980b, p. 92; 1989, pp. 57-9)

Wallerstein has interpreted the prevalence of Britain over France not as a 'triumph of liberalism', but as a 'triumph of the strong state'. (1980b, p. 268) According to Wallerstein, the British emphasis on trade and the government's attempt to expand British shares of world metallurgical and textile production by the enactment of mercantilist measures has led to Britain's emphasis on the navy and the colonies. In the end, this policy enabled Britain to outstrip France militarily.

The downturn of the seventeenth century caused a reduction of production in the world system's periphery. Parts of former peripheral activities (cereals production, pasturage) were relocated to the core. Peripheral producers of export crops reacted to this reduction in one of two ways. They tried to increase their income either by expanding the volume of exports or by increasing the intensity of exploitation of the labourers. (1980b, pp. 129-31) In the Eastern European periphery, *corvée* labour was increased and competition was reduced by the buying out of producers. In Hispanic America, the introduction of the *hacienda* enabled landowners to adjust production to changing demand on the world market. (1980b, pp. 136-57) In addition to these changes, a new peripheral region was created in the Caribbean (according to Wallerstein, this concerned the area from Northwest Brazil to Maryland) for the production of sugar, tobacco and gold. (1980b, pp. 166-7)

The former great powers, Spain and Portugal, suffered from deindustrialization and had become too weak to develop into mercantilist states. These countries were therefore relegated to a semiperipheral position as 'conveyor belts for the interests of the core powers in the peripheral regions'. (1980b, p. 158) Sweden was an 'upwardly mobile' semiperipheral country. The Swedish state encouraged the production of copper, iron and tar, and obtained a stronger political-military position in the seventeenth-century world economy. (1980b, pp. 209-18) Prussia also gradually developed into a semiperipheral state, mainly by the activities of the *Junkers*, who wanted to create a strong state bureaucracy in order to provide themselves with employment opportunities. (1980b, pp. 230-1) The American settler colonies (New England and the middle Atlantic colonies) were involved in so-called triangular trade with Africa and the West Indies and achieved their semiperipheral position by their trading activities.

The second era of great expansion of the capitalist world economy, according to Wallerstein, is the period between, roughly, 1730 and the 1840s. In this era, two revolutions - the industrial revolution in Great Britain and the French Revolution - took place. Contrary to commonly accepted explanations, Wallerstein interprets these revolutions as two representatives of one development. (1989, p. 3) As to the industrial revolution, Wallerstein writes that it has not been a sudden change, but instead a series of innovations in the English textile and iron industries, based on the development of new and improved machines and the organization of factories. This fits into the evolution of capitalism, since 'cumulative, self-sustaining change in the form of the endless search for accumulation has been the leitmotiv of the capitalist world-economy ever since its genesis in the sixteenth century'. (1989, p. 22)

France had been the principal industrial power in the seventeenth and eighteenth centuries, but it was not in this country that the industrial revolution took place, since its position in the capitalist world economy was not favourable. Wallerstein argues that '[i]t is the world-economy which develops over time and not subunits within it' (1989, p. 33), and therefore the relative competitive strength of France and Britain is a prime explanatory factor in his account of the industrial revolution. The French Revolution is, in his view, part and parcel of the development of the capitalist world economy: it is interpreted as 'the moment when the ideological superstructure finally caught up with the economic base. It was the consequence of the transition, not its cause nor the moment of its occurrence.' (1989, p. 52) According to Wallerstein, the French Revolution occurred *as a consequence of* France's sense of imminent defeat in the struggle for hegemony with Britain. (1989, p.94) He sees the Revolution as 'a relatively conscious attempt by a diverse group of the ruling capitalist strata to force through urgently needed reforms of the French state in light of the perceived British leap forward to hegemonic status in the world-economy'. (1989, p. 111) The Revolution was also the first important antisystemic or anticapitalist movement in the modern world system; it was the rise of the popular masses - the peasants and the *sans-culottes* - against the feudal ruling classes. (1989, pp. 104-5, 111)

The beginning of the nineteenth century witnessed a 'double movement' in the world economy. On the one hand, new zones, such as the Indian subcontinent, the Ottoman and Russian empires and West Africa, were incorporated into the world system. On the other hand, parts of Western Europe - France, Belgium, the western parts of 'Germany', and Switzerland - and the northern states of the United States began their industrialization and gradually developed into core states. (1989, pp. 122, 137)

Wallerstein has indicated three major consequences of the incorporation of previously external areas into the periphery of the world economy. In the first place, he has pointed out the development of a new pattern of exports and imports. The new peripheral areas became part of the global division of labour as producers of raw materials and agricultural cash-crops. Local manufacturing was reduced or even destroyed by relatively cheap imports of manufactured products from the core. (1989, pp. 138-52) In the second place, Wallerstein has argued that incorporation into the world economy necessitated the creation of larger 'economic decision-making entities' in order to assure market-responsive production. The two most common means were the establishment of plantations and the creation of dependency relations between local producers and merchants, for instance through debt bondage. (1989, p. 152) In the third place,

Wallerstein has mentioned the increased coercion of the labour force as a consequence of incorporation. Enhanced coercion of labour, implying enslavement, serfdom and the like, appeared to be necessary to achieve competitive production. (1989, p. 157)

France, Spain and Portugal lost their role in the Western Hemisphere with the decolonization of the Americas at the end of the eighteenth and the beginning of the nineteenth century. Although Great Britain also lost many of its possessions in America, its hegemonic position in the world economy enabled it to retain its commercial ties. The United States, according to Wallerstein, 'was able to carve itself out a role as lieutenant and, therefore, potential and eventual rival to Britain'. (1989, p. 255)

V THE THEORY OF CAPITALIST CRISES AND ANTISYSTEMIC MOVEMENTS

The starting point of Wallerstein's theory of capitalist crises is the assumption that the fundamental drive of capitalism toward 'ceaseless accumulation' occasionally encounters 'bottlenecks'. (1982a, pp. 13-16) The long-term development of the world economy shows a cyclical pattern of upswings or A-phases and downswings or B-phases, together forming so-called Kondratieff waves of about fifty years' duration. (E.g. Hopkins, Wallerstein et al. 1982a)

The bottlenecks of accumulation are the consequences of a continuing antinomy between supply and demand, which are the expression of two different logics. World supply is primarily the result of 'market-oriented "individual" production decisions', while demand is predominantly a 'function of "socially" determined allocations of income'. (Hopkins, Wallerstein et al. 1982b, p. 58) Supply tends to be increased as long as markets can be found and entrepreneurs expect to get a profit by producing additional quantities of commodities. Wallerstein does not believe in 'Say's Law', which holds that supply creates demand. According to Wallerstein, the level of demand is the result of a particular income distribution, which is determined, in its turn, by power processes inside private enterprises and by political decisions at the level of the state. The contradiction between supply and demand under capitalism is summarized by Wallerstein in the following way:

> [W]orld demand, the sum of the consequences of political decisions taken in each state, tends to remain stable over the middle run while world supply is hurtling toward ever greater production. Sooner or later, usually after about twenty-five years, there comes a point where there are insufficient buyers for the additional supply and

the capitalist world-economy finds itself in one of its recurring 'bottlenecks of accumulation'. We are in the most recent such bottleneck today, and have been since about 1967. (1982a, p. 16)

Wallerstein has mentioned several short-term solutions to the problem of accumulation. In the first place, some producers are forced into bankruptcy. This leads to a reduction of supply, a concentration of ownership and a concomitant increase of profit for the surviving producers. Secondly, the total sum of wages is reduced by increasing the capital intensity of production. Furthermore, production processes are transferred to low-income countries in the semiperiphery and the periphery. Finally, technological innovations are stimulated in order to rationalize production. (1982a, pp. 17-18)

These short-term reactions do not, however, solve the fundamental accumulation problem. Historically, solutions to this problem have been found in either of two directions: further commodification of social transactions and geographical expansion of the world economy. Commodification is the result of the combination of political pressure by the workers, who want to increase their salaries, and the interests of the producers, who want to stimulate demand. (1983c, pp. 36-7) Commodification, however, puts additional pressure on the level of profit. This is where geographical expansion of the world economy offers a way out. Expansion, which has also shown a cyclical pattern (E.g. 1980a, pp. 21-2), has meant the inclusion into the world economy of new zones having 'levels of real remuneration which were at the bottom of the world-system's hierarchy of wage-levels'. (1983c, p. 39) According to Wallerstein,

the policies of the colonial states (and of the restructured semi-colonial states in those incorporated zones that were not formally colonized) seemed designed precisely to promote the emergence of the very semi-proletarian household which, as we have seen, made possible the lowest possible wage-level threshold. [...] If we add to this analysis the observation that new incorporations into the world-system of capitalism tended to correlate with phases of stagnation in the world-economy, it becomes clear that geographical expansion of the world-system served to counterbalance the profit-reducing process of increased proletarianization, by incorporating new workforces destined to be semi-proletarianized. (1983c, p. 39)

The overall structural problem of the modern world system can no longer, according to Wallerstein, be solved by such measures. In his view, '[t]he two asymptotes of geographical expansion and commodification have reached the level where they have begun to act as structural constraints on the survival of capitalism as an historical system'. (1982a, p. 25) The constraints mentioned by Wallerstein concern the facts that all parts of the world have already been integrated into the capitalist world system and that transactions have nearly all become subject to market considerations.

As a corollary of the 'economic squeeze' that has been described in the previous paragraphs, Wallerstein has analysed a so-called 'political squeeze'. This political squeeze appears to find its expression in two phenomena: the increase of internal conflicts among the upper strata in the world system and the growing importance of antisystemic movements.

Wallerstein has distinguished three groups within the upper class: a small group of 'superaccumulators', who control the economic sources of power, the enterprises; the 'bulk of the cadres', who have gained control of most of the political sources of power, the state machineries; and the 'supplicants to cadre status and rewards'. (1983b, p. 24) In times of crisis, when the pressure on the rate of profit increases, the upper strata start to fight among themselves in order to retain their claim to a certain part of the surplus.

The struggle among the upper strata is accompanied by the increased vehemence of antisystemic activities. The characteristic of all antisystemic movements is that they do not accept the claims to legitimacy of the economic and/or political system. The most important antisystemic movements in the history of the modern world system, according to Wallerstein, were the socialist and nationalist movements, in recent times supplemented by 'new social movements'. (1984b, pp. 123-6; Arrighi, Hopkins and Wallerstein 1989, p. 88)

The socialist movement, which was created in the nineteenth century, 'was rooted in the intensification of the processes of capitalist centralization, and rationalization of economic activities'. (Arrighi, Hopkins and Wallerstein 1989, p. 77) At first this movement had a revolutionary aim, the overthrow of the capitalist system. In the West, the movement gradually became reformist and participated in the political process. According to Arrighi, Hopkins and Wallerstein (1989, pp. 85-8), the social-democratic parties in Western Europe achieved a large number of their objectives in the two decades after the Second World War. The working class experienced a substantial rise in its standard of living and its organizations obtained an equal position in the political structure.

The causes of the success of the socialist and social-democratic movement offer a partial explanation of the rise, in the West, of the 'new social movements', which comprise the peace/ecology/alternative lifestyle movement, the women's movement and the 'minority' rights/'Third World within' movement. Apart from protesting against the ideology of progress propagated by the defenders of the capitalist system, these groups complained about the social-democratic movements, which 'had lost their "oppositional" quality precisely as a result of their successes in achieving partial state power'. (Arrighi, Hopkins and Wallerstein 1989, p. 88)

The third important antisystemic movement mentioned by Wallerstein is the nationalist movement. Also being a product of the nineteenth century, this movement focused on the domination of one ethno-national group over others. The aim of nationalist movements is the liberation of the oppressed groups by obtaining equal status within or, more commonly, outside the existing national entity. (Arrighi, Hopkins and Wallerstein 1989, pp. 30-3) In many countries, especially in the Third World, nationalist movements have come to power over the last several decades. Although some people have stressed the common antisystemic character of socialist and nationalist movements, Arrighi, Hopkins and Wallerstein have rejected the analogy between the two, since national liberation 'has not eliminated the relational conditions through which the accumulation process operates'. (1989, p. 70) In their view, elimination of the conditions of capitalist accumulation requires the prolongation of the class struggle.

NOTES

1. In line with the practice in the rest of this book, terms such as 'world system' and 'world economy' will be written without hyphen.
2. The problems of operationalizing the concepts used in Wallerstein's world system theory become clear from the discussion of data sources and modes of measurement in Hopkins, Wallerstein et al. 1982b, esp. pp. 72-80.

7. Operationalization

I INTRODUCTION

In this chapter a research design will be developed that will be used in the ensuing empirical assessment of dependency theory. This research design will consist of some different, but clearly related elements. First, in section II, some methodological considerations relating to quantitative research in dependency theory and in the study of international relations in general will be presented.

Secondly, the units of research, both in time and space, will be defined in section III. In order to do so in a justifiable manner, a short discussion of previous research will be followed by an outline of the units in the present study.

Thirdly, in section IV, some attention will be paid to choosing the correct research technique for the problem under study. As in section III, a discussion of previous research will be accompanied by a choice of techniques that appear to fit the research problem of this study.

Finally, and perhaps most importantly, ample space will be devoted to the choice of variables that are to represent the theoretical concepts used in the variants of dependency theory (section V). Since this is a crucial undertaking, which might to some extent determine the value of the empirical assessment, this section will discuss several problems connected with the operationalization of the variables and the selection of indicators.

II METHODOLOGICAL CONSIDERATIONS

At several instances in the previous chapters it has been stressed that this study will apply a quantitative-empirical methodology. The choice of this methodology, instead of one of comparative case-studies, is based on both theoretical and pragmatic arguments. First of all, a quantitative approach is preferred because of the possibility to include a far larger number of countries than a comparative case-study design would allow.

Secondly, the *external validity* of a quantitative design comprising a large number of countries is superior to that of a case-study or even of a series of case-studies. This implies that it is possible to arrive at more general statements about international reality. Obviously, case-studies, which can take into account many more variables influencing the objects under study, can lay claim to superior *internal validity*. (Hagenaars and Segers 1980, pp. 39-60)

A third methodological reason leading to the adoption of a quantitative-empirical design is that the dependency theories that have been dealt with in the previous three chapters contain broad and general statements about the developments in the capitalist world system. A quantitative-empirical design appears to be the most feasible one for scrutinizing these types of statements. With respect to this issue, Jackson et al. have followed a similar reasoning:

> The above remarks should *not* be interpreted to mean that case studies of dependence ought to be avoided. Quite the contrary. Given the richness of their findings, their exploration of those micro-level hypotheses assumed in the macro-level theories referred to above, and their ability to research subtle, long-term changes, case studies possess great scholarly value. However, the preceding analysis suggests that future studies of dependence should (1) be designed to take into account the effects of context and of long-term trends, and (2) have their propositions couched in precise, systematic terms. Both of these conditions can be satisfied by a set of case studies (obviously, a single country will not suffice); however, they also suggest that a many-country, more formal analysis might be fruitful. (1979, p. 18)

A pragmatic reason for choosing a quantitative-empirical research design is that it is almost impossible for a single researcher to perform a number of case-studies sufficiently large to warrant conclusions about the empirical value of dependency theory.

All this is not meant to say, of course, that the performance of case-studies is useless. As Chase-Dunn has argued, 'both historical interpretive studies and quantitative comparative studies can be useful approaches to the world-system' (1989, p. 312), because both answer different questions: 'Historical studies are useful because some things really are conjunctural and impossible to analyse structurally, and also because they often generate hypotheses and conceptualizations which stimulate the formulation of structural theories.' (1989, p. 312) Robert W. Jackman has indicated that the quantitative-empirical research design is best suited for evaluating the *implications* of an approach with an obvious historical component, as is dependency theory: 'The evaluation of such implications is surely important, even though it does not concern the *origins* of those implications. [...] If the world system does seem to be organized along the lines anticipated in the dependency literature, then we have more confidence in the approach; if not, our confidence is weakened.' (1985, p. 178)

The debate about the empirical research of dependency theory's central tenets exhibits some clear disagreements which, according to Charles Ragin, 'cannot be settled by debating the relative merits of statistical and qualitative historical methodologies'. (1985, p. 453) Both approaches possess, in his view, 'unique strengths'. Yet there often is an extra-scientific element in scholars' choice for either of the two approaches. As Ragin indicates:

> Scholars in Third World countries are major proponents of the interpretive research strategy [...] The primary explanation of their preference [...] is the fact that scholars in noncore countries are interested in concrete problems of dependency and development faced by their own countries. Moreover, they seek specific knowledge relevant to the identification of local obstacles to development and the actions necessary to overcome these obstacles. The generalizing research strategy practiced by many North American social scientists is not directly relevant to these concerns. (1985, pp. 470-1; cf. Chase-Dunn 1985, p. 446)

Ragin's analysis of the methodologies used in the research of dependency theory implies that considerations about the usefulness of knowledge influence the choice of methods and techniques. Rosenau's conclusion that the 'considerable division over whether scientific or dialectic methods best lend themselves to analysis of the world-system' implies that 'efforts spent developing appropriate methodologies that will facilitate proof or disproof of propositions about the world-systems may be wasted energy' (1982, pp. 361-2), may, however, be drawn too hastily. The rejection of quantitative-empirical methods by some adherents of dependency theory might tell more about their values and about the specific uses they want to make of the theory than about the usefulness of the methods. An independent evaluation of quantitative-empirical research will still be needed.

From the literature criticizing the quantitative-empirical research of dependency Ragin (1985, pp. 454-9) has distilled and countered seven major lines of attack. These lines of attack lead to the following positions: dependency is all-encompassing in the Third World and not just a variable that can be measured; the research ignores the tentative and dialectical nature of dependency theory; the research is ahistorical; the techniques that are used imply a special causal metatheory that is irrelevant to the theory; the data that are used relate to countries that are not comparable; the research accords too much explanatory power to forces external to the dependent countries; and the research produces knowledge that is irrelevant to the problems confronted by progressive groups in the dependent countries.

Ragin (1985, pp. 454-9) does not consider these criticisms to be sufficiently strong arguments against applying quantitative methods to the generalizations that were formulated by the dependency theorists. The perception of dependency as either an all-encompassing or a dialectical process does not imply that the concept cannot be specified and measured; if the content of the concept changes over time, there is no reason why the operationalization in empirical research would stay identical. (Cf. Chase-Dunn 1989, p. 305) Furthermore, quantitative methods are not inherently ahistorical: quantitative methods can be applied to historical phenomena if these phenomena can be quantified. The techniques that are applied in quantitative research do not presuppose a specific causal process, nor do they assume identical units of analysis. The existing research stresses certain external forces only because the theories themselves have placed much emphasis on those factors. Finally, the knowledge produced by quantitative research offers some insight into the characteristics of the world economic system that influence poverty in the developing countries.

The conclusion of this section must be, then, that a quantitative approach can be helpful in evaluating the empirical value of dependency theory. Obviously, this should not lead one to deny the value of other methodological designs. It is apt to quote Jackman, who has argued that 'the cross-national statistical method is only one of several methods in comparative politics, and for some substantive problems it is not necessarily an appropriate one'. (1985, p. 179)

III UNITS OF ANALYSIS

Most quantitative studies focusing on dependency theory have chosen developing countries as their units of analysis. (See Bornschier, Chase-Dunn and Rubinson 1978; Bornschier and Chase-Dunn 1985, pp. 68-79; Hirsch 1986; Mahler 1980, pp. 16-27; Rubinson and Holtzman 1981) Some of these studies are limited to a regional sub-group of developing countries, while others have considered all or most developing countries for which data are available.

Some scholars have performed analyses in which both developed and developing countries are taken as the units of analysis. (Bollen 1983; Peacock, Hoover and Killian 1988; Snyder and Kick 1979) Since the object of these studies has been to analyse the core-periphery division *as such*, the choice of a heterogeneous population is justified. Most dependency theorists have argued or assumed that dependence, which is seen as a basic characteristic of the capitalist world system, does not imply a *quantitative*, but a *qualitative* difference between the units. In their view, the relative dependence of, say, Canada or the Netherlands has an implication fundamentally different from the dependence of India, Peru or Ghana. A comparison of developed and developing countries in one analysis of levels of dependence does not appear to be justifiable.

Hirsch has argued against limiting the analysis of dependency theory to a regional sub-group of developing countries. In his view, 'there is no theoretical reason provided to explain why region - or shared historical traits - should greatly affect a relationship of hierarchical control within the world system'. (1986, p. 106) Moreover, from a statistical-technical point of view, the limitation of the sample that would be the result of this approach is less satisfactory.

Chase-Dunn has warned against the dangers connected with the use of data on the level of the nation state. He argues that other units, such as classes or modes of production, might be theoretically relevant in theories of the world system, so that 'data which are aggregated from information on nation states may misrepresent the operation of world-system processes'. (1989, p. 319) Yet, data representing these elements are generally not available. Moreover, as Chase-Dunn has indicated, nation state data are useful tools in the research of certain problems. It is felt that data collected on the national level of developing countries are suited for the research undertaken in the context of the present study.

On the basis of his overview of previous analyses of dependency theory, Mahler (1980, p. 26) has formulated several *caveats* that seem relevant for the selection of units of analysis. First, cases should be eliminated when they might result in 'misleading findings'. This might be the case with countries having a very small population, extensive oil production, or both. Secondly, a sample should be composed of countries from all of the world's major regions; nevertheless, 'region' is a characteristic that may be used in further analysis. Thirdly, the sample should include a large number of developing countries.

For this study, data have been collected on developing countries in the period from 1965 until 1985. This period offers the possibility of controlling for differences in the world economic situation: the period encompasses the upswing of the 1960s, the recession of the 1970s, and the debt crisis of the 1980s. In order to limit the number of countries in the sample only those developing countries - i.e., countries with a *per capita* income below a certain minimum, as defined by, for instance, the World Bank - with a population of at least one million people in 1967 will be considered; the *Compendium of data for world-system analysis*, which has been edited by Bornschier and Heintz (1979), will serve as a guideline. The countries that will be considered in the subsequent analyses are listed in Appendix A.

In the subsequent analyses, a so-called 'pooled cross-sectional' or 'pooled panel' research design has been chosen. According to Chase-Dunn, this design 'is particularly useful for world-system studies'. (1989, p. 326) Chase-Dunn has characterized the benefits of this research design in the following insightful way:

> This design employs data on countries measured at several time points and uses both countries and time points as the unit of comparison (country-times). It throws together in one analysis the cross-sections (or panels) from different periods of time. This design is particularly appropriate for studying structural variables which change slowly [...]. The number of datum-points is increased considerably, thus overcoming one of the limitations of other crossnational research designs: a rather small number of cases. [...] If a process of theoretical interest changes only slowly a short time lag contains mostly measurement error. Pooled panel analysis allows the use of more widely-spaced measurement points and the specification of longer time lags, because the number of 'cases' is increased when 'country-times' are analyzed. (1989, p. 326)

The pooled cross-sectional analysis in this study will contain 242 cases. For each of the units of analysis listed in Appendix A three observations are included: 1965, 1975 and 1985. 'Country-times' having more than forty per cent of missing values on the original variables are excluded from the analyses.[1] Because of the relatively long distance between the time points in the analysis (ten years), it seems justifiable to treat the 242 cases as independent observations. The variation of the units of analysis over time is analysed in conjunction with the changing situation of the world system. In order to study time-specific effects, the pooled cross-sectional analysis is complemented by analyses for each of the three time points.

IV METHODS OF ANALYSIS

By far most quantitative-empirical studies of dependency theory have applied multiple regression analysis in their attempt to establish relationships between variables. A clear majority of these studies uses multiple regression analysis as the single technique, while some studies use it in combination with other techniques. Techniques that have also been employed are: path analysis, cluster analysis, correlation analysis, factor analysis, variance and covariance analysis, and canonical correlation analysis.

It seems that the use of regression techniques has become 'normal science'. Scholars using these techniques hardly ever feel the need to justify their choice, since the techniques have been used so often. Multiple regression analysis will not be employed in this study, because the models that have been derived from the dependency theories in chapters 3, 4 and 5 imply another research design.

The models that will be scrutinized in the next chapter are of a causal nature. Therefore, causal modelling techniques fit the problem much better than techniques such as multiple regression analysis, which allow for only one dependent variable. A technique such as canonical correlation analysis, which can be considered to be the most general variant of the linear model, offers the possibility of analysing more than one dependent variable. Yet, this type of analysis does not suit the present research problem in that it does not distinguish among dependent variables: it is only possible to study the relation between one *set* of independent and one *set* of dependent variables. (See Pedhazur 1982, pp. 720-71)

In the context of the models that were presented in the previous three chapters it is difficult to speak of dependent and independent variables. Most variables in the models are influenced by one or several others, while they, in their turn, influence other variables. The causal flow of the models is from the 'left' to the 'right'.

Elazar J. Pedhazur (1982, pp. 637-8) has indicated that LISREL (the acronym of Linear Structural Relations modelling) is a very versatile approach for the analysis of causal models. LISREL is suited for the analysis of causal models containing both manifest, or observed, and latent, or non-observed, variables. LISREL would have been an appropriate research technique for the purpose of this study. The number of cases and model parameters to be estimated, are not, however, in balance; at best, the ratio between the number of cases and the number of parameters is 4:1. In some cases, the number of missing values is quite large. As a consequence of these two factors, the LISREL analyses resulted in instable solutions, with variances being larger than 1.0 (in analyses based on correlation matrices the theoretical minimum of the variances is 0.0, and the maximum, 1.0), and covariance matrices being non-positive definite.

Another research technique that has been developed to estimate causal models is so-called *path analysis*. In order to judge whether this technique is suitable for the present study, the assumptions underlying path analysis must be taken into consideration. According to Pedhazur (1982, p. 582), the assumptions underlying the application of path analysis are fivefold. First, the relations among the variables in the model should be linear, additive and causal; curvilinear, multiplicative or interaction relations are excluded by path analysis. Secondly, each residual should be uncorrelated with the variables preceding it in the model; as a consequence, 'exogenous' variables (that is, variables not explained by other variables in the model, but by variables outside the model) are treated as 'givens'. Thirdly, the model should be recursive, i.e., the causal flows in the model should be unidirectional. Fourthly, the variables should be measured on at least interval scale. Finally, the variables should be measured without error.

Probably there is no model in the social sciences that could be set up entirely in accordance with these five assumptions. Nevertheless, a tradition of using causal modelling techniques has developed in the social sciences. In the past, a number of scholars have successfully applied path analysis in their studies of dependency theories. (E.g. Bornschier 1982; Bornschier and Ballmer-Cao 1979; Bornschier and Chase-Dunn 1985; Evans and Timberlake 1980; Kentor 1981; Meyer-Fehr 1980; Van Puijenbroek 1984; Walleri 1978a) The dependency models developed in chapters 3, 4 and 5 can be argued to be, on the whole, in accordance with the assumptions underlying path analysis. The first, third and fourth assumptions apply to the dependency models. It is not clear *a priori* whether the second assumption applies to the models; this might not be, on the whole, too much of a problem, since the path analyses will not be used for exploratory purposes, but for assessing theoretical constructions. Because of the nature of the data used in this study, some uncertainty with respect to the fifth assumption is bound to remain. Yet, the best guarantee for the reliability of these data is that they have been collected by reputable international organizations. (Cf. the remarks on reliability made in section V)

V OPERATIONALIZATION OF THE VARIABLES

In the previous sections, choices have been made about the units of research and the research methods. In this section the operationalization of the variables in the study will be dealt with. Some very specific problems might arise with respect to the indicators that will be used as empirical representatives of the theoretical concepts. These problems concern, respectively, the availability and reliability of data on developing countries.

In the first place, many developing countries do not possess the instruments needed for a regular collection of data concerning different aspects of their society, and their political and economic system. In some cases, the publication of these data is discouraged because of the potential harm to purported security interests. For these reasons it is nearly impossible to collect a complete set of data (i.e., containing data on all countries and all periods needed).

In the second place, and connected with the previous point, the reliability of the data might be less than desired. The lack of adequate data-gathering instruments in the developing countries might be partly responsible for this situation. The tendency of developing countries to have a relatively large 'informal' sector is also a factor in reducing the reliability of the data.

Notwithstanding these problems, in this section an attempt will be made to operationalize the concepts that have been used in modelling the dependency theories of Andre Gunder Frank, Samir Amin and Johan Galtung in chapters 3, 4 and 5. First, a summary of all the concepts used in the models will be presented. Subsequently, each of the concepts will be operationalized.

A The Concepts

The model that has been formulated on the basis of *Andre Gunder Frank's* theory of dependency contains seven theoretical concepts. These concepts are the following:

- the state of the capitalist world system;
- the degree of dependence;
- the concentration of production;
- internal polarization;
- the degree of exploitation;
- the nature of the political regime, the extent of repression;
- the level of development.

The model of *Samir Amin's* dependency theory contains eight theoretical concepts. These are:

- the degree of dependence;
- the conjunctural situation in the world system;
- the degree of extroversion;
- the degree of social and political inequality;
- the degree of exploitation;
- the economic distortions;
- the level of democracy;
- the level of development.

The analysis of *Johan Galtung's* theory of dependency has resulted in the formulation of a model containing nine theoretical concepts. These are:

- the position in the world structure (centre/periphery);
- the position in the world division of labour;
- the degree of power;

- the degree of inequality;
- the degree of exploitation;
- the degree of fragmentation/marginalization;
- the degree of penetration/dependence;
- the degree of spin-offs;
- the level of development.

In the remainder of section V an operational definition will be given for each of these concepts. Where possible, discussion of the concepts from the three variants will be combined.

B The Degree of Dependence (Frank, Amin, Galtung)

In all variants of dependency theory, the concept of dependence is used. The variants that have been dealt with in the previous three chapters appear to use the concept in roughly the same way: as the extent to which developing countries have to rely on other actors for the provision of certain values (goods, services, etc.) relevant for their economic, political and social situation. In this context, Frank, Amin and Galtung refer to imports and exports, the provision of capital through investments, loans and aid, the reliance on externally provided technology, and the concentration on a small number of trade partners. (E.g. Frank 1972b, chapters 7 and 8; 1969b, pp. 152-4, 171, 380 ff.; Amin 1976, pp. 246 ff.; Galtung 1971, p. 90)

In section III it has already been argued that dependence is, almost by definition, a crucial variable in all theories of dependency. It is with respect to this variable that the qualitative difference between countries belonging to the core and those in the periphery is argued to be most evident. Nevertheless, some researchers have included both developed and developing countries in their studies and have compared these countries using a scale of dependence, ranging from less to more dependent. In this study an attempt will be made at constructing a scale of dependence on the basis of data on developing countries.

Several researchers have used intricate operationalizations of dependence, while others have chosen only one or two indicators. From previous research it is clear that dependence is not a *unidimensional* concept. Instead, several dimensions can be discerned, the most important of which appear to be: the *dependence on international trade* and the *dependence on foreign finance and technology.*

In order to operationalize the concept of dependence, data have been collected on four trade-related variables and three financial and technological variables.[2] The following seven variables are used as indicators of dependence (see Appendix B for definitions and sources):[3]

- relative dependence on exports;
- relative dependence on imports;
- export partner concentration;
- import partner concentration;
- government external debt;
- foreign direct investment;
- dependence on development assistance.

The dimensionality of the concept of dependence can be tested by applying factor analysis to the indicators of dependence. The object of this technique is to discover 'clusters' of variables that, together, account for a substantial portion of the variance in all the variables, and that can be labelled as a theoretically separate dimension. Apart from the so-called *factor loadings*, indicating the relative position of the variables on the resulting factors, *factor scores* can be computed.[4] The factor scores represent the position of the units of analysis with respect to the factors. These scores will be used in subsequent analyses to indicate the degree of dependence experienced by individual countries.

Table 7.1: Factor Analysis of Dependence

Variables	*Factors* 1	2	3	*Communality*
Exports	.84	.02	-.41	.88
Imports	.93	.04	-.13	.89
Export partner concentration	-.02	.87	.00	.76
Import partner concentration	-.10	.87	-.12	.78
Government debt	.41	-.11	.72	.69
Foreign investment	-.17	-.05	.28	.11
Development aid	.31	.29	.70	.67
Eigenvalue	1.88	1.62	1.29	
Percentage of variance explained	26.9	23.1	18.4	

Factor analysis of the dependence variables on the basis of the *principal-components* procedure (Cf. Tacq 1991, pp. 295-6) results in the extraction of three factors, together accounting for nearly seventy per cent of the variance in the original seven variables. The three factors are theoretically interpretable as 'trade dependence' (Factor 1), 'trade partner dependence' (Factor 2) and 'financial dependence' (Factor 3). The results of the solution are summarized in table 7.1.

C The Level of Development (Frank, Amin, Galtung)

Each overview of the relevant literature indicates that there is no generally accepted definition of the concept of *development*. Scholars have enumerated elements that, if combined, might operationalize development. Economists have often considered the *per capita* gross national product (GNP) of a country to be a correct indicator of its level of development. GNP is easily quantifiable and interpretable, but its value as an indicator of development has been widely criticized. According to a good number of scholars, other factors than GNP determine a country's development. Bill Warren is one of several authors who have defined development broader than GNP; Warren (1980, pp. 225-35) has mentioned the following possible indicators: the quality of nourishment, the quality of education, the eradication of illiteracy, the health situation of the population and the quality of housing.

In the three variants of dependency theory that were discussed in the previous chapters several interpretations of development and its opposite, underdevelopment, have been encountered. Andre Gunder Frank has offered the most elaborate 'definition' of the concept. Some of the elements he considers to be part of the concept of development are: (per capita) income, food production and consumption, the availability of capital, the presence of capital goods industries, the differentiation of production, and the level of employment. (1969a, pp. 59, 84, 284, 304; 1969b, pp. 167, 173, 225, 355-7; 1972b, pp. 108 ff.) Samir Amin has mentioned several elements of development that are closely related to those mentioned by Frank: the level of employment, social equality, the level of education, the productivity of different sectors of the economy, and the degree of integration of the economic system. (1976, pp. 190-1, 202, 292, 381; 1974, pp. 16-28; 1972a) Johan Galtung has been more specific with respect to the concept of development; he has pointed at indicators such as the satisfaction of fundamental needs (food, clothes, shelter, health and education), GNP per capita, the part of the population that is employed in the non-primary (industrial and service) sector, the degree of urbanization, and the quality of transport and communication infrastructure. (1971, pp. 101-2; 1980j, pp. 442-5)

These considerations imply that the concept of development should not be operationalized in exclusively economic terms. (Cf. Delacroix 1977; Delacroix and Ragin 1978; Gasiorowski 1988; Gonick and Rosh 1988; Mahler 1981; McGowan 1976; Nemeth and Smith 1985; Prechel and Sica 1987; Van Puijenbroek and Van Snippenburg 1985; Wimberley 1990) Therefore, data have been collected on seven indicators which can all be considered as distinct elements of development. These indicators are:

- gross national income per capita;
- gross domestic investment per capita;
- the contribution of industry to the gross domestic product;
- the rate of infant mortality;
- life expectancy at birth;
- the level of educational enrolment;
- energy consumption per capita.

In order to test whether these seven indicators can be considered a unidimensional representation of the variable of development, principal-components analysis will be used. The factor scores of the countries will be used in the subsequent analyses as the expression of their level of development.

Factor analysis on the seven variables of development results in the extraction of one meaningful factor, containing nearly seventy-two per cent of all variance. The first factor can thus be interpreted as a meaningful representation of the development variable. The results of the analysis are summarized in table 7.2.

Table 7.2: Factor Analysis of Development

Variables	*Factor 1*	*Communality*
National income	.87	.75
Domestic investment	.85	.73
Industrial contribution	.69	.47
Infant mortality	-.85	.73
Life expectancy	.91	.83
Educational enrolment	.84	.71
Energy consumption	.90	.81
Eigenvalue	5.03	
Percentage of variance explained	71.9	

D The Degree of Exploitation (Frank, Amin, Galtung)

Exploitation is probably the most difficult concept in the operationalization of dependency theory. An initial problem is that scholars do not agree on the exact meaning of the term. Even if they do agree on the meaning of exploitation, their definition often lacks empirical content and sometimes is outright metaphysical.

The definition of exploitation as *unequal exchange*, which has been given by Andre Gunder Frank (1979a, pp. 103-10) and Samir Amin (1977b, pp. 128-31, 187-218; 1976, pp. 138-54), suffers from the latter problem. The idea behind unequal exchange is that a situation is possible in which exchange between trading partners takes place *on equal terms*. In this context, equality connotes equity, and a situation of exchange where 'just' prices are being paid. (Cf. Visser 1981)

Other elements of exploitation that have been mentioned by Frank, Amin and Galtung include the deterioration of the developing countries' terms of trade *vis-à-vis* the developed countries (Frank 1979a, pp. 101-3; 1975, pp. 66-7; Amin 1976, pp. 163-71; Galtung 1980j, pp. 449-50; 1973, pp. 38-47) and the outflow of capital from the Third World to the West. (Frank 1969b, pp. 162-74; 1972b, pp. 94-102; 1971, pp. 237-48; Amin 1976, pp. 185-91)

The deterioration of the developing countries' terms of trade has often been interpreted as an indication of the extent of exploitation of these countries. It has been argued that, as the price level of primary products decreases while the price level of manufactured goods increases, the developed countries are paying less and less for their imports of raw materials and agricultural products. The consequence of this tendency for the developing countries would be reduced export revenues.

An important *caveat* with respect to the use of figures expressing fluctuations in the terms of trade is connected with the real, i.e., economic-statistical meaning of these figures. Since terms of trade figures are basically *ratios of price changes*, they do not necessarily correspond with the welfare consequences of a simple rise of export prices or a fall of import prices. In order to grasp the implications for a country's welfare, it is also necessary to have access to data expressing the reactions of supply and demand to these price fluctuations. For example, an increase of export prices might prove to be a benefit for a Third World country - although it results in a deterioration of the terms of trade - when it leads to a shift of demand away from imported to locally manufactured goods.

A related weakness of terms of trade data is that they do not reflect whether a deterioration is the result of an improvement of productivity. In the case of productivity increases there is a problem similar to the one referred to above: as production prices tend to fall when a certain amount of products is made with less labour, export prices may fall, too. This development is reflected as a deterioration of the terms of trade, although it need not, and usually does not, result in a worsening of the economic position of the country concerned. For the reasons mentioned here, the development of the terms of trade will not be used in operationalizing the concept of exploitation.

From dependency and related literature it is obvious that 'exploitation' is a fundamentally contested concept. It is therefore extremely difficult to develop an operationalization of the concept that would be agreed upon by all dependency theorists. An additional problem inherent in operationalizing exploitation is the non-availability of data. The measurements of concepts such as 'surplus value' or 'unequal exchange' would require specific insight in production processes and price formation in developing countries. At present there is no statistical report available listing data with such specificity that 'surplus value' or 'unequal exchange' can be quantified in a meaningful way.

Nevertheless, at least one element of what is considered as exploitation is available for a relatively long period of time. Data on the debits on investment by foreign companies and interest payments on loans have been collected by the International Monetary Fund in its *Balance of Payments Statistics*. These statistics can be considered a reliable source. Following previous researchers, data on investment debits and interest payments, expressed as a percentage of a country's merchandise exports, will be used as the indicator of the concept of exploitation. (Cf. Alschuler 1976; Chase-Dunn 1975; Evans and Timberlake 1980; Fiala 1983; Gobalet and Diamond 1979; Kentor 1981; Rubinson 1976 and 1977; Szymanski 1976)

E The Degree of Inequality and Internal Polarization (Frank, Amin, Galtung)

All three variants of dependency theory that have been dealt with so far contain statements about the *inequality* and/or *internal polarization* in the countries of the periphery. The meaning of these terms is not exactly the same in all three variants, but they show enough similarity to be treated in one section.

In a discussion of internal polarization in developing countries, Andre Gunder Frank has emphasized the distribution of income, the 'town-countryside division' with respect to employment and the possession of land, and the concentration of capital in a few hands. (1969a, pp. 248-53; 1969b, pp. 221-68; 1975, pp. 72-80; 1984a, pp. 125-36, 208-29)

With respect to the concept of inequality/polarization, Samir Amin has written about the social and political inequality in Third World countries.

The concept, as Amin uses it, refers to the social and political domination of certain groups in periphery countries ('compradorization') and to the level of inequality in their social and economic systems. (1974, pp. 360-95; 1976, pp. 343-50; 1987a)

Johan Galtung has focused his discussion of inequality on the distribution of income and the possession of land in developing countries. (1971, p. 101; 1980j, pp. 445-7; 1985a, pp. 38-41)

Because of the difficulty of collecting data on the distribution of income and other possessions, and perhaps also because of the data's potential political sensitivity, no available sources contain relatively complete distributional data for a longer period. For this reason, this indicator cannot be used in the present study. As Bradshaw (1987), Gidengil (1978), London (1987), and London and Smith (1988) have argued, an alternative indicator of inequality might be constructed by comparing the earnings in different sectors of the economy with the labour force in those sectors. In this study, the so-called 'rural-urban disparity ratio' will be used as the indicator of structural inequality and internal polarization. This indicator is the expression of the disparity in the distribution of earnings, measured by gross domestic product, over the agricultural and other sectors of the economy.

F The Concentration of Production, the Degree of Extroversion, the Position in the World Division of Labour (Frank, Amin, Galtung)

The *concentration of production*, the *degree of extroversion* and *the position in the world division of labour* are concepts that have been used, respectively, in modelling the dependency theories of Andre Gunder Frank, Samir Amin and Johan Galtung. Despite dissimilar terminologies, the concepts denote almost the same phenomenon. In using these terms the three authors refer to the existence, in many developing countries, of 'monocultures'. This concept stands for the extreme reliance of peripheral economies on the production of a small number of goods, usually for the purpose of export. It might be considered as the 'internal' analogue of dependence. (Frank 1969a, pp. 260-1; 1969b, 168-72; 1972b, pp. 138-45; Amin 1973)

Galtung has developed a so-called *trade composition index* to express the extent of reliance on certain commodities. (1971, pp. 101-2; 1980j, pp. 451-2) According to him, it is possible to group countries on the basis of their trade composition: a high value on the index implies a 'central' position in the world division of labour, and a low value implies a 'peripheral' position.

In order to express a country's orientation toward a small number of, usually primary, products, several measures have been developed. Factor analysis has been applied in order to discover whether three possible indicators can be considered as one dimension of the concentration of production, the degree of extroversion, and the position in the world division of labour. The indicators are:

- primary commodity orientation;
- commodity concentration;
- orientation of exports toward centre countries.

Factor analysis performed on these three variables results in two factors, respectively containing forty-three and thirty-four per cent of total variance; two variables, commodity concentration and orientation toward centre countries, have high loadings on the first component, while only primary commodity orientation has a high loading on the second component. These results indicate that general commodity concentration and orientation towards centre countries together form a dimension independent from primary commodity orientation. It is felt that the latter indicator should be used in subsequent analyses, since it is a better expression of Third World countries' orientation toward agricultural and raw material production.

G The State of the World System (Frank, Amin)

Andre Gunder Frank and Samir Amin have, in their respective theories, paid attention to the overall *state of the world system* at a given moment. In their view, the situation of the system at large (expansion versus contraction or crisis, 'A phases' versus 'B phases') is an important factor co-determining the relative position of the developing countries. Frank and Amin have not themselves provided specifically clear indicators of the different conjunctural phases characterizing the world system. Yet, some indications of the operational meaning of this concept can be derived from the work of Frank and Amin.

In Frank's view, the capitalist world system is inherently characterized by periodic crises, the occurrence of which is related to problems of capital accumulation. These crises of accumulation exhibit some or all of the following features: a decline of production, world trade, profitability and investment, and a sharp increase in the level of unemployment. A corollary of these tendencies is the declining importance of industrial production relative to the production of raw materials. (Frank 1981b, pp. 7-16, 23-38, 39-52, 111-42; 1982, pp. 109-19)

According to Samir Amin the crises characterizing the history of the capitalist world system are structural by definition. They are the most visible features of underlying tensions in the process of capital accumulation and the international division of labour. The so-called 'A phases' are periods of economic upswing, typified by a stable international division of labour and a relatively rapid growth of production. 'B phases' are characterized by a slowdown of economic growth, intensification of international competition and the weakening of social and class alliances. (Amin 1981; 1982b; 1983)

Among dependency theorists there appears to be widespread consensus that the post-World War II development of the world system has known some clearly distinct phases. Different interpretations notwithstanding, Frank, Amin and Galtung seem to agree on the following periodization of the three most recent decades: the period until 1967 has been characterized by growth and expansion, the phase from 1967 until, roughly, 1981 has seen a recession, and the final period, from 1981 onward, has witnessed a recovery in the world economy. (See Amin 1982b; Frank 1982; Wallerstein 1982a) In order to express this periodization, the variable 'state of the world system' will be scored '+1' for 1965, '-1' for 1975 and '0' for 1985.

H The Political Regime, the Level of Democracy and Repression (Frank, Amin)

In their respective theories of dependency, Frank and Amin have paid some attention to political factors. In their view, these political variables have a meaning beyond the purely political realm and are, at least partly, the expression of processes occurring at the level of the world system. The most important indicators of the political effects of world system processes are the way in which interests are represented in the political system, the extent of democracy and the level of repression.

It is assumed that working class interests will find no or only slight translation into political demands. The bourgeoisie is seen as the dominant political (and socio-economic) force in peripheral countries because of its presumed link with the elites in the developed countries. In such a situation of inequality, it is felt, the political system will necessarily be undemocratic. (Frank 1969b, pp. 318-49, 393-402; 1972b, pp. 133-7; Amin 1976, pp. 333-69; 1987a, pp. 1130-40)

Political repression is seen as the *ultima ratio*, to be used by the ruling groups in the periphery to maintain order and stability. Disorder and instability are thought to be detrimental to the accumulation of capital. Especially in periods of crisis in the world system, when the economic situation worsens, political repression is interpreted as a prerequisite for the adequate functioning of the world system. (Frank 1977; 1984a, pp. 222-9)

The abundance of economic data that can be used for analysing the development of the world system is not matched, unfortunately, by a comparable wealth of political data. Gastil's *Freedom in the world* project is one of a very few studies attempting to collect comparative longitudinal data on the nature of the world's political systems.[5] Since Gastil's project has run from 1973 onward, data on political and civil rights in independent states have become available for the two most recent decades. There is no identical scaling of political systems for the 1960s. For this reason, Gastil's *Political and civil rights index* has been combined with a comparable one, namely, Bollen's *Political democracy index*, which is available for 1965. (Gastil 1978 and 1985; Bollen 1980) In his original research report Bollen has shown that his index correlates highly with other indices measuring the level of political democracy. It is assumed that Bollen's and Gastil's indices are two expressions of one measure, so that they can be used in combination.[6]

I Economic Distortions (Amin)

In Amin's variant of dependency theory, *economic distortions* are the result of the extroversion of peripheral societies and of the conjunctural situation in the capitalist world system. As Amin (1973, pp. 155-8) has indicated, a near-permanent crisis of the government budget and the balance of payments as well as a very limited 'public saving capacity' are important elements of the economic distortions facing the developing countries.

The operationalization of the variable 'economic distortions' involves a less complicated procedure than the one that proved to be necessary in the case of some other variables. Data on the balance of payments and domestic savings are readily available. In order to operationalize the variable 'economic distortions', data on the current account position (surplus or deficit in relation to a country's merchandise exports) and the amount of domestic savings as a percentage of gross domestic product will be used. (Cf. Bornschier 1983; Bornschier and Ballmer-Cao 1979; Kaufman, Chernotsky and Geller 1975; Vengroff 1977b)

J The Position in the World Structure (Galtung)

In a certain way it is not correct to discuss the *position of countries in the world structure* in a chapter on the operationalization of *variables*. As it has been indicated in chapter 5, Galtung takes the structural position of countries as *given*. The specific history of countries might explain why one country has become part of the centre and another has fallen back to or remained in a peripheral position. In this way, the differences among, for example, the United States, Mexico and Portugal can be explained. Such an explanation will be a useful element of historical studies of long-term processes in the world system. (Cf. section II)

In the present study, following Galtung's interpretation, the structural position of countries will be taken as given. The selection of countries included in the present study (described in section III) has been such that it does not make sense to include a variable 'position in the world structure'.

Several researchers have tried to group countries according to their position in the world system. (E.g. Snyder and Kick 1979; Bollen 1983; Peacock, Hoover and Killian 1988) Their classifications will not be used here, because these are the result of inductive-empirical research and do not necessarily correspond with the theoretical categories that have been used by the authors considered in this study.

K The Degree of Power (Galtung)

According to Galtung (1973, p. 38), the *degree of structural power* of a country is built into the international structure. In other words, structural power is derived from the position in the world division of labour. Galtung has explicitly differentiated between this form of power and so-called *resource power*, which, in its turn, can be split up into ideological power (power derived from ideology, culture and language), remunerative power (derived from population, land and capital) and punitive power (derived from military capabilities).

Galtung's definition of structural power makes it difficult, if not outright impossible, to measure the degree of power as a variable distinct from position in the division of labour. For this reason, it will be assumed that this variable is identical with the position in the division of labour.

L The Degree of Fragmentation and Marginalization (Galtung)

Apart from being exploited and penetrated, developing countries, in Johan Galtung's view, suffer from fragmentation and marginalization. The *degree of fragmentation and marginalization* is one of the effects of the position taken in by developing countries in the world capitalist system. Although Galtung has differentiated between the two concepts, they appear to point at quite similar phenomena. Fragmentation and marginalization mean that there is much less interaction and cooperation among peripheral countries than among countries in the centre of the world system. (Galtung 1979a, pp. 8-9; 1980j, pp. 120-5)

A suitable indicator for fragmentation and marginalization is found by Galtung in the so-called *Eigenhandelsquote*. (1980j, p. 457; cf. Snyder and Kick 1979) This indicator expresses the relative tendency of a country to export to countries of its own kind. The *Eigenhandelsquote* is the percentage of a peripheral country's export directed at other peripheral countries.

M The Degree of Spin-offs (Galtung)

According to Johan Galtung, the extent to which countries experience *spin-offs* is dependent on their position in the world system. Countries that are relatively more oriented towards the production of primary goods benefit from fewer spin-offs than countries emphasizing the production of processed or finished commodities. Spin-offs include, in Galtung's view, economic, political, military, communicative and cultural effects. Significant spin-offs are: the build-up of research facilities, universities, infrastructure and technologically advanced production processes. (Galtung 1971, p. 87)

In this study, three indicators will be used in operationalizing the variable 'degree of spin-offs'. A fourth potential indicator, the number of scientists engaged in research and development, appeared to be available only for a minority of the countries in this study. For this reason, the following three indicators will be used (Cf. Delacroix and Ragin 1981; London 1987; McGowan 1976; Van Puijenbroek and Van Snippenburg 1984):

- the relative number of commercial vehicles;
- the relative importance of railway traffic;
- the relative number of telephones available.

In order to test the dimensionality of the data, the three indicators have been used in a principal-components analysis. The results indicate that one main factor can be extracted, containing nearly sixty per cent of total variance. This component can meaningfully be interpreted as the empirical representative of the theoretical variable 'degree of spin-offs'. The results of the factor analysis are summarized in table 7.3. The factor scores will be used in the subsequent analyses.

Table 7.3: Factor Analysis of Degree of Spin-offs

Variables	*Factor 1*	*Communality*
Commercial vehicles	.89	.79
Railway traffic	.42	.17
Telephones	.90	.81
Eigenvalue	1.77	
Percentage of variance explained	59.1	

NOTES

1. If data were unavailable for 1965, 1975 or 1985, data have been collected for other years in roughly the same period. In the analyses, the following 'country-times' have not been considered because more than forty per cent of the values were missing: Angola (1985), Cambodia (1975 and 1985), Cuba (1965), Guinea (1965, 1975 and 1985), Laos (1965 and 1975), Lebanon (1985), North Vietnam (1965) and Vietnam (1975 and 1985). Because of its creation after this date, no data on Bangladesh could be collected for 1965.
2. Most quantitative studies of dependence include variables of these two types. For lack of adequate data, the stock of investments by multinational firms and multinational corporation headquarter status are not included. Studies using data on multinational corporations are, for example, Bornschier 1981, Bornschier and Ballmer-Cao 1979, Meyer-Fehr 1980 and Ward 1978.
3. All variables in this study have been logarithmically transformed if the skewness was larger than 1 (adding a constant if a variable has negative values); all scores have been used as standardized or Z-scores.
4. In order to obtain factor scores for all units of analysis, missing data have been substituted by the mean, using SPSS-X option meansubstitution.
5. The data produced in this project have been reported, on a regular basis, in the journal *Freedom at Issue* and in the yearbooks, annually published under the title *Freedom in the world: Political rights and civil liberties*.
6. Alternative indicators of political democracy have been used by, for example, Ballmer-Cao 1980, Chan 1989, Delacroix and Ragin 1978, Gasiorowski 1988, Gonick and Rosh 1988, Kaufman, Chernotsky and Geller 1975, London and Robinson 1989, Timberlake and Williams 1984 and Weede 1983a.

8. Path Analyses of the Dependency Models

I INTRODUCTION

In this chapter the results of the empirical analyses of the dependency models of Andre Gunder Frank, Samir Amin and Johan Galtung, which were developed in chapters 3, 4 and 5, will be presented. In order to assess the empirical value of the theories, several so-called path analyses have been performed. In the terms of chapter 1, where a meta-theoretical, philosophy-of-science framework has been developed, this implies that the central question of this chapter will be: does dependency theory, in its different variants, present an adequate, or approximate, statement of the problem the theory claims to solve?

Many issues regarding the way in which the analyses have been performed have already been described in detail in chapter 7. For this reason, a rather brief description of the analyses of the respective models of dependency will suffice.

In the next three sections, the results of the path analyses will be reported. Initially, the focus will be on the pooled cross-sectional analyses. Subsequently, the results of separate analyses for the three periods will be described.

Section V will contain a brief conclusion with respect to the results. A broader conclusion, including a discussion of the theoretical implications of the analyses presented here, will be drawn in chapter 9.

II A PATH MODEL OF ANDRE GUNDER FRANK'S DEPENDENCY THEORY

On the basis of Andre Gunder Frank's dependency theory a theoretical model has been constructed, which contains seven theoretical concepts. In chapter 7, these seven concepts have been operationalized by using ten variables. On the basis of a factor analysis the concept of dependence has been laid out into three separate factors, namely, trade dependence, trade partner dependence and financial dependence. It has proven to be impossible to obtain a single factor for the concept of concentration of production; in the subsequent path analyses this concept will be represented by the variable primary commodity concentration.

In the process of operationalization the theoretical model has been transformed into an operational one; the operational model of Andre Gunder Frank's dependency theory is displayed in figure 8.1 on page 154. The arrows denote the theoretically expected relations among the variables in the model; the pluses and minuses express the expected nature of these relations.

The model of figure 8.1 has been the basis for several path analyses. In the first place, as described in chapter 7, a pooled cross-sectional analysis has been performed in order to present a general estimation of the relations among the variables, that is, an estimation for the entire 1965-85 period. Secondly, in an attempt to control for possible time-specific developments, separate path models have been estimated for the three years for which data have been collected: 1965, 1975 and 1985. The results of the path analyses are presented in table 8.1.[1]

It can be read from table 8.1 on page 155 that the proportion of variance (R^2) accounted for by Frank's dependency model is .53. The value of R^2 for the three limited-period models is .43 (model 1965), .53 (model 1975) and .62 (model 1985). These results make clear that the explanatory value of the Frank model is moderately, and certainly not exceptionally, high.

A comparison of the path coefficients resulting from the analysis of Frank's dependency model (reported in table 8.1) with the theoretical expectations makes clear that there are several instances where the results do not correspond with theoretical predictions. The most notable contradictions between the theoretical model and the empirical findings are to be found in the relations between, respectively, the situation of the capitalist world system and dependence (*b* in figure 8.1); the state of the system and internal polarization (*d*); dependence and concentration of production (*e*); dependence and exploitation (*f*); financial dependence and internal polarization (g_3); commodity concentration and exploitation (*h*); exploitation and development (*l*); and democracy and development (*m*). Each of these contradictions between model and results will be discussed in the following paragraphs.

The relation between the state of the capitalist world system and dependence (*b*) was expected to be *positive*. This expectation has been formulated on the basis of Andre Gunder Frank's explanation of the incorporation of developing countries into the capitalist world system.

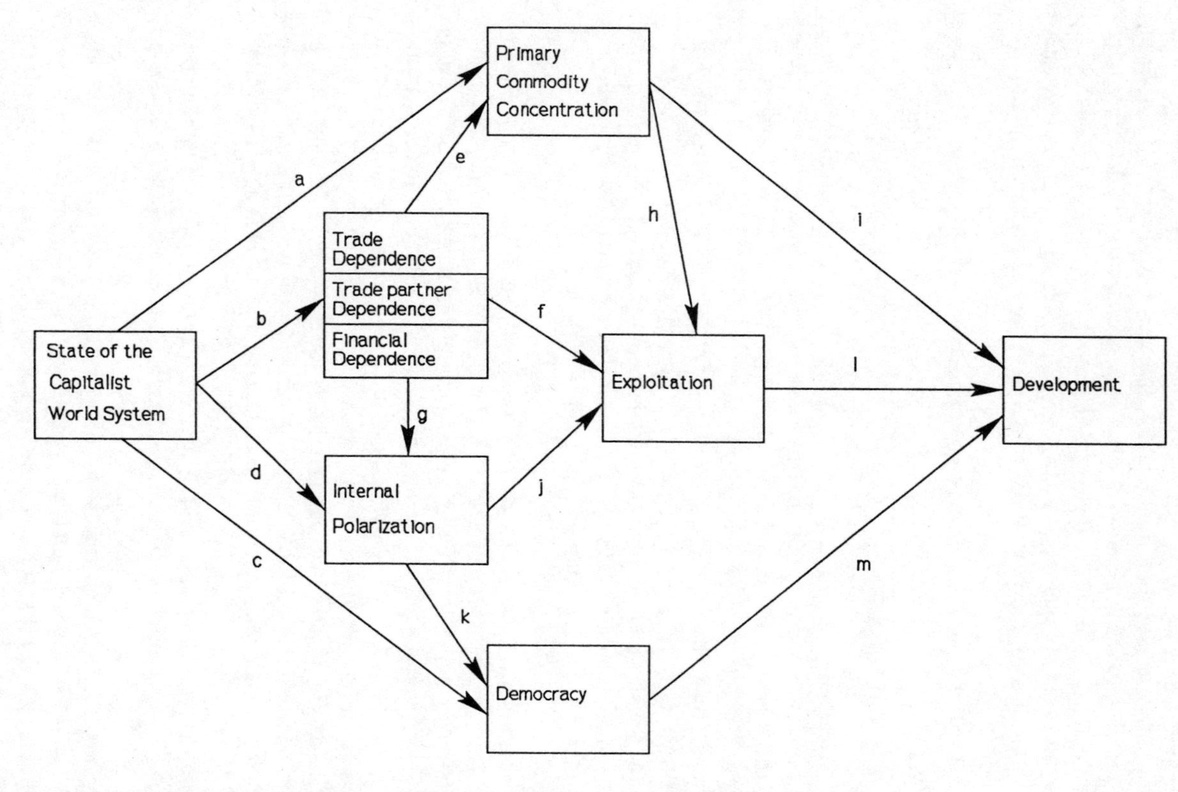

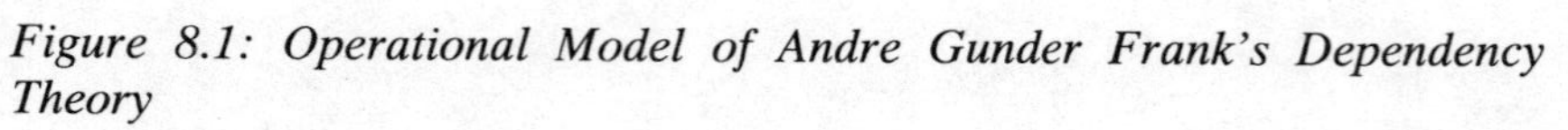

Figure 8.1: Operational Model of Andre Gunder Frank's Dependency Theory

Table 8.1: Path Coefficients of Frank's Dependency Model

Relation	Expected	1965-85	1965	1975	1985
a	+	.13*	N.a.	N.a.	N.a.
b_1	+	-.15**	N.a.	N.a.	N.a.
b_2	+	.22**	N.a.	N.a.	N.a.
b_3	+	.00	N.a.	N.a.	N.a.
c	+	.27**	N.a.	N.a.	N.a.
d	-	.01	N.a.	N.a.	N.a.
e_1	+	.00	.00	-.08	.38**
e_2	+	.09	-.01	.26**	-.13
e_3	+	.25**	.03	.38**	-.29**
f_1	+	.01	-.03	.03	-.07
f_2	+	.05	.16	.21*	.08
f_3	+	.29**	-.11	-.07	-.02
g_1	+	.03	.34**	.07	-.06
g_2	+	.16**	.03	.04	.10
g_3	+	-.12*	-.14	-.16	-.04
h	+	-.16**	-.34**	.03	.25*
i	-	-.36**	-.21*	-.33**	-.43**
j	+	.03	.06	.07	-.06
k	-	-.07	-.14	-.08	-.02
l	-	.20**	-.01	.25**	.22**
m	-	.33**	.40**	.35**	.38**
R^2		.53	.43	.53	.62

Notes to the table: The subscripts of relations *b*, *e*, *f* and *g* refer to the dimensions of dependence: trade (1), trade partner (2) and financial (3).
N.a. means that coefficients cannot be computed.
Significance: * denotes coefficients significant at the .10 level, ** at the .05 level (two-tailed).

In Frank's view, a situation of crisis would enable countries from the periphery to pursue relatively self-reliant development strategies, thereby reducing their dependence on the core. On the other hand, the relations of dependence would become tighter in periods of economic expansion. The present analysis shows that these expectations are not fully borne out by the data: the state of the world system appears to have a *negative* impact on trade dependence (the path coefficient is -.15 and significant), and no influence on financial dependence. The path analysis has only resulted in a positive, and significant, coefficient for the relation between the situation of the world system and trade partner dependence. These results indicate that the influence of world economic trends on dependence is more complex than was hypothesized by Andre Gunder Frank.

The relation between state of the world system and internal polarization (*d*) was expected to be *negative*: this implies that dependency theorists - and Andre Gunder Frank, in particular - assume that a worsening of the situation of the system at large will lead to the enhancement of inequality in the countries of the periphery. The results of the path analysis point to the absence of a relation between these two variables. This means that, on the whole (that is, in all 242 cases in the analysis), no clear pattern can be detected in the influence of the world system situation on internal polarization.

The relation between dependence and concentration of production (*e*) has been assumed to be *positive*, implying that a higher degree of dependence causes a higher concentration of primary commodity production. Summarizing the *concentration syndrome*, it is argued that more dependent countries tend to be focused on the production and export of a relatively small number of primary products. Of all coefficients relating to relation *e*, four bear a negative sign where a positive one was expected; of these, one is significant at the .05 level. On the other hand, four of eight positive coefficients are significant. The findings, however, seem to indicate a pattern: for the entire 1965-85 period, as well as for 1965 and 1975, there is a dominantly positive influence of dependence on concentration of production. The 1985 analysis results in two negative and one positive coefficient. It is interesting to note that the coefficient pertaining to financial dependence (e_3) is negative and significant: in this period, which was characterized by the so-called *debt crisis*, more dependent countries appear to have been less focused on primary products than other countries. This tendency might reflect that the policies of developing countries, which were aimed at diversification of production, were relatively successful when compared with the insistence of creditor countries and international organizations on structural adjustment. On the whole, the results of the path analysis offer support for Frank's expectations with respect to the influence of dependence on production concentration.

The results on relationship *f*, between dependence and exploitation, do not offer full support for Frank's theory. In this case, five out of twelve coefficients bear a sign different from the expected one. Only three coefficients show a moderately strong positive influence of dependence on exploitation. Trade dependence and exploitation are, on the whole, unrelated. The overall tendency of the coefficients, however, seems to indicate a positive influence of dependence on exploitation, meaning that, on the whole, more dependent countries experience more exploitation.

The analysis of the relation between financial dependence and internal polarization (g_3) leads to a conclusion different from the one concerning the other two dimensions of dependence. The results show that financial dependence has a consistently negative impact on internal polarization.

The coefficients of the relation between production concentration and exploitation (*h*) present a less clear-cut picture. These results do not support Frank's hypothesis of a positive causal relation: the highly significant coefficients for 1965-85 and 1965 point in the opposite direction, while the 1975 coefficient is very small. Only in the case of the third period do the results support Frank's hypothesis.

The path coefficients of the final two relations, between exploitation and development, and democracy and development (relations *l* and *m*, respectively), do not support Andre Gunder Frank's contention that there is a negative causation between the variables mentioned. Exploitation and development appear to be positively correlated, and in three out of four cases significantly so. This means that, on the whole, countries that, in the dependency theorists' view, suffer from the most intense exploitation exhibit the highest levels of development. Democracy and development do also appear to be positively related, with all four path coefficient being significant at the .05 level. This finding is in sharp contrast with Frank's hypothesis that less democratic Third World states would be more developed than their democratic counterparts.

III A PATH MODEL OF SAMIR AMIN'S DEPENDENCY THEORY

The model formulated on the basis of Samir Amin's dependency theory is displayed in figure 8.2 on page 160. As was the case with the model of Andre Gunder Frank's theory, this is an operational model; the theoretical model constructed on the basis of Amin's theory has been presented in figure 4.2.

The results of the path analysis performed with the 1965-85 data show that the proportion of variance (R^2) accounted for by Amin's model is .55. This R^2 is slightly higher than the R^2 of the comparable Frank model. A similar pattern is shown by the results of the 1965, 1975 and 1985 models: in these models, R^2 is, respectively, .62, .58 and .77.

In the previous section the path coefficients belonging to the relations in the model have been compared with the theoretical expectations, in order to formulate substantive conclusions about the dependency model. In this section, a similar approach will be followed.

The analysis of Andre Gunder Frank's dependency model has made clear that, in several instances, the empirical results do not correspond with the theoretical predictions. In the case of the Amin model, the most significant contradictions between theory and findings are to be found in relations between: dependence and extroversion (*a* in figure 8.2); dependence and exploitation (*b*); financial dependence and internal polarization (c_3); the state of the capitalist world system and economic distortions (*d*); extroversion and domestic savings capacity (h_2); extroversion and exploitation (*j*); exploitation and development (*k*); and democracy and development (*n*). These contradictions will be discussed in the ensuing paragraphs.

The relation between dependence and extroversion (*a* in figure 8.2) has been hypothesized by Amin as a positive one. Most path coefficients support the predictions, while some are only weakly negative. There appears to be one significant exception to Amin's expectations. Since this relation is equivalent to relation *e* in the Frank model, the same conclusion may be drawn here: the findings indicate that the relation between dependence and extroversion is more complex than hypothesized by the dependency theorists. In some periods some Third World countries appear to be able to reduce their extroversion despite their structural dependence on the centre countries in the world system.

The results with respect to relation *b*, between dependence and exploitation, are identical to the results reported on relation *f* in the Frank model. Above, it was argued that the path coefficients indicate that, generally speaking, trade dependence and exploitation are unrelated. There appears to be a generally positive influence of trade partner dependence on exploitation, but only one of the four path coefficients is significant at the .10 level. For the whole 1965-85 period, the relation between financial dependence and exploitation is positive, the path coefficient being significant at the .05 level. The general impression is that countries that are more dependent will experience more exploitation.

As in the case of the Frank model, the analysis of the Amin model shows that the relation between financial dependence and internal polarization (c_3) is consistently negative. This means that the degree of financial dependence has an altogether different impact on the level of inequality in developing countries than the other two dimensions of dependence.

The analysis of the relation between the situation of the world system and economic distortions in periphery countries (*d*) points out that these two variables are nearly unrelated: the path coefficients are .03 (d_1) and .02 (d_2). The economic situation of the world system appears to have no consistent influence on the balance of payments position and the domestic savings capacity of the developing countries.

The analysis of relation *h* indicates that the hypothesized positive influence between extroversion and the extent of economic distortions receives only partial support from the data. Where the current account position of Third World countries is concerned (relation h_1), the path coefficients are dominantly positive, with one being significant at the .10 level. Samir Amin's expectations with respect to the influence of primary commodity concentration on domestic savings are not supported by the data: all four path coefficients bear a negative sign and two are significant. The latter result implies that countries specializing in the production of primary commodities have, on the whole, more limited savings.

A somewhat different result has been found for the relation between extroversion and exploitation (relation *j* in figure 8.2). Amin has supposed this relation to be positive - as has Frank: see section II. Only the 1985 path coefficient, however, appears to be positive and significant. The analysis has resulted in highly significant negative coefficients for both the entire 1965-85 period and for 1965. The conclusion that might be drawn from these results is that the general influence of primary commodity concentration on exploitation is negative: countries that are specialized in the production of agricultural products and raw materials generally experience less exploitation than non-specialized countries. For 1985, the results of the analysis point in another direction: it might be under the influence of the international debt crisis that specialized countries have become relatively more vulnerable to exploitation than others. Non-specialized countries had more possibilities to escape the increasing pressure of debts and repayments.

With respect to relation *k*, summarizing the influence of exploitation on development, the results of the analysis do not offer support for Samir Amin's theoretical prediction. The path analyses show, as they did in the case of relation *l* in the Frank model, that exploitation and development are positively related; three out of four coefficients are significantly positive. Amin's contention that countries that are subject to exploitation lose an important part of their resources to the countries of the centre does not appear to be supported by the data.

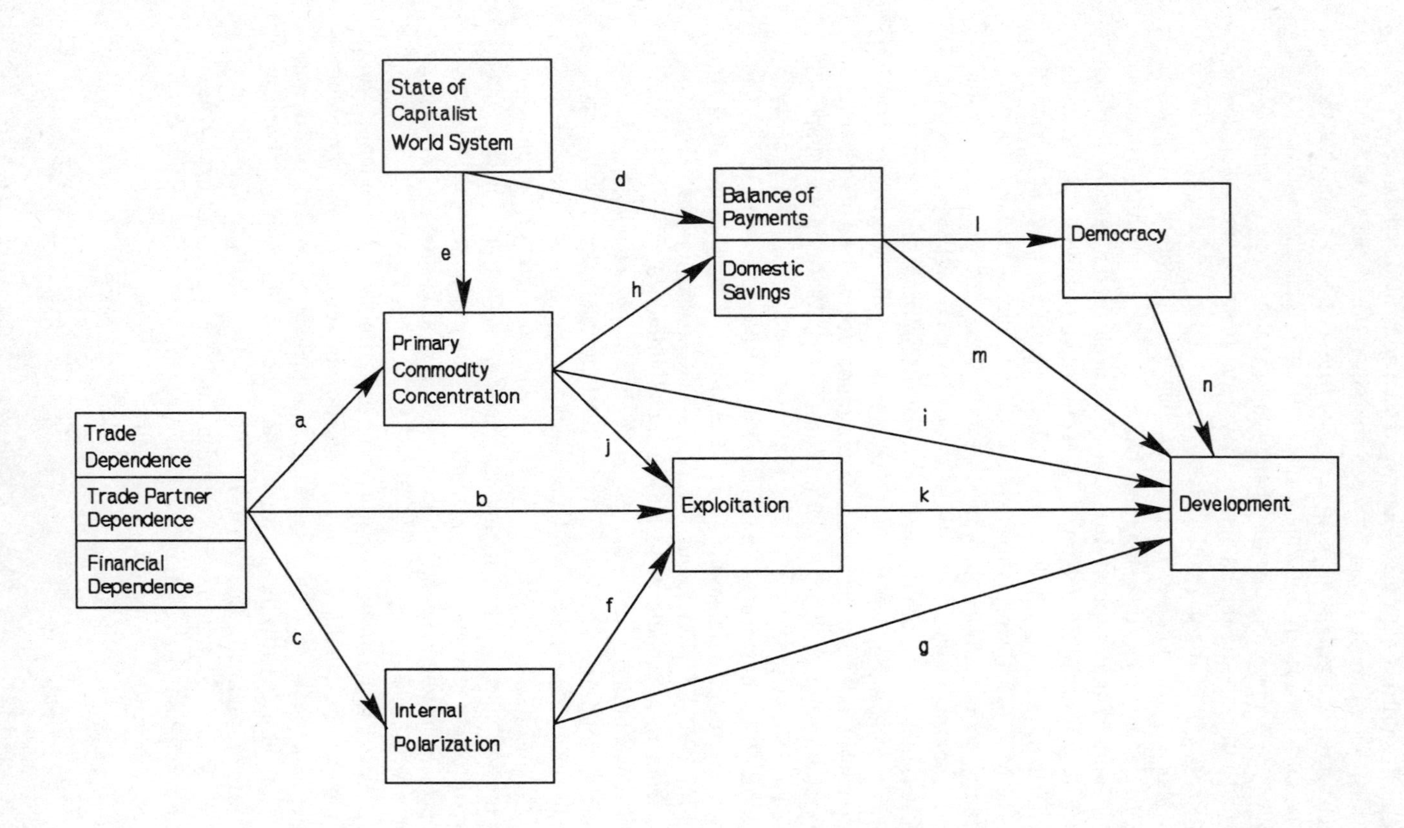

Figure 8.2: Operational Model of Samir Amin's Dependency Theory

Table 8.2: Path Coefficients of Amin's Dependency Model

Relation	Expected	1965-85	1965	1975	1985
a_1	+	.00	.00	-.08	.38**
a_2	+	.09	-.01	.26**	-.13
a_3	+	.25**	.03	.38**	-.29**
b_1	+	.01	-.03	.03	-.07
b_2	+	.05	.16	.21*	.08
b_3	+	.29**	-.11	-.07	-.02
c_1	+	.03	.34**	.07	-.06
c_2	+	.16**	.03	.04	.10
c_3	+	-.12*	-.14	-.16	-.04
d_1	+	.03	N.a.	N.a.	N.a.
d_2	+	.02	N.a.	N.a.	N.a.
e	+	.13*	N.a.	N.a.	N.a.
f	+	.03	.06	.07	-.06
g	-	-.09*	-.28**	-.08	.03
h_1	+	.11*	-.01	.09	.15
h_2	+	-.20**	-.14	-.16	-.37**
i	-	-.33**	-.16	-.33**	-.33**
j	+	-.16**	-.34**	.03	.25*
k	-	.20**	.00	.25**	.24**
l_1	+	.12**	-.17*	.14	.13
l_2	+	.29**	.39**	.25**	.32**
m_1	+	.03	.25**	-.01	.01
m_2	+	.13**	.10	.05	.34**
n	-	.29**	.37**	.33**	.27**
R^2		.55	.62	.58	.77

Notes to the table: The subscripts of relations *a*, *b* and *c* refer to the dimensions of dependence: trade (1), trade partner (2) and financial (3). The subscripts of relations *d*, *h*, *l* and *m* refer to the dimensions of economic distortions: balance of payments position (1) and domestic savings (2). N.a. means that coefficients cannot be computed.
Significance: * denotes coefficients significant at the .10 level, ** at the .05 level (two-tailed).

The final contradiction between Amin's theoretical formulations and the empirical findings relates to relation *n* in figure 8.2. The assumed negative relation between democracy and development is not supported by the data. All four path coefficients calculated for this relation bear a positive sign and are significant at the .05 level. There appears to be insufficient support for Amin's contention that less democratic countries would possess more capabilities than democracies to force the people to abstain from direct consumption and devote means to general development.

IV A PATH MODEL OF JOHAN GALTUNG'S DEPENDENCY THEORY

The approach of this section will be the same as that of the previous two sections. Figure 8.3 on page 164 is the operational model of Johan Galtung's dependency theory; this operational model is the result of the operationalization of the theoretical model, which has been presented in chapter 5. The model in figure 8.3 has been the basis for the ensuing path analyses, the results of which are summarized in table 8.3.

The results of the path analyses show that the overall fit of Johan Galtung's model is not incomparable to that of the Frank and Amin models. Where the 1965-85 data are concerned, the proportion of variance accounted for by the Galtung model is .56. From this it may be concluded that this model fits the data comparatively well; the R^2 of this model is somewhat higher than the R^2s of the Frank and Amin models. The results for the 1965, 1975 and 1985 estimates show a slightly different picture: the R^2 for the three limited-period models is, respectively, .53, .67 and .70.

A comparison of the theoretically expected outcomes with the path coefficients resulting from the analyses of Galtung's dependency model makes clear that some results do not correspond with the theory. Contradictions between the theoretical expectations and the empirical findings are to be found in the relations between, respectively, division of labour and exploitation (relation *a* in figure 8.3), division of labour and Eigenhandel (*b*), exploitation and development (*e*), Eigenhandel and development (*f*), and dependence and development in 1985 (*g*).

The analysis of the relation between the position in the world division of labour and exploitation (relation *a*) leads to a mixed result: two path coefficients are positive, and supportive of Galtung's hypothesis, while the remaining two bear a negative sign. These results seem to indicate the existence of a time-effect: for the entire 1965-85 period, as well as for 1965, the position in the division of labour, operationalized by the concentration of primary production, has a negative influence on the level of exploitation, although the path coefficient for 1965-85 is not significant. The analyses performed on the 1975 and 1985 data suggest a positive influence. These results seem to indicate that the boom of the 1960s, the crisis of the 1970s and the recession of the 1980s have all had a different impact on the relation between division of labour and exploitation. In periods of relative economic decline, countries specializing in primary commodities appear to suffer from more exploitation than other countries, while these countries tend to be exploited less during economic upswings.

Johan Galtung's hypothesis of a negative causal relation between Third World countries' position in the division of labour and Eigenhandel (relation *b* in figure 8.3) is not supported by the data. The path coefficients resulting from all four analyses point out that the two variables are almost unrelated. In two cases, the path coefficient has a positive sign, while it is negative in the remaining two cases. All four coefficients are weak and non-significant.

The path analytical results with respect to relation *e* (the influence of exploitation on development) do not correspond with the hypothesis derived from Johan Galtung's dependency theory. Three out of four path coefficients indicate that the level of exploitation positively influences Third World countries' development; this finding is in accordance with the outcome of the analyses of the Frank and Amin models.

Galtung's expectations concerning the relation between Eigenhandel and development (*f* in figure 8.3) are not confirmed. The two variables are almost unrelated, the path coefficients being very small and non-significant.

The final contradiction between empirical results and theoretical predictions is to be found in the relation between dependence and development in 1985 (*g* in figure 8.3). Galtung has hypothesized a negative influence of dependence on development; this prediction is supported by the data for 1965-85, 1965 and 1975. In the case of the 1985 analysis, the path coefficients of relations g_2 and g_3 indicate a positive and significant relation between trade partner and financial dependence, on the one hand, and the level of development, on the other. The results of this analysis suggest that, on the whole, dependence is negatively related to development. The period of the debt crisis is an exception to the general trend: during this period, countries that were more dependent on a small number of trade partners and/or on foreign finance tended to be relatively more developed than others.

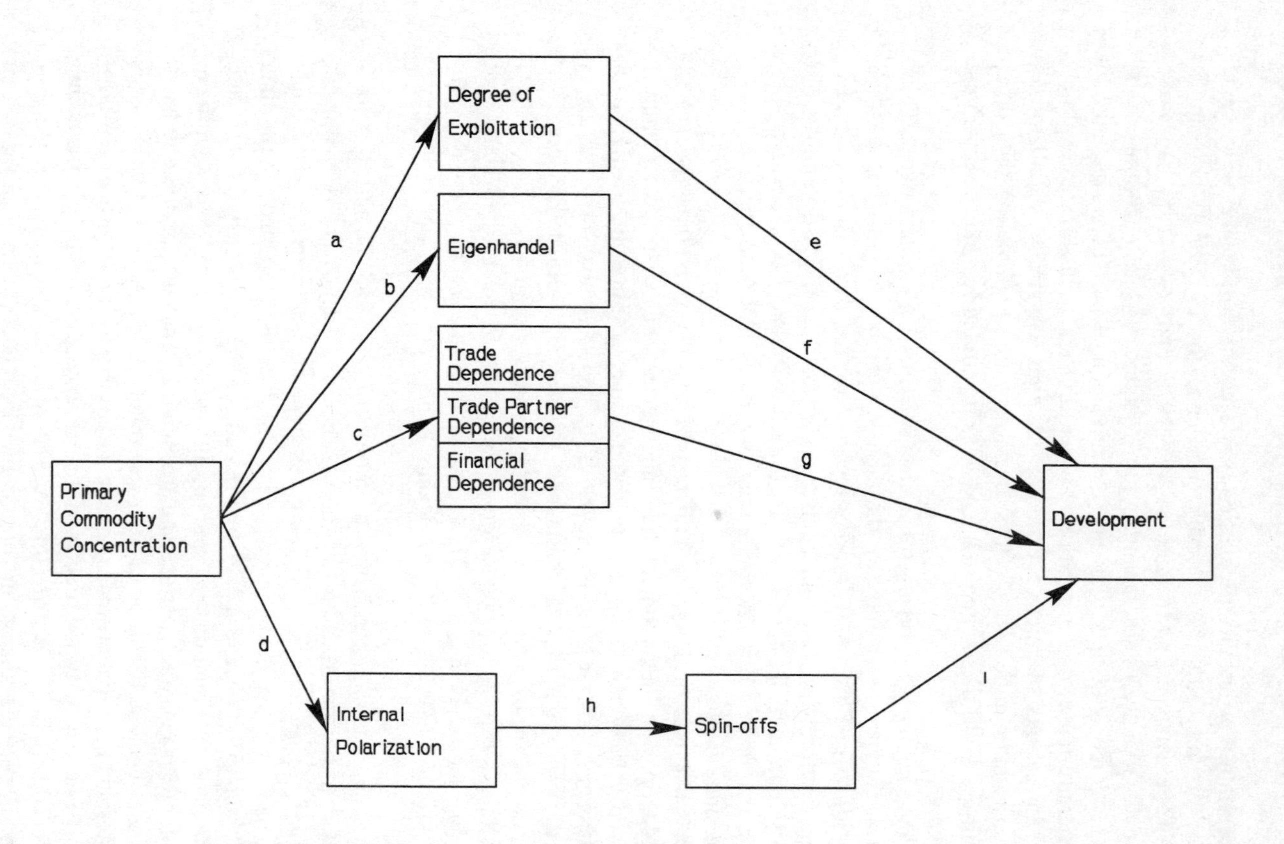

Figure 8.3: Operational Model of Johan Galtung's Dependency Theory

Table 8.3: Path Coefficients of Galtung's Dependency Model

Relation	Expected	1965-85	1965	1975	1985
a	+	-.08	-.34**	.05	.21*
b	-	-.05	.05	.04	-.01
c_1	+	.00	.00	-.06	.41**
c_2	+	.11*	-.01	.24**	-.14
c_3	+	.24**	.03	.36**	.33**
d	+	.09	.12	-.01	.09
e	-	.22**	-.05	.23**	.24**
f	+	.04	-.05	.00	.09
g_1	-	.03	-.14	-.01	-.06
g_2	-	-.12**	-.12	-.21**	.16**
g_3	-	-.26**	-.10	-.23**	.42**
h	-	-.08	-.13	.05	-.11
i	+	.56**	.61**	.61**	.40**
R^2		.56	.53	.67	.70

Notes to the table: The subscripts of relations *c* and *g* refer to the dimensions of dependence: trade (1), trade partner (2) and financial (3).
Significance: * denotes coefficients significant at the .10 level, ** at the .05 level (two-tailed).

V CONCLUSION

The focus of sections II, III and IV has been on the results of the path analyses of the three dependency models formulated in chapters 3, 4 and 5. Above, the main contradictions between the theoretical predictions, contained in the models, and the empirical findings have been outlined. In this section, a general conclusion regarding the empirical value of the three dependency theories will be formulated.

The path analyses of the dependency models do not offer conclusive results. Some elements of the models can be criticized, while other elements are to be supported. Given the complexity of (international) reality, this result might have been foreseen from the start. The metatheoretical position assumed in chapter 1 requires a discussion of the empirical anomalies alongside an indication of the supportive elements.

Several elements belonging to the 'hard core' of dependency theory have not been supported by the path analyses in the previous sections. Most notably, the relations between exploitation and development, the state of the world system and internal polarization, the state of the world system and economic distortions in the periphery, and democracy and development have not found support in the data.

Mixed results have been found for the following 'hard core' elements of dependency theory: the relations between primary commodity concentration/extroversion/division of labour, on the one hand, and exploitation and dependence, on the other; the state of the world system and dependence; dependence and exploitation; dependence and internal polarization; primary commodity concentration and economic distortions; primary commodity concentration and Eigenhandel; and dependence and development.

The path analyses have also resulted in support for a good number of statements contained in dependency theory. The most significant elements of the 'hard core' of dependency theory receiving support from the empirical analyses are the following (the nature of the relation is mentioned in brackets): the relation between state of the capitalist world system and democracy (positive); primary commodity concentration and development (negative); spin-offs and development (positive); situation of the world system and primary commodity concentration (positive); internal polarization and democracy (negative); absence of economic distortions and development (positive); trade and trade partner dependence and internal polarization (positive); and lack of economic distortions and democracy (predominantly positive).

The first conclusion that might be drawn on the basis of these findings is that the integration of developing countries in the international trade system does not hamper, but, on the contrary, stimulates their development. On the whole, dependence has a positive influence on the level of exploitation, while exploitation positively influences development. This result is clearly irreconcilable with dependency theory's thesis that dependence makes developing countries more vulnerable to exploitation and that this situation leads to underdevelopment.

The second conclusion can be that reliance on the production of a small number of primary commodities is potentially harmful to developing countries. The results of the analyses in this chapter show that dependence enhances primary commodity concentration, while the latter variable negatively influences the level of development.

Additionally, the positive relation between the state of the world system and concentration of production/extroversion supports the dependency theorists' assertion that periods of recession and crisis offer more opportunities for the developing countries to loosen the ties with the centre.

The final conclusion on the basis of the empirical analyses might be that the dependency theorists appear to be correct in emphasizing the internal political effect of dependence. The path analyses show that dependence enhances the internal polarization in the countries of the periphery. The latter variable, in its turn, appears to have a negative influence on the extent of democracy and spin-offs and on the level of development in the developing countries.

NOTE

1. In order to limit the number of missing cases, a procedure of including cases with missing data has been applied to the path analyses. This procedure is analogous to the one which has been applied to the factor analyses in chapter 7: missing data have been replaced by the mean score of variables under consideration.

9. Conclusions

I INTRODUCTION

The result of this study of dependency theory and its claims to scientific progress is less clear cut than aspired at the beginning. The aspiration of achieving final answers has been nourished, in the case of much social scientific research, by Popper's ideal-typical image of science as a process of *'conjectures and refutations'*. The Popperian idea is implicit in many textbooks on social science methodology; and with many social scientists worrying about the 'falsifiability' of their statements, committing oneself to 'hypothesis testing' and trying to 'corroborate' their expectations, it is not easy not to respond favourably to this inclination.

The initial choice for a philosophy-of-science framework different from the mainstream (quasi-) Popperian one has had several important consequences for this study. In the first place, the overall objective of the study has not been the 'empirical testing' of dependency theory; in chapter 1, following the logic of Larry Laudan's methodology, it has been argued that such testing is impossible and, even if it were not impossible, not very worthwhile. Nor has the intention of this study been to reformulate or specify dependency theory. The aim of the study has been to provide a meta-theoretical evaluation of dependency theory as one of the approaches in the discipline of international relations.

Not all variants of dependency theory have been studied above. Yet, the works of four important authors working in the dependency tradition (Andre Gunder Frank, Samir Amin, Johan Galtung and Immanuel Wallerstein) have been analysed; on the basis of these analyses, three theoretical models have been formulated and these were used in the subsequent empirical analysis. The empirical analysis has served to indicate if, and to what extent, dependency theory can be considered as an 'approximate statement of the problem' it wants to solve.

The results of the theoretical and empirical analyses are clear enough to warrant several conclusions. First, some conclusions will be formulated about the theorizing on international inequality. Secondly, some attention will be paid to the relevance of this study for policies trying to attack these inequalities. In this respect, only partial answers can be expected, since the intention of the study has not been to provide explanations of or solutions to international inequality.

II THEORETICAL IMPLICATIONS

The theoretical conclusions of this study with respect to dependency theory are mixed. On the one hand, it has been argued, in chapter 2, that dependency theory has solved some important problems that were left unsolved by its main predecessors and competitors. On the other hand, the results of chapter 8 have pointed at some shortcomings in dependency theory's 'statement of the problem'.

In the final section of chapter 2, the central or 'hard core' elements of dependency theory have been summarized in three points. First, the focus of dependency theory is on the development of a capitalist world system and a concomitant international division of labour. Secondly, dependency theory concentrates on dependence and exploitation and on the resulting division of the world into developed and underdeveloped areas. Thirdly, dependency theory emphasizes the derivative nature of political units and the pre-eminence of capital movements across the world.

The main theoretical and empirical problems left unsolved by the theories of chapter 2 and for which dependency theory appeared to have offered a solution were the following. With respect to the traditional economic and neo-Marxist theories of imperialism two important and unsolved problems have been mentioned: the survival of the capitalist world system in a situation of increased Third World opposition to imperialist relations, and the lack of development in the Third World despite the supposedly progressive nature of capitalism. Two crucial problems that were left unsolved by the liberal theories of international trade were: the failure of the expansion of international trade to benefit the majority of Third World countries, and the lack of development of Third World countries with evident comparative advantages. Some serious problems left open by the E.C.L.A. approach appeared to be: the incompatibility of import substitution policies with the contemporary capitalist world economic order, and the failure of changes in the international trade structure to have a positive effect on Third World development. Finally, two problems can be mentioned that were left unsolved by the modernization theories: the similarity in level of development of countries with differing internal characteristics or policies, and the absence of association between traditional order and underdevelopment, on the one hand, and modernity and development, on the other.

All this is not to say, of course, that the dependency approach has produced no anomalies and has left no problems unsolved. In the final section of chapter 2 two serious theoretical problems have been mentioned. First, the dependency theorists have allowed too little variation in their explanations. The fact that the capitalist world system has an important influence on Third World countries does not inevitably mean that these countries will remain underdeveloped for ever. Policies pursued by individual countries, such as the Newly Industrializing Countries, can be shown to have beneficial effects in stimulating development. The second serious problem is dependency theory's neglect of political factors. As a consequence of this neglect, economic circumstances have been assumed to have political effects, and political situations have been explained in exclusively economic terms.

The path analyses of chapter 8 have offered partial support for the dependency theories. A good number of the relations laid down in the dependency models, which were formulated in chapters 3, 4 and 5, have been 'confirmed'. The most obvious contradiction between the results of the path analyses and the theoretical predictions of the dependency scholars can be found in the dependence-exploitation-development nexus. Several findings have pointed out that there is no unequivocal relation between dependence and exploitation, and that exploitation and development are positively related. The analyses have also shown, however, that the dependence on a small number of primary commodities is potentially harmful to the development of Third World countries.

The dependency theories have received support from the analyses on internal polarization. Broadly speaking, more dependent countries (with the possible exception of countries that are heavily dependent on foreign finance) tend to experience a higher degree of internal polarization; countries with a higher degree of internal polarization tend to be less democratic, have fewer spin-offs, and obtain a lower level of development.

The theoretical implications of the results summarized above are not *prima facie* obvious. Indeed, the theoretical proliferation in the study of international relations in general, and in the study of the causes and consequences of international inequality in particular, renders impossible the presentation of one clear-cut answer.

The discussion in this book has made clear that further theorizing and research is necessary in order to develop a more complete understanding of inequality in the context of international relations. This study has attempted to evaluate the implications of one theoretical perspective that pretends to offer such understanding. The study has made clear that the discipline of international relations would benefit by taking account of, more explicitly than in the past, the characteristics of the world system and their implications for the (structural) relations among states. The further development of a focus on structural power (Cf. Strange 1989, pp. 24-6; Gilpin 1987, chapter 3) instead of relational power would enhance the value of international relations theory. By focusing on structural power, scholars are likely to pay more attention to the underlying stability of international relations than to the diplomatic intercourse among states.

Moreover, the consideration of world system characteristics would bring 'historical awareness' back into international relations theory. On the one hand, scholars will be more aware of the fact that great power status and core position are not eternal givens, but the results of long-term developments in the world system at large. On the other hand, students of international relations will become more aware of the circumstance that positions in the world system take a very long time to change, and that profound structural changes in the society, economy, and polity of a country are necessary in order to bring about changes in the international position.

For the reasons outlined above, this conclusion has to be limited to delineating several elements that can be used in further theorizing. Most notably, the following discussion will focus upon seven elements: the nature and development of the (capitalist) world system; the international division of labour, and imperialism; the presumed role of exploitation; the influence of the world system on relations of dependence and concentration of production; the role of trade in international relations; the link between the international division of labour and internal characteristics of developing countries, especially the internal polarization and the democratic nature of the political system; and, finally, the factors stimulating and hampering development.

A The Capitalist World System

The presumed existence and influence of the *capitalist world system*, which is a crucial element of the dependency approach in all its variants, is a fiercely contested issue in the discipline of international relations. Although many scholars tend to agree about the globalizing influence of capitalism on relations between states (See Reich 1991), a good deal of them hold different opinions about the integration of all states into the capitalist world system, and about the structures it imposes upon the states in the system.

The very nature of the concept will probably keep scholars divided about the capitalist world system: the concept is an encompassing one, requiring explanations at the system level rather than at the level of the individual states. The previous chapter contains three attempts to assess the value of a world system perspective; the analyses there could only be indirect, since the capitalist world system cannot be studied as such. The capitalist world system is a theoretical concept *pur sang*. Although it is generally applied in the clarification of empirical problems, the way in which the concept is used is not always devoid of metaphysical connotations.

The world system concept can best be used in a historical and structural sense. First of all, it indicates that the countries of the world are not separate entities, taking positions in international political and economic relations in the way billiard balls do on a billiard table. Countries have become linked in many ways during the past few centuries, and these links have often been of a hierarchical nature. The integration of non-European countries in the European, and later also American, based capitalist world system has relegated these countries to a subordinate position, in the so-called periphery. In most cases, the non-European countries were economically, politically, militarily and culturally the weaker partners. Occasionally, countries have succeeded in moving from a peripheral to a core position in the world system; the most spectacular examples are, no doubt, the United States of America, Australia and Japan. In more recent times, steady risers have been countries such as Singapore, South Korea, Hong Kong and Taiwan.

Despite its ongoing integration, the capitalist world system is still characterized by huge inequalities between 'North' and 'South'. These inequalities are fed by the structural features of the countries of the world system, in the economic realm (production structures and financial structures), in the social realm (class structures and regional inequalities) and in the political realm (power structures). These structural features are sometimes reinforced by the interactions among countries from different parts of the world system. For many countries in the periphery, it is difficult, if not impossible, to set up new production processes (for instance, of industrial goods), because their populations do not possess adequate purchasing power to buy the products. On the other hand, they can only sell small quantities of their manufactured products to the core countries, because the latter have put up barriers to foreign products, and also because they prefer more sophisticated manufactured goods from other core countries. Moreover, the concentration of production in developing countries on relatively unsophisticated industrial goods or agricultural products and raw materials is often in the interests of the dominant classes. Frequently, these classes have occupied the central positions in the political system and thereby resist a possible restructuring of the national economy, which might harm their interests. The success of their resistance cannot be predicted from a world system perspective - and this, it needs to be stressed, should also not be its intention - because such a prediction requires knowledge on the specific internal power balance among competing groups in developing countries.

B The International Division of Labour and Imperialism

Above, some things have already been written about the *international division of labour* and *imperialism*. In a certain way, the division of labour can be seen as the central element of the idea of the capitalist world system. The capitalist world system, as it has developed during the last several centuries, is characterized by a division of labour in which some parts (the core countries) engage in technologically sophisticated, capital-intensive and knowledge-intensive production, requiring scientific research at the cutting edge, while other parts (the periphery) produce relatively unsophisticated, labour-intensive goods. The division of labour can be seen as given, in the sense that the division of labour and the resulting structure of production determine the place of countries in the capitalist world system. The fact that, during the last four or five centuries, the centre of the world system has been in Europe rather than in Asia, must be explained by reference to the features of the European social, political and cultural order. (Jones 1981; Kay 1991) The results of the path analyses in chapter 8 indicate that the division of labour exerts some influence on the level of dependence of the developing countries: in general, countries specializing in the production of primary goods tend to be more dependent than other countries. Moreover, there appears to be a consistently negative relation between the concentration on primary commodities and on commodities in general, on the one hand, and the level of development on the other.

Some theories consider imperialism to be a direct result of capitalism. Most notably, these are the traditional economic and neo-Marxist theories of imperialism. To a certain extent, the dependency theorists also adhere to this view. The identification of imperialism with capitalism is not a necessary element of structural theories of the world system, however. Many authors are led to believe that the coincidence of the spread of capitalism and the heyday of imperialism during the nineteenth century is not accidental, but that one factor (capitalism) caused the other (imperialism).

Many studies show that there certainly is no one-to-one relationship between capitalism and imperialism. First, not all capitalist states exhibit the drive to imperialism. Secondly, there are non-capitalist states that can aptly be characterized as imperialist. Thirdly, many actions of the imperialist nations cannot be explained as economically inspired. (See Cohen 1973; Fieldhouse 1984; Doyle 1986; Ray 1973)

The identification of imperialism with capitalism is not only wrong, but also unnecessary. As Benjamin Cohen (1973, pp. 231-45) has shown, it is possible to analyse imperialism without taking recourse to this identification thesis. In Cohen's view, imperialism is the expression of *unequal power relations*: powerful countries tend to use their resources *vis-à-vis* less powerful ones in order to have the latter comply with their demands. It is therefore possible, and indeed preferable, to interpret imperialism as a political consequence of differences in power, rather than study the economic advantages of imperialism, as many neo-Marxists and dependency theorists have done, to try to 'prove' the economic foundation of imperialism.

C Exploitation

One of the central elements in many works on the relationship between developed and developing countries has been the question of *exploitation*. Nourished by the traditional economic and Marxist analyses of imperialism, many authors have focused on the economic causes and consequences of imperialist relations and on their presumed exploitative nature. The neo-Marxist scholar Bill Warren (1973 and 1980) has attacked the negative interpretation of imperialism and has argued that the contact between the developed and developing countries would lead to an increase of the wealth of the latter countries. In the same vein, the Keynesian economist Joan Robinson has argued that 'the misery of being exploited by capitalists is nothing compared to the misery of not being exploited at all'. (1964, p. 46)

The results of the path analyses of the dependency models have shown that the expectation of a positive relationship between dependence and exploitation has only received partial support. The supposition that exploitation and development are negatively related has not been borne out by the data. The analyses show that countries experiencing a higher degree of exploitation are more developed than countries that are exploited less. This possibly puzzling outcome can be explained in a rather straightforward manner. The starting point of the explanation has to be the realization that exploitation is a relative concept. The operationalization of the concept as the transfer of debits on investments and interest payments has stayed close to the empirical interpretation of exploitation that has been provided by the dependency theorists. Exploitation in this meaning will be more intense if more interest payments or investment debits are transferred from a developing country to the developed countries. For these transfers to become possible, first of all, investments have to be made or loans have to be provided. These investments and loans will generally be put to productive uses and may be expected to stimulate economic activity and, eventually, enhance economic development. Foreign investment would not, in this interpretation, be a strictly *zero-sum* activity, the only beneficiaries of which are the Western investors. (Warren 1980, pp. 139-57) The investment of capital has effects that go beyond the direct spending of money: investments can be shown to have both 'multiplier' and 'accelerator' effects. The results of the path analyses lend partial support to this explanation: the path coefficient of the relation between financial dependence and exploitation in the entire 1965-85 period is strongly positive and highly significant. The three remaining analyses have not produced significant coefficients.

The historical dimension of the repatriation of investment debits has been studied by, among others, Patrick O'Brien and Bela Balassa. O'Brien (1982) has shown that the average historical rates of profit earned in the periphery appear to be normal and are not likely to have been an excessively large source of capital for European countries. Balassa (1986, pp. 267-8) has calculated that, for the period 1979-84, the profit of United States' manufacturing firms located in the developing countries averaged ten per cent, with the profits of firms based in Latin America - by far the most important area for U.S. corporations - being a mere eight per cent. By contrast, the profits gained from domestic investments averaged thirteen per cent during the same period. About forty per cent of the profits have been reinvested in the developing countries, enhancing the spending effects of the investments even further.

D The Capitalist World System and Dependence

The *influence of the world system on relations of dependence* is another important problem that has been raised in the dependency theories. In general, the assumption has been that developing countries, during periods of crisis, can loosen their ties with the developed countries and attempt to diversify their economic activities. This prediction draws heavily on the experience of some Latin American countries during the Great Depression of the 1930s. In that period, Latin American countries have successfully pursued import substitution policies, resulting in the development of local industries.

The path analyses of chapter 8 have resulted in mixed support for the predictions made by the dependency theorists in this respect. Two of the three path coefficients of the relation between the state of the world system and the dimensions of dependence appear to be positive and significant. The significantly positive coefficient of the relation between the situation of the world economy and trade partner dependence points to the fact that the extent of dependence on a small number of trade partners will generally be less in periods of crisis, and will be enhanced in times of expansion. The negative coefficient of the relation between world system situation and trade dependence presents a different picture: the dependence on general trade relations will be reduced during economic upswings, and enhanced during economic recessions. The results on general trade relations are qualified by those on the developing countries' primary commodity concentration; it appears that this concentration will, on the whole, be less in periods of crisis in the world system.

The results summarized in the previous paragraphs suggest that the dynamics of the world system might have an important influence on developing countries. Most path coefficients of the relation between concentration of production and development appear to be significantly negative. Moreover, there is a moderately negative correlation between the state of the world system and development of -.14 (significant at the .05 level). These findings imply that periods of crisis in the world system offer developing countries the opportunity of reducing their trade partner dependence and their concentration of production, thereby stimulating their own development.

E The Role of Trade in International Relations

The *role of trade in international relations* is a hotly debated issue, not only by the dependency theorists, but also, as chapter 2 has shown, by many other scholars dealing with international inequality. The position of the dependency theorists has been, in general, that the dependence on trade would make a country vulnerable to outside influences. In their view, the mechanisms of unequal exchange and terms-of-trade deterioration work to the detriment of the countries of the Third World.

The dependency position has come under heavy attack by the proponents of so-called export-led growth. Scholars who have advised developing countries to stimulate growth by focusing on export have often presented the example of the South East Asian 'four little dragons' (Singapore, South Korea, Taiwan and Hong Kong). These newly industrializing countries have succeeded in their policy of export promotion and have thus been able to build a large industrial capability. (Cf. Lee 1981; Harris 1987; Dixon 1991)

In the path analyses of chapter 8, the effects of trade dependence on exploitation and development have proven to contradict the dependency theorists' expectations. In general, trade dependence can be concluded to have almost no influence on the level of exploitation and development of Third World countries. Moreover, the generally positive, though weak, influence of the height of the *Eigenhandelsquote* on the level of development points at the possibly positive contribution of trade for the Third World. Too much reliance on a small number of developed trade partners could, however, be detrimental.

A conclusion analogous to the one about exploitation can be formulated here. Trade is not a *zero-sum* activity, in which one trading partner reaps all benefits and the other suffers all losses. The neo-classical interpretation of comparative advantages as the foundation of trade is heavily flawed: international 'markets' are not characterized by a situation of perfect competition, in which market power does not play any role; consequently, prices are not the sole, and sometimes not even the most important, factor in the choice of certain products. Yet, the neo-classical insight that trade involves transactions that are potentially beneficial to all trading partners, and enhance the welfare of all partners, has been discarded too quickly by the dependency theorists. The experience of the NICs shows that the production of high-tech products, on the basis of very cheap labour, has stimulated the growth of the South East Asian countries to an unprecedented extent. During the crisis of the 1970s and 1980s, these countries have, by far, outrivalled the West in terms of economic growth, with some South East Asian countries even achieving a double-digit percentage of growth. (Lee 1981; Harris 1987; Dixon 1991)

F Internal Polarization and Democracy

Although the influence of the international division of labour on *internal characteristics* of the developing countries should not be exaggerated, this influence should nevertheless be recognized. It is important, as Tony Smith has argued, to avoid dependency theory's 'chief methodological error', which is 'to deprive local histories of their integrity and specificity, thereby making local actors little more than the pawns of outside forces'. (1979, pp. 257-8)

A first link between the international division of labour and internal characteristics of developing countries can be discerned in the aspect of *internal polarization*. In the view of the dependency theorists, the international division of labour produces specific structures of interests. The dominant classes in the developing countries are considered as having an interest in the maintenance of the *status quo*, which offers them a good deal of advantages they would not possess otherwise. It is assumed that this interest dictates the exploitation, and consequent impoverishment of a large part of the population, especially of the people living and working in the countryside. Therefore, a sharp dichotomy between the rural and urban areas is expected to develop.

In general, the existence of a link between the structure of the world system and the internal polarization in the periphery has been confirmed in the path analyses. Generally speaking, there are positive relations, although not always as strong as expected, between trade and trade partner dependence and concentration of production, on the one hand, and internal polarization, on the other. As it has been stressed above, the concentration of developing countries' production on relatively unsophisticated manufactured goods or agricultural products is often in the interest of the dominant classes. In most cases, developing countries lack a strong and wealthy industrial elite. As a consequence, the social and political system tends to be dominated by the landowning and trading classes.

The policies favoured by these dominating classes will not always - some might argue: almost never - be in the interest of the poor in the developing countries. The emphasis of landowners and traders will tend to be on the 'competitiveness' of their countries' produce; this is often felt to be incompatible with increasing the income of the poorer groups. Phenomena such as the massive migration to the urban areas, the resulting growth of shantytowns around the cities, and the explosive growth of the informal sector might partly be interpreted as means to overcome the urban-rural disparity that is growing in many developing countries.

This general explanation of polarization does not apply equally to all developing countries. In many African countries, polarization appears to have other roots. As Goran Hyden (1983, p. 8) has indicated, African societies are dominated by the 'economy of affection', that is, by networks of support, communication and interaction among people linked by family, community, religious or other ties. These countries are characterized by 'the existence of a state with no structural roots in society which, as a balloon suspended in mid-air, is being punctured by excessive demands and unable to function without an indiscriminate and wasteful consumption of scarce societal resources'. (Hyden 1983, p. 19) As a result, 'clan politics' permeates society and causes the politicization of the public service: people controlling the public service (politicians and civil servants, usually sharing a common background) can use social and economic resources for their own benefit at the expense of the general public, while those lacking access to the centre of power tend to be neglected and lack the economic and social means needed to improve their situation. (Hyden 1983, pp. 57-63)

The polarization in the developing countries seems to have not only social, but also political consequences. The connection between the internal polarization and the *level of democracy of the political system* in the developing countries has appeared to be weakly negative. This means that the degree of polarization will have a somewhat detrimental influence on the democratic rights of the citizens.

G Development

The ultimate dependent variable of all three dependency models has been the *level of development of Third World countries.* Above, some things have already been said about the factors causing development. First of all, primary commodity concentration appears to have a negative influence on development, as does trade partner dependence and financial dependence. Dependence on a small number of Western trading partners or on a small number of goods can be seen to reduce the development potential of developing countries.

The effect of exploitation has, almost counterintuitively, manifested itself as a variable contributing to development. Above it has been argued that this result, strange as it seems, is explainable if the investment debits transferred to other countries are interpreted as the payment for past investments or loans which, in the meantime, have had their effects on the economy.

The contribution of spin-offs of economic activity to development is rather obvious. As economic activity increases, and the spin-offs of this activity are considerable, it will become easier to transport goods and communicate. This will by itself have a positive influence on economic activity, thereby creating more spin-offs, and so on.

About the same holds for economic distortions. When the economic distortions, such as a deficit on the current account balance or a shortage of savings, become worse, a negative effect on the overall level of development will probably be the result. A reduction of the economic distortions would result in a higher level of development.

The polarization of society, especially the rural-urban disparity, exerts a negative influence on development, both directly and by affecting the democratic nature of the political system. It can be argued that a polarized society will allow less benefits, such as income, education, and health care, to 'trickle down' to the poor. As these are considered essential elements of development, countries restricting them to the better-off parts of society will be ranked less on development.

The effect of democracy on development can best be understood when democracy is seen as the 'bridge' between polarization and development. A higher level of democracy is, then, the expression of a less repressive, more open society, in which the disadvantaged, often rural groups are given the same rights to representation as other social groups.

III POLICY IMPLICATIONS

The link between dependency theory and certain policy preferences has been quite direct. It has been emphasized in chapters 3, 4 and 5 that Andre Gunder Frank, Samir Amin and Johan Galtung have seen their respective pleas for delinking as the logical consequence of their theories about the development and nature of the capitalist world system. To an important extent, dependency theory has been the main inspirator of Third World nationalism or *Third Worldism*, which stresses the need for new, less inequality-prone, international economic structures.

The present study has produced several results that might have some policy relevance. The objective of this section is to deal with two aspects of policy: first, the policy of the Western countries towards the Third World will be focused upon, and secondly, the development policies of the developing countries themselves will be discussed.

Several authors have argued that dependency theories have encouraged the idea of *rectification* as the normative basis of Third World claims to wealth transfers from the Western countries. (See Bauer 1981, pp. 66-85; 1991, pp. 38-55; Smith 1981, pp. 232-49; Van Benthem van den Bergh 1980, pp. 7-46) The present unequal distribution of wealth across the countries of the world is often perceived as a direct consequence of colonialism and imperialism. Therefore, arguments based on or related to dependency theories have often been used as scientific support for claims to rectification. Claims to rectification do not, however, provide adequate guiding principles for Western policies *vis-à-vis* the developing countries. (Cf. Hout 1988) There are at least two reasons why they are not good guides.

First, the concept of rectification is based on empirical judgments that are fundamentally flawed. It is assumed that all contacts between developed and developing countries have been and still are of an exploitative nature. Trade, foreign investment, aid and lending have all been considered as mechanisms of exploitation. Many studies, including the present one, have presented results that cast heavy doubt upon the general validity of this proposition. Although it is undeniable that some relations have harmed and still harm the Third World, it is equally unquestionable that many groups have benefited from their relations with the presently developed countries.

Secondly, the argumentation supporting the claims to rectification is based upon a *counterfactual* assumption. It is assumed that Third World countries would be much more developed if they had not been exploited by the West. Although a counterfactual judgment can never be proven, at least some indications of its explanatory power are required. The present assumption is extremely implausible, however, since some countries (for instance, Thailand, Ethiopia, Afghanistan and Iran) which, during the history of the modern capitalist world system, have never had close ties with the countries of the core have not become noticeably more developed than countries having such ties. At the same time, there are some important examples of countries (such as Australia and New Zealand) that have been fully integrated into the capitalist world system as producers of primary products, and nevertheless have attained a high level of development.

A related problem connected with the claims to rectification is the difficulty of linking compensations to historical wrongs. Following George Sher's approach, one might suppose that in the *actual* world, W_a, a country X has been exploited and, as a consequence, does not have the potential nor the incentive to be economically active. In the actual world such a country might end up being underdeveloped. In a *rectified* world, W_r, where the exploitation of W_a would not have occurred, country X would possess both the potential and the incentive to be economically active. In this rectified world, X might attain a higher level of development and a higher average income. If W_a and W_r are separated by several centuries it is not at all clear that X, after such a long time, is entitled to all that it would have achieved in W_r, since there can be, and probably are, more circumstances responsible for its lack of development. As Sher has formulated it:

> Where the initial wrong was done many hundreds of years ago, almost all of the difference between the victim's entitlements in the actual world and his entitlements in a rectified world can be expressed to stem from the actions of various intervening agents in the two alternative worlds. Little or none of it will be the automatic effect of the initial wrong itself. Since compensation is warranted only for disparities in entitlements which are the automatic effect of the initial wrong act, this means that there will be little or nothing left to compensate for. (1981, p. 13)

For the reasons mentioned above, arguments of rectification do not provide an adequate normative foundation for policies of the presently developed countries towards the Third World. Instead, concepts of distributive justice should be applied to international inequality. Charles Beitz (1979, pp. 69-123) has argued that the state is not a significant *moral* actor in international relations. State borders should not, therefore, be the borders of distributive justice. As in the case of national welfare states, a redistribution of wealth and development should take place on a world scale, so as to counter the most extreme inequalities. Following the logic of Rawls' theory of justice, Beitz (1979, pp. 127-76) has argued that inequalities should only be allowed if their reduction would harm those who are living in the poorest conditions. (Cf. O'Neill 1991)

In this context, the situation of the poorest groups in the Third World is most alarming. They are the ones who suffer most from the extreme inequalities still existing in the world at large and in the developing countries in particular. The ideas about what should be done to further the situation of the poorest differ, however. According to Gary S. Fields (1988, p. 468), research on income distribution and economic growth has produced the insight that rapid economic growth is a good means to reduce absolute poverty. In the *World Development Report 1990*, the World Bank has emphasized that the critical trade-off in developing countries is not between growth and poverty reduction: 'Switching to an efficient, labor-intensive pattern of development and investing more in the human capital of the poor are not only consistent with faster long-term growth; they contribute to it.' (1990, p. 3) According to the World Bank, the principal trade-off involved in the reduction of poverty is between the interests of the poor and those of the 'nonpoor'. The acceptability of this trade-off depends, to a large extent, on the political situation in developing countries; countries where the poor have a say in decision-making are more likely to adopt policies combating poverty than countries where the poor have no influence. (World Bank 1990, pp. 51-2)

The present state of the debate on development assistance makes clear that aid as it has been provided over the last three decades is not the solution to the distress of the poorest groups in the developing countries. Many writers have indicated that foreign policy aims other than the redistribution of wealth have entered into the policy making processes of the Western countries. Even if development assistance is provided with the best intentions, most aid is given to *governments*, not directly to the poorest groups. Moreover, the experience of development projects indicates that many of the projects fail to reach the objectives that were formulated at the outset. (Bauer 1991, pp. 38-55; cf. Hayter 1971; Lebovic 1988; McKinlay and Little 1977 and 1979; Stokke 1984)

Structural measures appear to be much more important in furthering developing countries' wealth and development. The destruction of barriers to trade might be more helpful to developing countries than all kinds of aid. The World Bank (1991, p. 105) has reported that the cost of protection (in 1990 dollars) to developing countries in terms of forgone exports was $55 billion in 1980, an amount almost equal to that year's total official development assistance. The results of the analyses in chapter 7 seem to support this contention. By means of the Lomé Treaties, the member states of the European Community have subscribed to the need for structural reforms in the relations between developed and developing countries. Yet, instead of reducing all barriers to imports from developing countries, large economic entities such as the European Community have tried, in cases such as the Multi-Fibre Agreement, to set limits to these imports. (Hine 1985, pp. 100-13) Hine (1985, pp. 59-99) has described the trade policy of the European Community as a 'hierarchy of trade preferences' or a 'pyramid of privilege', thereby indicating that the granting of trade privileges to developing countries depends on economic and foreign policy considerations, and certainly does not occur automatically.

The asymmetric relations of dependence between the developed and developing countries impede the latter from bargaining on matters of trade preferences. (Cf. Krasner 1985, pp. 39-46; Murphy 1986, p. 249) Most developing countries have simply nothing to offer in return. An indication of this can be found in the negotiations on the so-called Uruguay Round of the G.A.T.T. (the General Agreement on Tariffs and Trade). These negotiations have resulted in a deadlock because of the inability of the United States and the European Community to reach agreement about the subsidization of agriculture. The position of the developing countries has barely been discussed in the Uruguay Round, and the demands of these countries regarding the liberalization of trade in services have hardly been heard.

The conclusion that is to be derived from the remarks above, indicates that the developing countries would be ill-advised to wait for structural changes in the international system. On the other hand, the development strategy proposed by the dependency theorists, which would lead them to delink or dissociate from the capitalist world system, does not offer a solution either. Many studies, including this one, suggest that withdrawal from the world system is not a viable development strategy, but that, instead, integration into the world system by pursuing a policy of export-led growth might prove more effective. These findings appear to be supported by the experiences of at least some Third World countries. (Cf. Furtado 1982, pp. 275-6) In a recent article, Robert Wade has indicated, however, that the chances for developing countries to successfully follow the example of Newly Industrializing Countries such as Korea and Taiwan are a good deal slimmer than many scholars have argued. Wade points at inhibiting factors such as the present lack of expansion in the world economy at large, and the absence in many countries of the political conditions required to establish and sustain 'the key policy combination of competition, dirigisme, and education'. (1992, p. 316)

The need to further trade has been supported by several scholars sympathetic to the dependency approach. (E.g. Kay 1991) In this context, it has been emphasized that developing countries should, at the same time, aim for a more differentiated, industrial production structure. The extreme reliance of these countries on primary products, and thus on heavily fluctuating prices on the world market, has proven to be detrimental to their development. The aiming at the production of certain labour-intensive industrial commodities, for which the developing countries possess undeniable 'comparative advantages', might turn out to be beneficial to these countries. The policy of governments in the developing countries could be focused at (partly) taking over the production of the goods that, in the West, are in the later phases of the 'product-life cycle', such as certain parts of microelectronics and automobiles, and that offer them significant value-added and positive external effects. (Cf. Lake 1987, p. 229)

A problem facing this policy is the lack of capital in many developing countries. The developing countries could follow one of several policies in order to obtain more capital. In the first place, they could invite foreign capital-owners to invest in their country. (World Bank 1991, pp. 88-96) As has been suggested above, the positive external effects of investments (on the quality of labour, know-how and technological innovation) might outweigh the negative consequences, such as the outflow of debits. The experiences of the NICs also seem to support this policy option.

A more hazardous way to obtaining capital is by borrowing on the international capital market. The debt crisis of the 1980s has made clear that the accumulation of too much foreign debt might have disastrous consequences since countries can become vulnerable to previously unforeseen exogenous developments. The sudden rise of interest at the beginning of the 1980s caused many developing countries to default. The necessity of adjustment, which often has been imposed by creditors such as the I.M.F. and the World Bank or by groups of creditors such as the Paris and London Clubs, caused many developing countries to change their policy priorities away from development. (See Polanyi Levitt 1989)

Although the policy options outlined in this section are widely supported by many scholars working on problems of international inequality and development, this does not mean that they offer the solution for all problems facing the developing countries. In the foreseeable future, many of the problems that have been discussed in this book will remain. The solving of these problems requires a change in structures as well as in policies. As history teaches us, it requires much time for structures to be changed.

Appendix A: Units of Analysis

Afghanistan (1965, 1975, 1985)
Algeria (1965, 1975, 1985)
Angola (1965, 1975)
Argentina (1965, 1975, 1985)
Bangladesh (1975, 1985)
Benin/Dahomey (1965, 1975, 1985)
Bolivia (1965, 1975, 1985)
Brazil (1965, 1975, 1985)
Burkina Faso/Upper Volta (1965, 1975, 1985)
Burma (1965, 1975, 1985)
Burundi (1965, 1975, 1985)
Cambodia (1965)
Cameroon (1965, 1975, 1985)
Central African Republic (1965, 1975, 1985)
Chad (1965, 1975, 1985)
Chile (1965, 1975, 1985)
Colombia (1965, 1975, 1985)
Costa Rica (1965, 1975, 1985)
Cuba (1975, 1985)
Dominican Republic (1965, 1975, 1985)
Ecuador (1965, 1975, 1985)
Egypt (1965, 1975, 1985)
El Salvador (1965, 1975, 1985)
Ethiopia (1965, 1975, 1985)
Ghana (1965, 1975, 1985)
Guatemala (1965, 1975, 1985)
Haiti (1965, 1975, 1985)
Honduras (1965, 1975, 1985)
Hong Kong (1965, 1975, 1985)
India (1965, 1975, 1985)
Indonesia (1965, 1975, 1985)
Iran (1965, 1975, 1985)
Iraq (1965, 1975, 1985)
Ivory Coast (1965, 1975, 1985)
Jamaica (1965, 1975, 1985)

Jordan (1965, 1975, 1985)
Kenya (1965, 1975, 1985)
Korea, Republic of (South) (1965, 1975, 1985)
Laos (1985)
Lebanon (1965, 1975)
Liberia (1965, 1975, 1985)
Libya (1965, 1975, 1985)
Madagascar (1965, 1975, 1985)
Malawi (1965, 1975, 1985)
Malaysia (1965, 1975, 1985)
Mali (1965, 1975, 1985)
Mauritania (1965, 1975, 1985)
Mexico (1965, 1975, 1985)
Morocco (1965, 1975, 1985)
Mozambique (1965, 1975, 1985)
Nepal (1965, 1975, 1985)
Nicaragua (1965, 1975, 1985)
Niger (1965, 1975, 1985)
Nigeria (1965, 1975, 1985)
Pakistan (1965, 1975, 1985)
Panama (1965, 1975, 1985)
Papua New Guinea (1965, 1975, 1985)
Paraguay (1965, 1975, 1985)
Peru (1965, 1975, 1985)
Philippines (1965, 1975, 1985)
Rwanda (1965, 1975, 1985)
Senegal (1965, 1975, 1985)
Sierra Leone (1965, 1975, 1985)
Singapore (1965, 1975, 1985)
Somalia (1965, 1975, 1985)
Sri Lanka (1965, 1975, 1985)
Sudan (1965, 1975, 1985)
Syria (1965, 1975, 1985)
Tanzania (1965, 1975, 1985)
Thailand (1965, 1975, 1985)
Togo (1965, 1975, 1985)
Trinidad and Tobago (1965, 1975, 1985)
Tunisia (1965, 1975, 1985)
Turkey (1965, 1975, 1985)
Uganda (1965, 1975, 1985)
Uruguay (1965, 1975, 1985)
Venezuela (1965, 1975, 1985)

Vietnam, Republic of (South) (1965)
Yemen, Democratic Republic of (South) (1965, 1975, 1985)
Yemen, Republic of (North) (1965, 1975, 1985)
Yugoslavia (1965, 1975, 1985)
Zaire (1965, 1975, 1985)
Zambia (1965, 1975, 1985)
Zimbabwe/Rhodesia (1965, 1975, 1985)

Appendix B: Data, Definitions and Sources

1. DEPENDENCE

a. Relative Dependence on Exports

Exports of goods and nonfactor services as a percentage of gross domestic product, at current market prices, in domestic currency.

Source 1965: Bornschier and Heintz 1979.

Source 1975 and 1985: World Bank 1989.

b. Relative Dependence on Imports

Imports of goods and nonfactor services as a percentage of gross domestic product, at current market prices, in domestic currency.

Source 1965: Bornschier and Heintz 1979.

Source 1975 and 1985: World Bank 1989.

c. Export Partner Concentration

Exports to the largest export partner as a percentage of total exports.

Source 1965, 1975 and 1985: United Nations 1969, 1976a, 1980, 1987a and 1988a.

d. Import Partner Concentration

Imports from the largest import partner as a percentage of total imports.

Source 1965, 1975 and 1985: United Nations 1969, 1976a, 1980, 1987a and 1988a.

e. Government External Debt

Public and publicly guaranteed long-term debt outstanding and disbursed, as a percentage of gross national product.

Sources 1967: Bornschier and Heintz 1979 (debt data); World Bank 1989 (GNP data).

Sources 1975 and 1985: World Bank 1988-89; UNCTAD 1985b.

f. Foreign Direct Investment

Direct investment, in millions of US dollars.

Source 1965: International Monetary Fund 1968, 1970 and 1971.

Source 1975: International Monetary Fund 1980.
Source 1985: International Monetary Fund 1989 and 1990.

g. Dependence on Development Assistance
Net receipts of official development aid (ODA) as a percentage of the receiving country's GNP.
Source 1967-9: Organisation for Economic Co-operation and Development 1970.
Source 1975: Organisation for Economic Co-operation and Development 1977.
Source 1985: World Bank 1987.

2. DEVELOPMENT

a. Gross National Income per Capita
The sum of gross national income estimates at market prices, in 1980 U.S. dollars, and the terms of trade adjustments, per capita.
Source 1967, 1975 and 1985: World Bank 1989.

b. Gross Domestic Investment per Capita
The sum of gross domestic fixed investment and the change in stocks.
Source 1967, 1975 and 1980: World Bank 1989.

c. Contribution of Industry to Gross Domestic Product
The contribution of value added in the manufacturing sector as a percentage of the total gross domestic product.
Source 1965: World Bank 1976.
Source 1975 and 1985: World Bank 1989.

d. Rate of Infant Mortality
The number of infants per thousand live births, in a given year, who die before reaching the age of one.
Source 1966: World Bank 1988.
Source 1975 and 1985: World Bank 1989.

e. Life Expectancy at Birth
The number of years a newborn infant would live if prevailing patterns of mortality for all people at the time of his or her birth were to stay the same throughout his or her life.
Source 1965: World Bank 1982.
Source 1975 and 1985: World Bank 1989.

f. Level of Educational Enrolment, Secondary Level

Gross enrolment of all ages at the secondary level (including students in vocational, or teacher-training secondary schools) as a percentage of children in the country's secondary school-age group.

Source 1965: World Bank 1982.

Source 1975 and 1985: World Bank 1989.

g. Energy Consumption per Capita

Consumption of commercial energy per capita, in kilogrammes of coal equivalent.

Source 1965: United Nations 1976c.

Source 1975 and 1985: United Nations 1982 and 1988b.

3. EXPLOITATION

Debits on Investment

The debits on investment by foreign companies and interest payments on official loans, as a percentage of merchandise export income, in current prices.

Source 1965 and 1975: International Monetary Fund 1970 and 1978.

Source 1985: International Monetary Fund 1990.

4. INEQUALITY AND INTERNAL POLARIZATION

Rural-urban Disparity Ratio

The inequality ratio of production per sector relative to the part of the total labour force working in that sector: the ratio of the gross domestic product of the non-agricultural sectors (as a percentage of total gross domestic product) and the percentage of the total labour force working in these sectors is divided by the ratio of the gross domestic product of the agricultural sector and the percentage of the labour force working in agriculture.

Sources 1965: United Nations 1970b and 1976b; International Labour Organization 1990.

Sources 1975 and 1985: United Nations 1990a and 1990b; International Labour Organization 1978, 1979, 1980, 1986, 1987 and 1988.

5. CONCENTRATION OF PRODUCTION, DEGREE OF EXTROVERSION AND POSITION IN THE WORLD DIVISION OF LABOUR

a. Primary Commodity Orientation

The export value of primary commodities as a percentage of total exports (excluding fuels).

Source 1966, 1975 and 1985: UNCTAD 1987 and 1989.

b. Commodity Concentration

The Hirschman Commodity Concentration Index, expressing the degree of concentration of exports. The index is equal to 1 if only one commodity is exported and its value decreases with the degree of diversification of exports.

Source 1966, 1976 and 1982: UNCTAD 1969, 1979 and 1985a.

c. Orientation of Exports toward Centre Countries

The percentage of total export value directed towards the industrial countries.

Source 1965: International Monetary Fund and International Bank for Reconstruction and Development undated.

Source 1975 and 1985: International Monetary Fund 1982 and 1988.

6. STATE OF THE WORLD SYSTEM

Expansion, Recession, Recovery

The situation of the world capitalist economy, scored as '+1' for 1965 (expansion phase), '-1' for 1975 (recession phase) and '0' for 1985 (recovery phase).

7. POLITICAL REGIME, DEMOCRACY AND REPRESSION

a. Political Democracy Index

The rating of political liberties and popular sovereignty (average) on a scale of 0 through 100, where 0 is the least democratic and 100 is the most democratic; the 0-100 scale has been transformed into a 1-7 scale to make it comparable with the one used for 1977 and 1985.

Source 1965: Bollen 1980.

b. Political and Civil Rights Index

The rating of political and civil freedom (average) on a scale of 1 through 7, where 1 is the least free and 7 is the freest.

Source 1977: Gastil 1978, pp. 10-3.

Source 1985: Gastil 1985.

8. ECONOMIC DISTORTIONS

a. Current Account Position

The deficit or surplus of the current account balance as a percentage of the country's merchandise exports.

Source 1965, 1975 and 1985: International Monetary Fund 1964-8, 1965-9, 1978 and 1989.

b. Gross Domestic Savings Rate

Gross domestic savings at current prices as a percentage of the country's gross domestic product.

Source 1967, 1975 and 1985: World Bank 1989.

9. FRAGMENTATION AND MARGINALIZATION

Eigenhandelsquote

The percentage of developing countries' total trade value (import and export) with other non-oil exporting developing countries.

Source 1965: International Monetary Fund and International Bank for Reconstruction and Development undated.

Source 1975: International Monetary Fund 1982.

Source 1985: International Monetary Fund 1986.

10. SPIN-OFFS

a. Vehicles

The number of commercial vehicles in use per thousand inhabitants.

Source 1965, 1975 and 1985: United Nations 1970a, 1979-80, 1985-6 and 1987b.

b. Railways

Net ton-kilometres: millions of freight net ton-kilometres including fast and ordinary goods services, excluding service traffic, mail, baggage and non-revenue governmental stores, per ten thousand inhabitants.

Source 1965, 1975 and 1985: United Nations 1970a, 1979-80, 1985-6 and 1987b.

c. Telephones

The number of public and private telephones in use, per hundred inhabitants.

Source 1965, 1975 and 1985: United Nations 1970a, 1979-80, 1985-6 and 1987b.

Bibliography

Almond, G.A. (1960), 'Introduction: A functional approach to comparative politics', in G.A. Almond and J.S. Coleman (eds), *The politics of the developing areas*, Princeton, Princeton University Press, pp. 3-64.

Almond, G.A. (1970), *Political development: Essays in heuristic theory*, Boston, Little, Brown.

Alschuler, L.R. (1976), 'Satellization and stagnation in Latin America', *International Studies Quarterly*, vol. 20, no. 1, March, pp. 39-82.

Amin, S. (1965), *Trois expériences africaines de développement: Le Mali, la Guinée et le Ghana*, Paris, Presses Universitaires de France.

Amin, S. (1966), *L'économie du Maghreb*, Paris, Les Editions de Minuit.

Amin, S. (1970), *The Maghreb in the modern world: Algeria, Tunisia, Morocco*, Harmondsworth, Penguin.

Amin, S. (1971), 'Development and structural changes: African experience', in B. Ward, J.D. Runnalls and L. d'Anjou (eds), *The widening gap*, New York, Columbia University Press, pp. 312-33.

Amin, S. (1972a), 'Le modèle théorique d'accumulation et de développement dans le monde contemporain: La problématique de transition', *Revue Tiers-Monde*, vol. 13, no. 52, October-December, Special issue 'Le capitalisme périphérique', pp. 703-26.

Amin, S. (1972b), 'Underdevelopment and dependence in Black Africa: Origins and contemporary forms', *Journal of Modern African Studies*, vol. 10, no. 4, pp. 503-24.

Amin, S. (1973), *Neo-colonialism in West Africa*, Harmondsworth, Penguin.

Amin, S. (1974), *Accumulation on a world scale: A critique of the theory of underdevelopment*, 2 vols, New York, Monthly Review Press.

Amin, S. (1976), *Unequal development: An essay on the social formations of peripheral capitalism*, New York, Monthly Review Press.

Amin, S. (1977a), 'Capitalism, state collectivism, and socialism', *Monthly Review*, vol. 29, no. 2, June, pp. 25-41.

Amin, S. (1977b), *Imperialism and unequal development*, Hassocks, Harvester Press.

Amin, S. (1977c), 'Self-reliance and the new international economic order', *Monthly Review*, vol. 29, no. 3, July/August, pp. 1-21.

Amin, S. (1977d), 'La structure de classe du système impérialiste contemporain', *L'Homme et la Société*, no. 45-6 (July-September/ October-December, pp. 69-87.

Amin, S. (1978a), *The Arab nation: Nationalism and class struggles*, London, Zed Press.

Amin, S. (1978b), *The law of value and historical materialism*, New York, Monthly Review Press.

Amin, S. (1979a), 'NIEO: How to put Third World surpluses to effective use', *Third World Quarterly*, vol. 1, no. 1, January, pp. 65-72.

Amin, S. (1979b), 'Les perspectives de l'Afrique australe', *Revue Tiers-Monde*, vol. 20, no. 77, January-March, Special issue 'Capitalisme et lutte des classes en Afrique australe', pp. 7-26.

Amin, S. (1980a), *Class and nation: Historically and in the current crisis*, London, Heinemann.

Amin, S. (1980b), *L'économie arabe contemporaine*, Paris, Les Editions de Minuit.

Amin, S. (1980c), 'Sous-développement et histoire: Le cas de l'Afrique', in L. Blussé, H.L. Wesseling and G.D. Winius (eds), *History and underdevelopment: Essays on underdevelopment and European expansion in Asia and Africa*, Leiden, Centre for the History of European Expansion; Paris, Editions de la Maison des Sciences de l'Homme, pp. 137-45.

Amin, S. (1981), 'The world crisis of the 1980s' (interview), *Monthly Review*, vol. 33, no. 2, June, pp. 33-43.

Amin, S. (1982a), 'After the New International Economic Order: The future of international economic relations', *Journal of Contemporary Asia*, vol. 12, no. 4, pp. 432-50.

Amin, S. (1982b), 'Crisis, nationalism, and socialism', in S. Amin, G. Arrighi, A.G. Frank and I. Wallerstein, *Dynamics of global crisis*, New York, Monthly Review Press, pp. 167-231.

Amin, S. (1983), 'Expansion or crisis of capitalism?', *Third World Quarterly*, vol. 5, no. 2, April, pp. 361-85.

Amin, S. (1984a), 'Income distribution in the capitalist system', *Review* vol. 8, no. 1, Summer, pp. 3-28.

Amin, S. (1984b), 'Introduction', in S. Amin (ed.), *Human resources, employment and development: Proceedings of the Sixth World Congress of the International Economic Association, Mexico, 1980*, vol. 5, London, Macmillan, pp. vii-xxiii.

Amin, S. (1985), 'Modes of production, history and unequal development', *Science and Society*, vol. 49, no. 2, Summer, pp. 194-207.

Amin, S. (1986), 'Is an endogenous development strategy possible in Africa?', in K. Ahooja-Patel, A. Gordon Drabek and M. Nerfin (eds),

World economy in transition: Essays presented to Surendra Patel on his sixtieth birthday, Oxford, Pergamon, pp. 159-72.

Amin, S. (1987a), 'Democracy and national strategy in the periphery', *Third World Quarterly*, vol. 9, no. 4, October, pp. 1129-56.

Amin, S. (1987b), 'A note on the concept of delinking', *Review*, vol. 10, no. 3, Winter, pp. 435-44.

Amin, S. (1987c), 'Preface', in S. Amin, D. Chitala and I. Mandaza (eds), *SADCC: Prospects for disengagement and development in Southern Africa*, London, Zed; Tokyo, The United Nations University, pp. 1-7.

Amin, S. (1988a), 'Comment on Senghaas', *Review*, vol. 11, no. 1, Winter, pp. 55-66.

Amin, S. (1988b), 'La région méditerranéenne dans l'histoire et le présent', in S. Amin and F. Yachir, *La Méditerranée dans le monde: Les enjeux de la transnationalisation dans la région méditerranéenne*, Paris, Editions de la Découverte; Casablanca, Editions Toubkal; Tokyo, Universités des Nations Unies, pp. 9-42.

Amin, S. (1989), 'Peace, national and regional security and development: Some reflections on the African experience', *Alternatives*, vol. 14, no. 2, April, pp. 215-29.

Amin, S. (1990), *Delinking: Towards a polycentric world*, London, Zed.

Amin, S. (1991), 'The state and development', in D. Held (ed.), *Political theory today*, Oxford, Polity Press, pp. 305-29.

Apter, D.E. (1967), *The politics of modernization*, First edition 1965, Chicago, University of Chicago Press.

Armstrong, A. (1981), 'The political consequences of economic dependence', *Journal of Peace Research*, vol. 25, no. 3, September, pp. 401-28.

Aronowitz, S. (1981), 'A metatheoretical critique of Immanuel Wallerstein's *The modern world system*', *Theory and Society*, vol. 10, no. 4, July, pp. 503-20.

Arrighi, G., Hopkins, T.K. and Wallerstein, I. (1989), *Antisystemic movements*, London, Verso.

Balassa, B. (1986), 'Dependency and trade orientation', *The World Economy*, vol. 9, no. 3, September, pp. 259-73.

Ballmer-Cao, T.-H. (1980), 'Politisches System, Einkommensverteilung und multinationale Konzerne', in V. Bornschier (ed.), *Multinationale Konzerne, Wirtschaftspolitik und nationale Entwicklung im Weltsystem*, Frankfurt, Campus, pp. 241-62.

Banaji, J. (1983), 'Gunder Frank in retreat?', in P. Limqueco and B. McFarlane (eds), *Neo-Marxist theories of development*, London, Croom Helm; New York, St Martin's Press, pp. 97-113.

Baran, P.A. (1957), *The political economy of growth*, New York, Monthly

Review Press.

Baran, P.A. and Sweezy, P.M. (1966), *Monopoly capital: An essay on the American economic and social order*, New York, Monthly Review Press.

Baran, P.A. and Sweezy, P.M. (1972), 'Notes on the theory of imperialism', in K.E. Boulding and T. Mukerjee (eds), *Economic imperialism: A book of readings*, Ann Arbor, University of Michigan Press, pp. 156-70.

Barratt Brown, M. (1970), *After imperialism*, Revised edition, London, Heinemann.

Barratt Brown, M. (1972), 'A critique of Marxist theories of imperialism', in R. Owen and B. Sutcliffe (eds), *Studies in the theory of imperialism*, London, Longman, pp. 35-70.

Barratt Brown, M. (1974), *The economics of imperialism*, Harmondsworth, Penguin.

Barone, C.A. (1982), 'Samir Amin and the theory of imperialism: A critical analysis', *Review of Radical Political Economics*, vol. 14, no. 1, Spring, pp. 10-23.

Barone, C.A. (1985), *Marxist thought on imperialism: Survey and critique*, Armonk, N.Y., M.E. Sharpe.

Bauer, P.T. (1981), *Equality, the Third World and economic delusion*, London, Weidenfeld and Nicolson.

Bauer, P.T. (1991), *The development frontier: Essays in applied economics*, London, Harvester Wheatsheaf.

Bauzon, K.E. and Abel, C.F. (1986), 'Dependency: History, theory, and a reappraisal', in M.A. Tétreault and C.F. Abel (eds), *Dependency theory and the return of high politics*, New York, Greenwood Press, pp. 43-69.

Beitz, C.R. (1979), *Political theory and international relations*, Princeton, Princeton University Press.

Benthem van den Bergh, G. van (1972), 'Theory or taxonomy? Some critical notes on Johan Galtung's "A structural theory of imperialism" ', *Journal of Peace Research*, vol. 9, no. 1, pp. 77-89.

Benthem van den Bergh, G. van (1980), *De staat van geweld en andere essays*, Amsterdam, Meulenhoff.

Bergesen, A. (1980), 'From utilitarianism to globology: The shift from the individual to the world as a whole as the primordial unit of analysis', in A. Bergesen (ed.), *Studies of the modern world-system*, New York, Academic Press, pp. 1-12.

Blomström, M. and Hettne, B. (1984), *Development theory in transition: The dependency debate and beyond: Third World responses*, London, Zed Books.

Bodenheimer, S.J. (1970), 'The ideology of developmentalism: American political science's paradigm-surrogate for Latin-American studies', *Berkeley Journal of Sociology*, vol. 15, pp. 95-137.

Bodenheimer, S.J. (1973), 'Dependency and imperialism: The roots of Latin American underdevelopment', *Politics and Society*, vol. 1, no. 3, May, pp. 327-57.

Bollen, K.A. (1980), 'Issues in the comparative measurement of democracy', *American Sociological Review*, vol. 45, no. 3, June, pp. 370-90.

Bollen, K.A. (1983), 'World system position, dependency, and democracy: The cross-national evidence', *American Sociological Review*, vol. 48, no. 4, August, pp. 468-79.

Bonnell, V.E. (1980), 'The uses of theory, concepts and comparison in historical sociology', *Comparative Studies in Society and History*, vol. 22, no. 2, April, pp. 156-73.

Booth, D. (1975), 'Andre Gunder Frank: An introduction and appreciation', in I. Oxaal, T. Barnett and D. Booth (eds), *Beyond the sociology of development: Economy and society in Latin America*, London, Routledge & Kegan Paul, pp. 50-85.

Bornschier, V. (1980), 'Multinational corporations and economic growth: A cross-national test of the decapitalization thesis', *Journal of Development Economics*, vol. 7, no. 2, June, pp. 191-210.

Bornschier, V. (1981), 'Dependent industrialization in the world economy: Some comments and results concerning a recent debate', *Journal of Conflict Resolution*, vol. 25, no. 3, September, pp. 371-400.

Bornschier, V. (1982), 'The world economy in the world-system: Structure, dependence and change', *International Social Science Journal*, vol. 34, no. 91, pp. 37-59.

Bornschier, V. (1983), 'World economy, level development and income distribution: An integration of different approaches to the explanation of income inequality', *World Development*, vol. 11, no. 1, January 1983, pp. 11-20.

Bornschier, V. and Ballmer-Cao, T.-H. (1979), 'Income inequality: A cross-national study of the relationships between MNC-penetration, dimensions of the power structure and income distribution', *American Sociological Review*, vol. 44, no. 3, June, pp. 487-506.

Bornschier, V., in association with Ballmer-Cao, T.-H. (1980), 'Multinationale Konzerne in der Weltwirtschaft und das Wirtschaftswachstum der Gastländer', in V. Bornschier (ed.), *Multinationale Konzerne, Wirtschaftspolitik und nationale Entwicklung im Weltsystem*, Frankfurt, Campus, pp. 51-105.

Bornschier, V. and Chase-Dunn, C. (1985), *Transnational corporations and underdevelopment*, New York, Praeger.

Bornschier, V., Chase-Dunn, C. and Rubinson, R. (1978), 'Cross-national evidence of the effects of foreign investment and aid on economic growth and inequality: A survey of findings and a reanalysis', *American Journal of Sociology*, vol. 84, no. 3, pp. 651-83.

Bornschier, V. and Heintz, P. (ed.) (1979), *Compendium of data for world-system analysis: A sourcebook of data based on the study of MNCs, economic policy and national development*, Special issue of the Bulletin of the Sociological Institute of the University of Zürich, Reworked and enlarged by Thanh-Huyen Ballmer-Cao and Jürg Scheidegger, Zürich, University of Zürich.

Bradshaw, Y.W. (1985), 'Dependent development in Black Africa: A cross-national study', *American Sociological Review*, vol. 50, no. 2, April, pp. 195-207.

Bradshaw, Y.W. (1987), 'Urbanization and underdevelopment: A global study of modernization, urban bias, and economic dependency', *American Sociological Review*, vol. 52, no. 2, April, pp. 224-39.

Bradshaw, Y.W. and Tshandu, Z. (1990), 'Foreign capital penetration, state intervention, and development in sub-Saharan Africa', *International Studies Quarterly*, vol. 34, no. 2, June, pp. 229-51.

Brewer, A. (1980), *Marxist theories of imperialism: A critical survey*, London, Routledge & Kegan Paul.

Brown, C. (1981), 'Galtung and the marxists on imperialism: Answers vs questions', *Millennium: Journal of International Studies*, vol. 10, no. 3, Autumn, pp. 220-8.

Brown, C. (1985), 'Development and dependency', in M. Light and A.J.R. Groom (eds), *International relations: A handbook of current theory*, London, Frances Pinter, pp. 60-73.

Bukharin, N. (1966), *Imperialism and world economy*, Originally published in Russian in 1917, New York, Howard Fertig.

Cain, P. (1979a), 'Capitalism, war and internationalism in the thought of Richard Cobden', *British Journal of International Studies*, vol. 5, no. 3, October, pp. 229-47.

Cain, P. (1979b), 'International trade and economic development in the work of J.A. Hobson before 1914', *History of Political Economy*, vol. 11, no. 3, pp. 406-24.

Cardoso, F.H. (1977), 'The originality of a copy: CEPAL and the idea of development', *CEPAL-Review*, no. 4, Second Half, pp. 7-40.

Carr, E.H. (1939), *The twenty years' crisis, 1919-1939: An introduction to the study of international relations*, London, Macmillan.

Chan, S. (1982), 'Cores and peripheries: Interaction patterns in Asia', *Comparative Political Studies*, vol. 15, no. 3, October, pp. 314-40.

Chan, S. (1989), 'Income inequality among LDCs: A comparative analysis of alternative perspectives', *International Studies Quarterly*, vol. 33, no. 1, March, pp. 45-65.

Chandra, N.K. (1986), 'Theories of unequal exchange: A critique of Emmanuel and Amin', *Economic and Political Weekly*, vol. 21, no. 30, July 26, pp. PE 77-PE 84.

Chase-Dunn, C. (1975), 'The effects of international economic dependence on development and inequality: A cross-national study', *American Sociological Review*, vol. 40, December, pp. 720-38.

Chase-Dunn, C. (1985), 'Introduction', *Review*, vol. 8, no. 4, Spring, pp. 445-9.

Chase-Dunn, C. (1989), *Global formation: Structures of the world-economy*, Oxford, Basil Blackwell.

Cheng, W.-Y. (1989), 'Testing the food-first hypothesis: A cross-national study of dependency, sectoral growth and food intake in less developed countries', *World Development*, vol. 17, no. 1, January, pp. 17-27.

Chilcote, R.H. (1974), 'A critical synthesis of the dependency literature', *Latin American Perspectives*, vol. 1, no. 1, Spring, Special issue 'Dependency theory: A reassessment', pp. 4-29.

Cobden, R. (1868), 'England, Ireland, & America', in *The political writings of Richard Cobden*, Second edition, vol. I, London, William Ridgway; New York, D. Appleton, pp. 1-153.

Cobden, R. (1878), *Speeches on questions of public policy*, Edited by J. Bright and J.E. Thorold Rogers, London, Macmillan.

Cohen, B. (1973), *The question of imperialism: The political economy of dominance and dependence*, New York, Basic Books.

Cohen, G.A. (1982), 'Functional explanation, consequence explanation, and Marxism', *Inquiry*, vol. 25, no. 1, March, pp. 27-56.

Coleman, J.S. (1960), 'Conclusion: The political systems of the developing areas', in G.A. Almond and J.S. Coleman (eds), *The politics of the developing areas*, Princeton, Princeton University Press, pp. 532-76.

Collier, D. (ed.) (1979), *The new authoritarianism in Latin America*, Princeton, Princeton University Press.

Corden, W.M. (1974), *Trade policy and economic welfare*, Oxford, Clarendon Press.

Corden, W.M. (1984), 'The normative theory of international trade', in R.W. Jones and P.B. Kenen (eds), *Handbook of international economics*, vol. I, Amsterdam, North-Holland, pp. 63-130.

Coppens, H.A.J. (1980), 'Imperialisme: Een nieuwe benadering', in Ph.P. Everts and H.W. Tromp (eds), *Tussen oorlog en vrede: Thema's in de polemologie*, Amsterdam, Intermediair, pp. 109-31.

Delacroix, J. (1977), 'The export of raw materials and economic growth: A cross-national study', *American Sociological Review*, vol. 42, no. 5,

October, pp. 795-808.

Delacroix, J., and Ragin, C. (1978), 'Modernizing institutions, mobilization, and Third World development: A cross-national study', *American Journal of Sociology*, vol. 84, no. 1, July, pp. 123-50.

Delacroix, J. and Ragin, C. (1981), 'Structural blockage: A cross-national study of economic dependency, state efficacy, and underdevelopment', *American Journal of Sociology*, vol. 86, no. 6, May, pp. 1311-47.

Denemark, R.A. and Thomas, K.P. (1988), 'The Brenner-Wallerstein debate', *International Studies Quarterly*, vol. 32, no.1, March, pp. 47-65.

Dixon, C. (1991), *South East Asia in the world-economy*, Cambridge, Cambridge University Press.

Dixon, W.J. (1985), 'Change and persistence in the world system: An analysis of global trade concentration, 1955-1975', *International Studies Quarterly*, vol. 29, no. 2, June, pp. 171-89.

Dobb, M. (1937), *Political economy and capitalism: Some essays in economic tradition*, London, George Routledge & Sons.

Dobb, M. (1963), *Economic growth and underdeveloped countries*, London, Lawrence and Wishart.

Dolan, M.B. and Tomlin, B.W. (1980), 'First World-Third World linkages: External relations and economic development', *International Organization*, vol. 34, no. 1, Winter, pp. 41-64.

Dougherty, J.E. and Pfaltzgraff, Jr, R.L. (1981), *Contending theories of international relations: A comprehensive survey*, Second edition, New York, Harper & Row.

Doyle, M.W. (1986), *Empires*, Ithaca, N.Y., Cornell University Press.

Dube, S.C. (1988), *Modernization and development: The search for alternative paradigms*, Tokyo, United Nations University; London: Zed.

Duvall, R., Jackson, S., Russett, B.M., Snidal, D. and Sylvan, D. (1981), 'A formal model of "dependencia theory": Structure and measurement', in R.L. Merritt and B.M. Russett (eds), *From national development to global community: Essays in honor of Karl W. Deutsch*, London, George Allen & Unwin, pp. 312-50.

Economic Commission for Latin America (1951), *Economic Survey of Latin America 1949*, New York, United Nations Department of Economic Affairs.

Edelstein, J.C. (1982), 'Dependency: A special theory within Marxian analysis', in R.H. Chilcote (ed.), *Dependency and marxism: Toward a resolution of the debate*, Boulder, Col., Westview, pp. 103-7.

Elguea, J.A. (1984), *Sociology of development and philosophy of science: A case study in contemporary scientific growth*, Ph.D. dissertation,

Stanford University, Stanford, Mimeo.

Elguea, J.A. (1985), 'Paradigms and scientific revolutions in development theories', *Development and Change*, vol. 16, pp. 213-33.

Emmanuel, A. (1972), *Unequal exchange: A study of the imperialism of trade*, New York, Monthly Review Press.

Emmanuel, A. (1974), 'Myths of development versus myths of underdevelopment', *New Left Review*, no. 85, May/June, pp. 61-82.

Evans, P. (1979), *Dependent development: The alliance of multinational, state, and local capital in Brazil*, Princeton, Princeton University Press.

Evans, P.B. and Timberlake, M. (1980), 'Dependence, inequality, and the growth of the tertiary: A comparative analysis of less developed countries', *American Sociological Review*, vol. 45, no. 4, August, pp. 531-52.

Fagen, R.R. (1977), 'Studying Latin American politics: Some implications of a dependencia approach', *Latin American Research Review*, vol. 12, no. 2, pp. 3-26.

Fiala, R. (1983), 'Inequality and the service sector in less developed countries: A reanalysis and respecification', *American Sociological Review*, vol. 48, no. 3, June, pp. 421-8.

Fieldhouse, D.K. (ed.) (1967), *The theory of capitalist imperialism*, London, Longman.

Fieldhouse, D.K. (1984), *Economics and empire, 1830-1914*, London, Macmillan.

Fields, G.S. (1988), 'Income distribution and economic growth', in G. Ranis and T.P. Schultz (eds), *The state of development economics: Progress and perspectives*, Oxford, Basil Blackwell, pp. 459-81.

Fitzgerald, F.T. (1983), 'Sociologies of development', in P. Limqueco and B. McFarlane (eds), *Neo-Marxist theories of development*, London, Croom Helm; New York, St Martin's Press, pp. 12-28.

Foster-Carter, A. (1976), 'From Rostow to Gunder Frank: Conflicting paradigms in the analysis of underdevelopment', *World Development*, vol. 4, no. 3, March, pp. 167-80.

Foster-Carter, A. (1980), 'Marxism versus dependency theory? A polemic', *Millennium: Journal of International Studies*, vol. 8, no. 3, Winter, pp. 214-34.

Frank, A.G. (1969a), *Capitalism and underdevelopment in Latin America: Historical studies of Chile and Brazil*, Revised and enlarged edition, First published in 1967, New York, Monthly Review Press.

Frank, A.G. (1969b), *Latin America: Underdevelopment or revolution: Essays on the development of underdevelopment and the immediate enemy*, New York, Monthly Review Press.

Frank, A.G. (1971), 'On the mechanisms of imperialism: The case of

Brazil', in K.T. Fann and D.C. Hodges (eds), *Readings in U.S. imperialism*, Boston, Porter Sargent, pp. 237-48.

Frank, A.G. (1972a), 'Economic dependence, class structure, and underdevelopment policy', in J.D. Cockroft, A.G. Frank and D.L. Johnson, *Dependence and underdevelopment: Latin America's political economy*, New York, Doubleday, pp. 19-45.

Frank, A.G. (1972b), *Lumpenbourgeoisie: lumpendevelopment: Dependence, class and politics in Latin America*, New York, Monthly Review Press.

Frank, A.G. (1975), *On capitalist underdevelopment*, Bombay, Oxford University Press.

Frank, A.G. (1977), 'Emergence of permanent emergency in India', *Economic and Political Weekly*, vol. 12, no. 11, March 12, pp. 463-75.

Frank, A.G. (1978a), 'Development of underdevelopment or underdevelopment of development in China', *Modern China*, vol. 4, no. 3, July, pp. 341-50.

Frank, A.G. (1978b), *World accumulation, 1492-1789*, London, Macmillan.

Frank, A.G. (1979a), *Dependent accumulation and underdevelopment*, New York, Monthly Review Press.

Frank, A.G. (1979b), *Mexican agriculture, 1521-1630: Transformation of the mode of production*, Cambridge, Cambridge University Press; Paris, Editions de la Maison des Sciences de l'Homme.

Frank, A.G. (1980a), *Crisis: In the world economy*, London, Heinemann.

Frank, A.G. (1980b), 'North-South and East-West Keynesian paradoxes in the Brandt report', *Third World Quarterly*, vol. 2, no. 4, October, pp. 669-80.

Frank, A.G. (1981a), *Crisis: In the Third World*, London, Heinemann.

Frank, A.G. (1981b), *Reflections on the world economic crisis*, London, Hutchinson.

Frank, A.G. (1981c), 'The world crisis: Theory and ideology', *Alternatives*, vol. 6, no. 4, Spring, pp. 497-523.

Frank, A.G. (1982), 'Crisis of ideology and ideology of crisis', in S. Amin, G. Arrighi, A.G. Frank and I. Wallerstein, *Dynamics of global crisis*, New York, Monthly Review Press, pp. 109-65.

Frank, A.G. (1983a), 'From Atlantic Alliance to Pan-European detente: Political economic alternatives', *Alternatives*, vol. 8, no. 4, Spring 1983, pp. 423-82.

Frank, A.G. (1983b), *The unequal and uneven historical development of the world economy*, Research Memorandum No. 8327, Amsterdam, University of Amsterdam.

Frank, A.G. (1984a), *Critique and anti-critique: Essays on dependence and reformism*, London, Macmillan.

Frank, A.G. (1984b), 'Defuse the debt bomb? When apparent solutions become real problems', *Economic and Political Weekly*, vol. 19, no. 27, July 7, pp. 1036-45.

Frank, A.G. (1984c), 'World economic crisis and Third World in mid-1980s', *Economic and Political Weekly*, vol. 19, no. 19, May 12, pp. 799-804.

Frank, A.G. (1986), 'Is the Reagan recovery real or the calm before a storm?', *Economic and Political Weekly*, vol. 21, no. 21, May 24, pp. 920-7 and no. 22, May 31, pp. 972-7.

Frank, A.G. (1987a), 'Crash course', *Economic and Political Weekly*, vol. 22, no. 46, November 14, pp. 1942-6.

Frank, A.G. (1987b), 'Debt where credit is due', *Economic and Political Weekly*, vol. 22, no. 42, October 17-24, pp. 1795-9.

Frank, A.G. (1988), 'A modest proposal', *Economic and Political Weekly*, vol. 23, no. 6, February 6, pp. 246-7.

Frank, A.G. (1990), 'Revolution in Eastern Europe: Lessons for democratic social movements (and socialists?)', *Third World Quarterly*, vol. 12, no. 2, April, pp. 36-52.

Furtado, C. (1982), 'Dependence in a unified world', *Alternatives*, vol. 8, no. 2, Fall, pp. 259-84.

Galtung, J. (1971), 'A structural theory of imperialism', *Journal of Peace Research*, vol. 8, no. 2, pp. 81-117.

Galtung, J. (1973), *The European Community: A superpower in the making*, Oslo, Universitetsforlaget; London, George Allen & Unwin.

Galtung, J. (1976a), 'Conflict on a global scale: Social imperialism and sub-imperialism - Continuities in the structural theory of imperialism', *World Development*, vol. 4, no. 3, March, pp. 153-65.

Galtung, J. (1976b), 'The Lomé Convention and neo-capitalism', *The African Review*, vol. 6, no. 1, pp. 33-42.

Galtung, J. (1978a), 'Grand designs on a collision course', *International Development Review*, vol. 20, no. 3-4, pp. 43-7.

Galtung, J. (1978b), 'The New International Economic Order and the Basic Needs Approaches: Compatibility, contradiction and/or conflict?', *Annales d'Etudes Internationales*, no. 9, pp. 127-48.

Galtung, J. (1978c), 'Perspectives on development: Past, present, future', in J. Galtung, *Peace and social structure*, Essays in peace research, vol. III, Copenhagen, Christian Ejlers, pp. 315-32.

Galtung, J. (1979a), *Development, environment and technology: Towards a technology for self-reliance*, Study prepared at the request of the UNCTAD secretariat and with the financial support of the United Nations Environment Programme, New York, United Nations.

Galtung, J. (1979b), 'Towards a new international technological order', *Alternatives*, vol. 4, no. 3, January, pp. 277-300.

Galtung, J. (1979c), 'The New International Economic Order and the Basic Needs Approach', *Alternatives*, vol. 4, no. 4, March, pp. 455-76.

Galtung, J. (1980a), 'Big powers and the world feudal structure', in J. Galtung, *Peace and world structure*, Essays in peace research, vol. IV, Copenhagen, Christian Ejlers, pp. 352-65.

Galtung, J. (1980b), 'The changing interface between peace and development in a changing world', *Bulletin of Peace Proposals*, vol. 11, no. 2, pp. 145-9.

Galtung, J. (1980c), 'Cuba: Anti-imperialism and socialist development', in J. Galtung, *Peace problems: Some case studies*, Essays in peace research, vol. V, Copenhagen, Christian Ejlers, pp. 206-18.

Galtung, J. (1980d), 'Development from above and the Blue Revolution: The Indo-Norwegian project in Kerala', in J. Galtung, *Peace problems: Some case studies*, Essays in peace research, vol. V, Copenhagen, Christian Ejlers, pp. 343-60.

Galtung, J. (1980e), 'The Latin American system of nations: A structural analysis', in J. Galtung, *Peace and world structure*, Essays in peace research, vol. IV, Copenhagen, Christian Ejlers, pp. 205-30.

Galtung, J. (1980f), 'On the technology of self-reliance', in J. Galtung, P. O'Brien and R. Preiswerk (eds), *Self-reliance: A strategy for development*, London, Bogle-L'Ouverture, pp. 223-46.

Galtung, J. (1980g), 'The politics of self-reliance', in J. Galtung, P. O'Brien and R. Preiswerk (eds), *Self-reliance: A strategy for development*, London, Bogle-L'Ouverture, pp. 355-83.

Galtung, J. (1980h), 'Self-reliance: Concepts, practice and rationale', in J. Galtung, P. O'Brien and R. Preiswerk (eds), *Self-reliance: A strategy for development*, London, Bogle-L'Ouverture, pp. 19-44.

Galtung, J. (1980i), ' "A structural theory of imperialism" - Ten years later', *Millennium: Journal of International Studies*, vol. 9, no. 3, Winter, pp. 181-96.

Galtung, J. (1980j), *The true worlds: A transnational perspective*, New York, Free Press.

Galtung, J. (1983), *Self-reliance: Beiträge zu einer alternativen Entwicklungsstrategie*, München, Minerva.

Galtung, J. (1985a), 'Global conflict formations: Present developments and future directions', in P. Wallensteen, J. Galtung and C. Portales (eds), *Global militarization*, Boulder, Col., Westview, pp. 23-74.

Galtung, J. (1985b), 'Military formations and social formations: A structural analysis', in P. Wallensteen, J. Galtung and C. Portales (eds), *Global militarization*, Boulder, Col., Westview, pp. 1-20.

Galtung, J. (1986), 'The winners and the losers: The rise of the South-East, the decline of the North-West', in K. Ahooja-Patel, A. Gordon Drabek and M. Nerfin (eds), *World economy in transition: Essays presented to Surendra Patel on his sixtieth birthday*, Oxford, Pergamon, pp. 37-46.

Galtung, J. (1989a), *Europe in the making*, New York, Crane Russak.

Galtung, J. (1989b), 'Predicting conflict dynamics', *Jerusalem Journal of International Relations*, vol. 11, no. 2, June, pp. 1-16.

Galtung, J., Preiswerk, R. and Wemegah, M. (1981), *A concept of development centred on the human being: Some Western European perspectives*, Itineraires, Notes et Travaux, No. 8, Troisième édition, Genève, Institut Universitaire d'Etudes du Développement.

Garst, D. (1985), 'Wallerstein and his critics', *Theory and Society*, vol. 14, no. 4, July, pp. 469-95.

Gasiorowski, M.J. (1986), 'Structure and dynamics in international interdependence', in M.A. Tétreault and C.F. Abel (eds), *Dependency theory and the return of high politics*, New York, Greenwood Press, pp. 71-99.

Gasiorowski, M.J. (1988), 'Economic dependence and political democracy: A cross-national study', *Comparative Political Studies*, vol. 20, no. 4, January, pp. 489-515.

Gastil, R.D. (1978), *Freedom in the world: Political rights and civil liberties 1978*, New York, Freedom House; Boston, G.K. Hall.

Gastil, R.D. (1985), 'The comparative survey of freedom 1985', *Freedom at Issue*, no. 82, January-February, pp. 3-16.

Gerami, S., Turner, C.G. and Hall, T.D. (1988), 'A symmetrical measure of financial dependency with an application to OPEC states', *Free Inquiry in Creative Sociology*, vol. 16, no. 1, May, pp. 51-6.

Gidengil, E.L. (1978), 'Centres and peripheries: An empirical test of Galtung's theory of imperialism', *Journal of Peace Research*, vol. 15, no. 1, pp. 51-66.

Gilpin, R. (1987), *The political economy of international relations*, Princeton, Princeton University Press.

Gobalet, J.G. and Diamond, L.J. (1979), 'Effects of investment dependence on economic growth: The role of internal structural characteristics and periods in the world economy', *International Studies Quarterly*, vol. 23, no. 3, September, pp. 412-44.

Golembiewski, R.T. (1977), *Public administration as a developing discipline*, Part 1: Perspectives on past and present, New York, Marcel Dekker.

Gonick, L.S. and Rosh, R.M. (1988), 'The structural constraints of the world-economy on national political development', *Comparative*

Political Studies, vol. 21, no. 2, July, pp. 171-99.

Griffin, K.B. and Enos, J.L. (1970), 'Foreign assistance: Objectives and consequences', *Economic Development and Cultural Change*, vol. 18, no. 3, April, pp. 313-27.

Griffin, K. and Gurley, J. (1985), 'Radical analyses of imperialism, the Third World, and the transition to socialism: A survey article', *Journal of Economic Literature*, vol. 23, no. 3, September, pp. 1089-143.

Gülalp, H. (1983), 'Frank and Wallerstein revisited: A contribution to Brenner's critique', in P. Limqueco and B. McFarlane (eds), *Neo-Marxist theories of development*, London, Croom Helm; New York, St Martin's Press, pp. 114-36.

Gülalp, H. (1987), 'Dependency and world-system theories: Varying political implications', *Journal of Contemporary Asia*, vol. 17, no. 2, pp. 131-9.

Hagenaars, J.A.P. and Segers, J.H.G. (1980), 'Onderzoeksontwerp', in J.H.G. Segers and J.A.P. Hagenaars (eds), *Sociologische onderzoeksmethoden*, vol. II: Technieken van causale analyse, Assen, Van Gorcum, pp. 27-91.

Harris, N. (1987), *The end of the Third World: Newly Industrializing Countries and the decline of an ideology*, Harmondsworth, Penguin.

Hartman, J. and Barnhouse Walters, P. (1985), 'Dependence, military assistance and development: A cross-national study', *Politics and Society*, vol. 14, no. 4, pp. 431-58.

Hartwell, R.M. (1971), 'Introduction', in D. Ricardo, *On the principles of political economy, and taxation*, Originally published in 1817, Harmondsworth, Penguin.

Hayter, T. (1971), *Aid as imperialism*, Harmondsworth, Penguin.

Hempel, C.G. (1962), 'Deductive-nomological vs. statistical explanation', in H. Feigl and G. Maxwell (eds), *Scientific explanation, space, and time*, Minnesota Studies in the Philosophy of Science, vol. III, Minneapolis, University of Minnesota Press, pp. 98-169.

Higgott, R.A. (1983), *Political development theory: The contemporary debate*, London, Croom Helm.

Hilferding, R. (1981), *Finance capital: A study of the latest phase of capitalist development*, Originally published in German in 1910, London, Routledge & Kegan Paul.

Hine, R.C. (1985), *The political economy of European trade: An introduction to the trade policies of the EEC*, New York, Harvester Wheatsheaf.

Hirsch, L.P. (1986), 'Incorporation into the world economy: Empirical tests of dependency theory', in M.A. Tétreault and C.F. Abel (eds), *Dependency theory and the return of high politics*, New York, Greenwood Press, pp. 101-21.

Hirschman, A.O. (1969), 'The political economy of import-substituting industrialization in Latin America', in C.T. Nisbet, *Latin America: Problems in economic development*, New York, Free Press; London, Collier-Macmillan, pp. 237-66.

Hobson, J.A. (1988), *Imperialism: A study*, Third edition, Originally published in 1938, First edition 1902, London, Unwin Hyman.

Holsti, K.J. (1985), *The dividing discipline: Hegemony and diversity in international theory*, Boston, Allen & Unwin.

Holsti, K.J. (1989), 'Mirror, mirror on the wall, which are the fairest theories of all?', *International Studies Quarterly*, vol. 33, no. 3, September, pp. 255-61.

Hoogvelt, A.M.M. (1982), *The Third World in global development*, London, Macmillan.

Hopkins, T.K. and Wallerstein, I. (1981), 'Structural transformations of the world-economy', in R. Rubinson (ed.), *Dynamics of world development*, Political economy of the world-system annuals, vol. 4, Beverly Hills, Sage, pp. 233-61.

Hopkins, T.K., Wallerstein, I. and associates (1982a), 'Cyclical rhythms and secular trends of the capitalist world-economy: Some premises, hypotheses, and questions', in T.K. Hopkins, I. Wallerstein, R.L. Bach, C. Chase-Dunn and R. Mukherjee, *World-systems analysis: Theory and methodology*, Explorations in the world-economy, vol. 1, Beverly Hills, Sage, pp. 104-20.

Hopkins, T.K., Wallerstein, I. and associates (1982b), 'Patterns of development of the modern world-system', in T.K. Hopkins, I. Wallerstein, R.L. Bach, C. Chase-Dunn and R. Mukherjee, *World-systems analysis: Theory and methodology*, Explorations in the world-economy, vol. 1, Beverly Hills, Sage, pp. 41-82.

Hoselitz, B.F. (1960), *Sociological aspects of economic growth*, Glencoe, Ill., Free Press.

Hoselitz, B.F. (1965), 'Unity and diversity in economic structure', in B.F. Hoselitz (ed.), *Economics and the idea of mankind*, New York, Columbia University Press, pp. 63-96.

Hout, W. (1984), *Frank en vrij in het zuiden? Een poging tot toetsing van de dependenciatheorie van Andre Gunder Frank*, Master's thesis, Erasmus Universiteit Rotterdam, Rotterdam, Mimeo.

Hout, W. (1987), 'Democratisering van het buitenlands beleid: De actualiteit van Richard Cobden', *Namens*, vol. 2, no. 1, January, pp. 52-6.

Hout, W. (1988), 'Rectification, exploitation and the Third World: A critique', *Acta Politica*, vol. 23, no. 4, October, pp. 437-60.

Hout, W. (1992), 'Centres and peripheries: An assessment of the contribution of dependency and world system theories to the study of international relations', *Acta Politica*, vol. 27, no. 1, January, Special issue 'Does theory matter? Dutch contributions to the study of international relations', pp. 71-92.

Huntington, S.P. (1968), *Political order in changing societies*, New Haven, Yale University Press.

Hyden, G. (1983), *No shortcuts to progress: African development management in perspective*, Berkeley, University of California Press.

International Labour Organization (1978, 1979, 1980, 1986, 1987 and 1988), *Yearbook of Labour Statistics*, Geneva, International Labour Organization.

International Labour Organization (1990), *Yearbook of Labour Statistics: Retrospective on national censuses, 1945-89*, Geneva, International Labour Organization.

International Monetary Fund (1964-8, 1965-9, 1968, 1970, 1971, 1978, 1980), *Balance of Payments Yearbook*, Washington, D.C., International Monetary Fund.

International Monetary Fund (1982, 1986 and 1988), *Direction of Trade Statistics: Yearbook*, Washington, D.C., International Monetary Fund.

International Monetary Fund (1989 and 1990), *Balance of Payments Statistics: Yearbook, Part 1*, Washington, D.C., International Monetary Fund.

International Monetary Fund and International Bank for Reconstruction and Development (undated), *Directory of Trade: Annual 1963-67*, Washington, D.C., International Monetary Fund and International Bank for Reconstruction and Development.

Jackman, R.W. (1982), 'Dependence on foreign investment and economic growth in the Third World', *World Politics*, vol. 34, no. 2, January, pp. 175-96.

Jackman, R.W. (1985), 'Cross-national statistical research and the study of comparative politics', *American Journal of Political Science*, vol. 29, no. 1, February, pp. 161-82.

Jackson, S.I. (1979), 'Capitalist penetration: Concept and measurement', *Journal of Peace Research*, vol. 26, no. 1, pp. 41-55.

Jackson, S., Russett, B., Snidal, D. and Sylvan, D. (1979), 'An assessment of empirical research on *dependencia*', *Latin American Research Review*, vol. 14, no. 3, pp. 7-28.

Jaffee, D. and Stokes, R. (1986), 'Foreign investment and trade dependence', *Sociological Quarterly*, vol. 27, no. 4, Winter, pp. 533-46.

Jagodzinski, W. and Weede, E. (1980), 'Weltpolitische und ökonomische Determinanten einer ungleichen Einkommensverteilung: Eine international vergleichende Studie', *Zeitschrift für Soziologie*, vol. 9, no. 2,

April, pp. 132-48.

Johnson, D.L. (1972), 'Dependence and the international system', in J.D. Cockroft, A.G. Frank and D.L. Johnson, *Dependence and underdevelopment: Latin America's political economy*, New York, Doubleday, pp. 71-111.

Jones, E.L. (1981), *The European miracle: Environments, economies and geopolitics in the history of Europe and Asia*, Cambridge, Cambridge University Press.

Junne, G. (1987), 'Benaderingen die uitgaan van klassentegenstellingen', in R.B. Soetendorp and A. van Staden (eds), *Internationale betrekkingen in perspectief*, Utrecht, Spectrum, pp. 65-99.

Kaufman, R.R., Chernotsky, H.I. and Geller, D.S. (1975), 'A preliminary test of the theory of dependency', *Comparative Politics*, vol. 7, April, pp. 303-30.

Kay, C. (1991), 'Reflections on the Latin American contribution to development theory', *Development and Change*, vol. 22, no. 1, January, pp. 31-68.

Keohane, R.O. and Nye, J.S. (eds) (1971), *Transnational relations and world politics*, Cambridge, Mass., Harvard University Press.

Keohane, R.O. and Nye, J.S. (1977), *Power and interdependence: World politics in transition*, Boston, Little, Brown.

Kemp, M.C. (1962), 'The gain from international trade', *Economic Journal*, vol. 72, no. 288, December, pp. 803-19.

Kentor, J. (1981), 'Structural determinants of peripheral urbanization: The effects of international dependence', *American Sociological Review*, vol. 46, no. 2, April, pp. 201-11.

Khalaf, N.G. (1979), 'Country size and economic growth and development', *Journal of Development Studies*, vol. 16, no. 1, October, pp. 67-72.

Kiernan, V.G. (1974), *Marxism and imperialism*, London, Edward Arnold.

Knorr, K. and Rosenau, J.N. (eds) (1970), *Contending approaches to international politics*, Princeton, Princeton University Press.

Kohli, A., Altfeld, M.F., Loftian, S. and Mardon, R. (1984), 'Inequality in the Third World: An assessment of competing explanations', *Comparative Political Studies*, vol. 17, no. 3, October, pp. 283-318.

Krasner, S.D. (1985), *Structural conflict: The Third World against global liberalism*, Berkeley, University of California Press.

Kuhn, T.S. (1970), *The structure of scientific revolutions*, Second edition, First published in 1962, Chicago, University of Chicago Press.

Laclau, E. (1971), 'Feudalism and capitalism in Latin America', *New Left Review*, no. 67, May/June, pp. 19-38.

Lakatos, I. (1970), 'Falsification and the methodology of scientific research programmes', in I. Lakatos and A. Musgrave (eds), *Criticism and the growth of knowledge: Proceedings of the International Colloquium in the Philosophy of Science, London, 1965*, vol. 4, Cambridge, Cambridge University Press, pp. 91-196.

Lake, D.A. (1987), 'Power and the Third World: Toward a Realist political economy of North-South relations', *International Studies Quarterly*, vol. 31, no. 2, June, pp. 217-34.

Lapid, Y. (1989), 'The third debate: On the prospects of international theory in a post-positivist era', *International Studies Quarterly*, vol. 33, no. 3, September, pp. 235-54.

Laudan, L. (1977), *Progress and its problems: Towards a theory of scientific growth*, Berkeley, University of California Press.

Leaver, R. (1983a), 'The debate on underdevelopment: "On situating Gunder Frank" ', in P. Limqueco and B. McFarlane (eds), *Neo-Marxist theories of development*, London, Croom Helm; New York, St Martin's Press, pp. 87-96.

Leaver, R. (1983b), 'Samir Amin on underdevelopment', in P. Limqueco and B. McFarlane (eds), *Neo-Marxist theories of development*, London, Croom Helm; New York, St Martin's Press, pp. 58-72.

Lebovic, J.H. (1988), 'National interests and U.S. foreign aid: The Carter and Reagan years', *Journal of Peace Research*, vol. 25, no. 2, June, pp. 115-35.

Lee, E. (ed.) (1981), *Export-led industrialization and development*, Singapore, International Labour Organization.

Lenin, V.I. (1964), *Imperialism, the highest stage of capitalism: A popular outline*, in V.I. Lenin, *Collected works*, vol. 22: December 1915-July 1916, Originally published in Russian in 1917, Moscow, Progress, pp. 185-304.

Lerner, D. (1964), *The passing of traditional society: Modernizing the Middle East*, First published in 1958, New York, Free Press; London, Collier-Macmillan.

Leurdijk, J.H. (1987), 'De analyse van de wereldsamenleving', in R.B. Soetendorp and A. van Staden (eds), *Internationale betrekkingen in perspectief*, Utrecht, Spectrum, pp. 37-64.

London, B. (1987), 'Structural determinants of Third World urban change: An ecological and political economic analysis', *American Sociological Review*, vol. 52, no. 1, February, pp. 28-43.

London, B. and Robinson, T.D. (1989), 'The effect of international dependence on income inequality and political violence', *American Sociological Review*, vol. 54, no. 2, April, pp. 305-8.

London, B. and Smith, D.A. (1988), 'Urban bias, dependence, and economic stagnation in noncore nations', *American Sociological Review*, vol. 53, no. 3, June, pp. 454-63.

Love, J.L. (1980), 'Raúl Prebisch and the origins of the doctrine of unequal exchange', *Latin American Research Review*, vol. 15, no. 3, pp. 45-72.

Luxemburg, R. (1975), *Die Akkumulation des Kapitals: Ein Beitrag zur ökonomischen Erklärung des Imperialismus*, in R. Luxemburg, *Gesammelte Werke*, vol. 5: Ökonomische Schriften, Originally published in 1913, Berlin, Dietz Verlag, pp. 5-411.

Magdoff, H. (1969), *The age of imperialism: The economics of U.S. foreign policy*, New York, Monthly Review Press.

Magdoff, H. (1972), 'Imperialism without colonies', in R. Owen and B. Sutcliffe (eds), *Studies in the theory of imperialism*, London, Longman, pp. 144-70.

Magdoff, H. (1978), *Imperialism: From the colonial age to the present*, New York, Monthly Review Press.

Maghroori, R. and Ramberg, B. (eds) (1982), *Globalism versus realism: International relations' third debate*, Boulder, Col., Westview.

Mahler, V.A. (1980), *Dependency approaches to international political economy: A cross-national study*, New York, Columbia University Press.

Mahler, V.A. (1981), 'Mining, agriculture, and manufacturing: The impact of foreign investment on social distribution in Third World countries', *Comparative Political Studies*, vol. 14, no. 3, October, pp. 267-97.

Maley, William (1985), 'Peace, needs and utopia', *Political Studies*, vol. 33, no. 4, December, pp. 578-91.

McGowan, P.J. (1976), 'Economic dependence and economic performance in Black Africa', *Journal of Modern African Studies*, vol. 14, no. 1, pp. 25-40.

McGowan, P.J. and Smith, D.L. (1978), 'Economic dependency in black Africa: An analysis of competing theories', *International Organization*, vol. 32, no. 1, Winter, pp. 179-235.

McKinlay, R.D. and Little, R. (1977), 'A foreign policy model of U.S. bilateral aid allocation', *World Politics*, vol. 30, no. 1, October, pp. 58-86.

McKinlay, R.D. and Little, R. (1979), 'The U.S. aid relationship: A test of the recipient need and the donor interest models', *Political Studies*, vol. 27, no. 2, June, pp. 236-50.

Meyer, J.W., Hannan, M.T., Rubinson, R. and Thomas, G.M. (1979), 'National economic development, 1950-70: Social and political factors', in J.W. Meyer and M.T. Hannan (eds), *National development and the world system: Educational, economic, and political change, 1950-1970*, Chicago, University of Chicago Press, pp. 85-116.

Meyer-Fehr, P. (1980), 'Technologische Kontrolle durch multinationale Konzerne und Wirtschaftswachstum', in V. Bornschier (ed.), *Multinationale Konzerne, Wirtschaftspolitik und nationale Entwicklung im Weltsystem*, Frankfurt, Campus, pp. 106-28.

Migdal, J.S. (1983), 'Studying the politics of development and change: The state of the art', in A.W. Finifter (ed.), *Political science: The state of the discipline*, Washington, D.C., American Political Science Association, pp. 309-38.

Mommsen, W.J. (1980), *Imperialismustheorien: Ein Überblick über die neueren Imperialismusinterpretationen*, Second edition, Göttingen, Vandenhoeck & Ruprecht.

Morgenthau, H.J. (1948), *Politics among nations*, New York, Alfred A. Knopf.

Muller, E.N. (1984), 'Financial dependence in the capitalist world economy and the distribution of income within nations', in M.A. Seligson (ed.), *The gap between rich and poor: Contending perspectives on the political economy of development*, Boulder, Westview, pp. 256-82.

Murphy, C.N. (1986), 'Toward transformation of dependency and high politics', in M.A. Tétreault and C.F. Abel (eds), *Dependency theory and the return of high politics*, New York, Greenwood Press, pp. 243-53.

Nemeth, R.J. and Smith, D.A. (1985), 'International trade and world-system structure: A multiple network analysis', *Review*, vol. 8, no. 4, Spring, pp. 517-60.

O'Brien, P. (1982), 'European economic development: The contribution of the periphery', *Economic History Review* (Second Series), vol. 35, no. 1, February, pp. 1-18.

O'Donnell, G.A. (1972), *Modernization and bureaucratic-authoritarianism: Studies in South American politics*, Berkeley, Institute of International Studies, University of California.

Olson, W.C. and Groom, A.J.R. (1991), *International relations then and now: Origins and trends in interpretation*, London, Harper Collins.

O'Neill, O. (1991), 'Transnational justice', in D. Held (ed.), *Political theory today*, Oxford, Polity Press, pp. 276-304.

Organisation for Economic Co-operation and Development (1970), *Development Assistance: Efforts and Policies of the Members of the Development Assistance Committee*, 1970 Review, Paris, Organisation for Economic Co-operation and Development.

Organisation for Economic Co-operation and Development (1977), *Development Co-operation: Efforts and Policies of the Members of the*

Development Assistance Committee, 1977 Review, Paris, Organisation for Economic Co-operation and Development.

Palma, G. (1978), 'Dependency: A formal theory of underdevelopment or a methodology for the analysis of concrete situations of underdevelopment?', *World Development*, vol. 6, no. 7/8, July/August, pp. 881-924.

Palma, G. (1979), 'Dependency and development: A critical overview', in D. Seers (ed.), *Dependency theory: A critical reassessment*, London, Frances Pinter, pp. 20-78.

Peacock, W.G., Hoover, G.A. and Killian, C.D. (1988), 'Divergence and convergence in international development: A decomposition analysis of inequality in the world system', *American Sociological Review*, vol. 53, no. 6, December, pp. 838-52.

Pedhazur, E.J. (1982), *Multiple regression in behavioral research: Explanation and prediction*, Second edition, New York, Holt, Rinehart and Winston.

Polanyi Levitt, K. (1989), 'Linkage and vulnerability: The 'debt crisis' in Latin America and Africa', in B.K. Campbell (ed.), *Political dimensions of the international debt crisis*, Basingstoke, Macmillan, pp. 15-50.

Popper, K.R. (1969), *Conjectures and refutations: The growth of scientific knowledge*, Third edition, First published in 1963, London, Routledge & Kegan Paul.

Prebisch, R. (1950), *The economic development of Latin America and its principal problems*, Lake Success, N.Y., United Nations Department of Economic Affairs.

Prebisch, R. (1959), 'Commercial policy in the underdeveloped countries', *American Economic Review, Papers and Proceedings*, vol. 49, no. 2, May, pp. 251-73.

Prechel, H. (1985), 'The effects of exports, public debt, and development on income inequality', *Sociological Quarterly*, vol. 26, no. 2, Summer, pp. 213-34.

Prechel, H. and Sica, A. (1987), 'Demonstrating dependency: A critique of ideologies, quantitative test, and educational misdevelopment', *Political Power and Social Theory*, vol. 6, pp. 239-76.

Puijenbroek, R.A.G. van (1984), *Enkele politieke en economische determinanten van economische groei*, Master's thesis, Katholieke Universiteit Nijmegen, Nijmegen, Mimeo.

Puijenbroek, R.A.G. van and Snippenburg, L.B. van (1984), 'Niveau van economische ontwikkeling in landenvergelijkend onderzoek: Constructie van een schaal', *Acta Politica*, vol. 19, no. 2, April, pp. 239-56.

Puijenbroek, R.A.G. van and Snippenburg, L.B. van (1985), 'Internationale arbeidsdeling, afhankelijkheid en economische groei: Een cross-

nationale studie', *Acta Politica*, vol. 20, no. 4, October, pp. 385-419.
Pye, L.W. (1966), *Aspects of political development*, Boston, Little, Brown.
Ragin, C. (1983), 'Theory and method in the study of dependency and international inequality', *International Journal of Comparative Sociology*, vol. 24, no. 1-2, January-April, pp. 121-36.
Ragin, C. (1985), 'Knowledge and interests in the study of the modern world-system', *Review*, vol. 8, no. 4, Spring, pp. 451-76.
Ragin, C. and Delacroix, J. (1979), 'Comparative advantage, the world division of labor, and underdevelopment', *Comparative Social Research*, vol. 2, pp. 181-214.
Ray, D. (1973), 'The dependency model of Latin American underdevelopment: Three basic fallacies', *Journal of Interamerican Studies and World Affairs*, vol. 15, February, pp. 4-20.
Ray, J.L. (1981), 'Dependence, political compliance, and economic performance: Latin America and Eastern Europe', in C.W. Kegley, Jr and P. McGowan (eds), *The political economy of foreign policy behavior*, Sage International Yearbook of Foreign Policy Studies, vol. 6, Beverly Hills, Sage, pp. 111-36.
Read, D. (1967), *Cobden and Bright: A Victorian political partnership*, London, Edward Arnold.
Reich, R.B. (1991), *The work of nations: Preparing ourselves for 21st-century capitalism*, New York, Alfred A. Knopf.
Ricardo, D. (1971), *On the principles of political economy, and taxation*, Originally published in 1817, Harmondsworth, Penguin.
Robinson, J. (1964), *Economic philosophy*, Harmondsworth, Penguin.
Rodríguez, O. (1977), 'On the conception of the centre-periphery system', *CEPAL-Review*, no. 3, First half, pp. 195-239.
Rosenau, J.N. (1982), 'Provocation and proof in world-system analysis', *Comparative Political Studies*, vol. 15, no. 3, October, pp. 357-63.
Rostow, W.W. (1960), *The stages of economic growth: A non-communist manifesto*, Cambridge, Cambridge University Press.
Rostow, W.W. (1971), *Politics and the stages of growth*, Cambridge, Cambridge University Press.
Rothgeb, J.M. (1986), 'Compensation or opportunity? The effects of international recessions upon direct foreign investment and growth in Third World states, 1970-1978', *International Studies Quarterly*, vol. 30, no. 2, June, pp. 123-52.
Rubinson, R. (1976), 'The world-economy and the distribution within states: A cross-national study', *American Sociological Review*, vol. 41, no. 4, August, pp. 638-59.
Rubinson, R. (1977), 'Dependence, government revenue, and economic

growth, 1955-1970', *Studies in Comparative International Development*, vol. 12, Summer, pp. 3-28.

Rubinson, R. and Holtzman, D. (1981), 'Comparative dependence and economic development', *International Journal of Comparative Sociology*, vol. 12, no. 1-2, March-June, pp. 86-101.

Rupert, M.E. (1990), 'Producing hegemony: State/society relations and the politics of productivity in the United States', *International Studies Quarterly*, vol. 34, no. 4, December, p. 427-56.

Samuelson, P.A. (1948), 'International trade and the equalisation of factor prices', *Economic Journal*, vol. 58, no. 230, June, pp. 163-84.

Samuelson, P.A. (1950), 'The gains from international trade', Originally published in 1939, in H.S. Ellis and L.A. Metzler (eds), *Readings in the theory of international trade*, London, George Allen and Unwin, pp. 239-52.

Samuelson, P.A. (1962), 'The gains from international trade once again', *Economic Journal*, vol. 72, no. 288, December, pp. 820-9.

Santos, T. dos (1970), 'The structure of dependence', *American Economic Review, Papers and Proceedings*, vol. 60, no. 2, May, pp. 231-6.

Schiffer, J. (1981), 'The changing post-war pattern of development: The accumulated wisdom of Samir Amin', *World Development*, vol. 9, no. 6, June, pp. 515-37.

Schröder, H.-C. (1973), *Sozialistische Imperialismusdeutung: Studien zu ihrer Geschichte*, Göttingen, Vandenhoeck & Ruprecht.

Sher, G. (1981), 'Ancient wrongs and modern rights', *Philosophy and Public Affairs*, vol. 10, no. 1, Winter, pp. 3-17.

Simon, L.H. and Ruccio, D.F. (1986), 'A methodological analysis of dependency theory: Explanation in Andre Gunder Frank', *World Development*, vol. 14, no. 2, February, pp. 195-209.

Simowitz, R. and Price, B.L. (1990), 'The expected utility theory of conflict: Measuring theoretical progress', *American Political Science Review*, vol. 84, no. 2, June, pp. 439-60.

Singer, H.W. (1950), 'The distribution of gains between investing and borrowing countries', *American Economic Review, Papers and Proceedings*, vol. 40, no. 2, May, pp. 473-85.

Skocpol, T. (1977), 'Wallerstein's world capitalist system: A theoretical and historical critique', *American Journal of Sociology*, vol. 82, no. 5, March, pp. 1075-90.

Smith, D.A. and Nemeth, R. (1988), 'An empirical analysis of commodity exchange in the international economy: 1965-80', *International Studies Quarterly*, vol. 32, no. 2, June, pp. 227-40.

Smith, S. (1980), 'The ideas of Samir Amin: Theory or tautology?', *Journal of Development Studies*, vol. 17, no. 1, October, pp. 5-21.

Smith, S. and Toye, J. (1979), 'Introduction: Three stories about trade and poor economies', *Journal of Development Studies*, vol. 15, no. 3, April, pp. 1-18.

Smith, T. (1979), 'The underdevelopment of development literature: The case of dependency theory', *World Politics*, vol. 31, no. 2, January, pp. 247-88.

Smith, T. (1981), *The pattern of imperialism: The United States, Great Britain, and the late-industrializing world since 1815*, Cambridge, Cambridge University Press.

Smith, T. (1985a), 'The dependency approach', in H.J. Wiarda (ed.), *New directions in comparative politics*, Boulder, Westview, pp. 113-26.

Smith, T. (1985b), 'Requiem or new agenda for Third World studies?', *World Politics*, vol. 37, no. 4, July, pp. 532-61.

Snyder, D. and Kick, E.L. (1979), 'Structural position in the world system and economic growth, 1955-1970: A multiple-network analysis of transnational interactions', *American Journal of Sociology*, vol. 84, no. 5, March, pp. 1096-126.

Staden, A. van (1987), 'De heerschappij van staten: Het perspectief van het realisme', in R.B. Soetendorp and A. van Staden (eds), *Internationale betrekkingen in perspectief*, Utrecht, Spectrum, pp. 13-36.

Stokes, R. and Jaffee, D. (1982), 'Another look at the export of raw materials and economic growth', *American Sociological Review*, vol. 47, no. 3, June, pp. 402-7.

Stokke, O. (ed.) (1984), *European development assistance*, Tilburg, European Association of Development Research and Training Institutes; Oslo, Norwegian Institute of International Affairs.

Strange, S. (1989), *States and markets: An introduction to international political economy*, London, Pinter.

Stumpp, M., Marsh, R.M. and Lake, D. (1978), 'The effects of international economic dependence on development: A critique', *American Sociological Review*, vol. 43, no. 4, August, pp. 600-4.

Sunkel, O. (1979), 'The development of development thinking', in J.J. Villamil (ed.), *Transnational capitalism and national development: New perspectives on dependence*, Hassocks, Harvester Press, pp. 19-30.

Sweezy, P.M. (1946), *The theory of capitalist development: Principles of Marxian political economy*, London, Dennis Dobson.

Sweezy, P.M. (1967), 'Obstacles to economic development', in C.H. Feinstein (ed.), *Socialism, capitalism and economic growth: Essays presented to Maurice Dobb*, Cambridge, Cambridge University Press, pp. 191-7.

Sweezy, P.M. and Magdoff, H. (1972), *The dynamics of U.S. capitalism: Corporate structure, inflation, credit, gold, and the Dollar*, New York,

Monthly Review Press.

Sylvan, D., Snidal, D., Russett, B.M., Jackson, S. and Duvall, R. (1983), 'The peripheral economies: Penetration and economic distortion, 1970-1975', in W.R. Thompson (ed.), *Contending approaches to world system analysis*, Beverly Hills, Sage, pp. 79-111.

Szymanski, A. (1976), 'Dependence, exploitation and economic growth', *Journal of Political and Military Sociology*, vol. 4, no. 1, Spring, pp. 53-65.

Tacq, J. (1991), *Van probleem naar analyse: De keuze van een gepaste multivariate analysetechniek bij een sociaal-wetenschappelijke probleemstelling*, De Lier, Academisch Boeken Centrum.

Terlouw, C.P. (1985), *Het wereldsysteem: Een interpretatie van het werk van I.M. Wallerstein*, CASP Serie Werkdocumenten, no. 8, Rotterdam, Comparative Asian Studies Programme.

Timberlake, M. and Williams, K.R. (1984), 'Dependence, political exclusion, and government repression: Some cross-national evidence', *American Sociological Review*, vol. 49, no. 1, February, pp. 141-6.

Townshend, J. (1988), 'Introduction', in J.A. Hobson, *Imperialism: A study*, London, Unwin Hyman, pp. [9]-[41].

Tromp, B. (1988), 'De theorie van het wereldsysteem: Een overzicht', *Sociologische Gids*, vol. 35, no. 1, January/February, pp. 4-23.

Tyler, W.G. and Wogart, J.P. (1973), 'Economic dependence and marginalization: Some empirical evidence', *Journal of Interamerican Studies and World Affairs*, vol. 15, no. 1, February, pp. 36-45.

UNCTAD (1969, 1979 and 1985a), *Handbook of International Trade and Development Statistics*, New York, United Nations.

UNCTAD (1985b), *Handbook of International Trade and Development Statistics*, Supplement 1985, New York, United Nations.

UNCTAD (1987 and 1989), *Commodity Yearbook*, New York, United Nations.

United Nations (1969, 1976a, 1980, 1987a and 1988a), *International Trade Statistics Yearbook*, New York, United Nations.

United Nations (1970a, 1979-80, 1985-6, 1987b), *Statistical Yearbook*, New York, United Nations.

United Nations (1970b and 1976b), *Yearbook of National Accounts Statistics*, vol. II: International Tables, New York, United Nations.

United Nations (1976c), *World Energy Supplies 1950-1974*, Statistical Papers, Series J, No. 19, United Nations, New York.

United Nations (1982 and 1988b), *Energy Statistics Yearbook*, New York, United Nations.

United Nations (1990a), *National Accounts Statistics: Analysis of main aggregates, 1987*, New York, United Nations.

United Nations (1990b), *National Accounts Statistics: Main aggregates and detailed tables, 1988*, New York, United Nations.

Valenzuela, J.S. and Valenzuela, A. (1979), 'Modernization and dependence: Alternative perspectives in the study of Latin American underdevelopment', in J.J. Villamil (ed.), *Transnational capitalism and national development: New perspectives on development*, Hassocks, Harvester Press, pp. 31-65.

Vengroff, R. (1977a), 'Dependency, development, and inequality in Black Africa', *African Studies Review*, vol. 20, no. 2, September, pp. 17-26.

Vengroff, R. (1977b), 'Dependency and underdevelopment in Black Africa: An empirical test', *Journal of Modern African Studies*, vol. 15, no. 4, pp. 613-30.

Visser, H. (1981), 'Uitbuiting van arme landen door rijke landen', *Maandschrift Economie*, vol. 45, no. 7-8, July-August, pp. 285-304.

Wade, R. (1992), 'East Asia's economic success: Conflicting perspectives, partial insights, shaky evidence', *World Politics*, vol. 44, no. 2, January, pp. 270-320.

Walleri, R.D. (1978a), 'Trade dependence and underdevelopment: A causal-chain analysis', *Comparative Political Studies*, vol. 11, no. 1, April, pp. 94-127.

Walleri, R.D. (1978b), 'The political economy literature on North-South relations: Alternative approaches and empirical evidence', *International Studies Quarterly*, vol. 22, no. 4, December, pp. 587-625.

Wallerstein, I. (1974), *The modern world-system: Capitalist agriculture and the origins of the European world-economy in the sixteenth century*, New York, Academic Press.

Wallerstein, I. (1976), 'The three stages of African involvement in the world-economy', in P.C.W. Gutkind and I. Wallerstein (eds), *The political economy of contemporary Africa*, Sage Series on African Modernization and Development, vol. 1, Beverly Hills, Sage, pp. 30-57.

Wallerstein, I. (1979), *The capitalist world-economy*, Cambridge, Cambridge University Press; Paris, Editions de la Maison des Sciences de l'Homme.

Wallerstein, I. (1980a), 'Imperialism and development', in A. Bergesen (ed.), *Studies of the modern world-system*, New York, Academic Press, pp. 13-23.

Wallerstein, I. (1980b), *The modern world-system II: Mercantilism and the consolidation of the European world-economy, 1600-1750*, New York, Academic Press.

Wallerstein, I. (1982a), 'Crisis as transition', in S. Amin, G. Arrighi, A.G. Frank and I. Wallerstein, *Dynamics of global crisis*, New York, Monthly Review Press, pp. 11-54.

Wallerstein, I. (1982b), 'World-systems analysis: Theoretical and interpretative issues', in T.K. Hopkins, I. Wallerstein, R.L. Bach, C. Chase-Dunn and R. Mukherjee, *World-systems analysis: Theory and methodology*, Explorations in the world-economy, vol. 1, Beverly Hills, Sage, pp. 91-103.

Wallerstein, I. (1983a), 'Capitalism and the world working class: Some premises and some issues for research and analysis', in I. Wallerstein (ed.), *Labor in the world social structure*, Explorations in the world-economy, vol. 2, Beverly Hills, Sage, pp. 17-21.

Wallerstein, I. (1983b), 'Crises: The world-economy, the movements, and the ideologies', in A. Bergesen (ed.), *Crises in the world-system*, Political economy of the world-system annuals, vol. 6, Beverly Hills, Sage, pp. 21-36.

Wallerstein, I. (1983c), *Historical capitalism*, London, Verso.

Wallerstein, I. (1984a), 'Household structures and the labor-force formation in the capitalist world-economy', in J. Smith, I. Wallerstein and H.-D. Evers (eds), *Households and the world-economy*, Explorations in the world-economy, vol. 3, Beverly Hills, Sage, pp. 17-22.

Wallerstein, I. (1984b), *The politics of the world-economy: The states, the movements, and the civilizations*, Cambridge, Cambridge University Press; Paris, Editions de la Maison des Sciences de l'Homme.

Wallerstein, I. (1989), *The modern world-system III: The second era of great expansion of the capitalist world-economy, 1730-1840s*, San Diego, Academic Press.

Wallerstein, I. (1991), *Geopolitics and geoculture: Essays on the changing world-system*, Cambridge, Cambridge University Press; Paris, Editions de la Maison des Sciences de l'Homme.

Waltz, K.N. (1979), *Theory of international politics*, Reading, Mass., Addison-Wesley.

Ward, M.D. (1978), *The political economy of distribution: Equality versus inequality*, New York, Elsevier.

Warren, B. (1973), 'Imperialism and capitalist industrialisation', *New Left Review*, no. 81, September/October, pp. 3-44.

Warren, B. (1980), *Imperialism: Pioneer of capitalism*, edited by John Sender, London, NLB and Verso.

Weede, E. (1981), 'Dependenztheorien und Wirtschaftswachstum: Eine international vergleichende Studie', *Kölner Zeitschrift für Soziologie und Sozialpsychologie*, vol. 33, no. 4, pp. 690-707.

Weede, E. (1982), 'Dependenztheorien und Einkommensverteilung: Eine international vergleichende Studie', *Zeitschrift für die gesamte Staatswissenschaft*, vol. 138, no. 2, pp. 241-61.

Weede, E. (1983a), 'The impact of democracy on economic growth:

Some evidence from cross-national analysis', *Kyklos*, vol. 36, no. 1, pp. 21-39.

Weede, E. (1983b), 'Military participation ratios, human capital formation, and economic growth: A cross-national analysis', *Journal of Political and Military Sociology*, vol. 11, no. 1, Spring, pp. 11-19.

Weede, E. and Tiefenbach, H. (1981a), 'Some recent explanations of income inequality: An evaluation and critique', *International Studies Quarterly*, vol. 25, no. 2, June, pp. 255-82.

Weede, E. and Tiefenbach, H. (1981b), 'Three dependency explanations of economic growth: A critical evaluation', *European Journal of Political Research*, vol. 9, pp. 391-406.

Weede, E. and Tiefenbach, H. (1982), 'Gesellschaftliche Machtverhältnisse und Einkommensverteilung: Ein kritischer Replikationsversuch zu einer Studie von Bornschier und Ballmer-Cao', *Zeitschrift für Soziologie*, vol. 11, no. 4, October, pp. 401-9.

Wehler, H.-U. (ed.) (1972), *Imperialismus*, Köln, Kiepenheuer & Witsch.

Wiarda, H.J. (1985), 'Toward a nonethnocentric theory of development: Alternative conceptions from the Third World', in H.J. Wiarda (ed.), *New directions in comparative politics*, Boulder, Westview, pp. 127-50.

Williams, G. (1978), 'Imperialism and development: A critique', *World Development*, vol. 6, no. 7/8, July/August, pp. 925-36.

Wimberley, D.W. (1990), 'Investment dependence and alternative explanations of Third World mortality: A cross-national study', *American Sociological Review*, vol. 55, no. 1, February, pp. 75-91.

World Bank (1976), *World Tables 1976*, Baltimore, Johns Hopkins University Press.

World Bank (1982), *World Tables*, Third edition, vol. 2: Social data, Baltimore, Johns Hopkins University Press.

World Bank (1987), *World Development Report 1987*, New York, Oxford University Press.

World Bank (1988), *World Tables 1987*, Fourth edition, Washington, D.C., World Bank.

World Bank (1988-9), *World Debt Tables: External Debt of Developing Countries*, Washington, D.C., World Bank.

World Bank (1989), *World Tables 1988-89*, Baltimore, Johns Hopkins University Press.

World Bank (1990), *World Development Report 1990*, Oxford, Oxford University Press.

World Bank (1991), *World Development Report 1991: The challenge of development*, Oxford, Oxford University Press.

Zolberg, A.R. (1981), 'Origins of the modern world system: A missing link', *World Politics*, vol. 33, no. 2, January, pp. 253-81.

Index